Cultural Interactions
in the Romantic Age

SUNY Series, The Margins of Literature
Mihai I. Spariosu, Editor

Cultural Interactions in the Romantic Age

Critical Essays in Comparative Literature

Edited by
GREGORY MAERTZ

STATE UNIVERSITY OF NEW YORK PRESS

Published by
State University of New York Press, Albany

© 1998 State University of New York

© Annette Wheeler Cafarelli, "Rousseau and British Romanticism: Women and
the Legacy of Male Radicalism"

For information, address the State University of New York Press,
State University Plaza, Albany, NY 12246

Production design by David Ford
Marketing by Anne M. Valentine

Library of Congress Cataloging-in-Publication Data

Cultural interactions in the Romantic Age : critical essays in
    comparative literature / edited by Gregory Maertz.
        p.   cm. — (SUNY series, the margins of literature)
    Includes bibliographical references and index.
        ISBN 0-7914-3559-8 (alk. paper). — ISBN 0-7914-3560-1 (pbk. :
alk. paper)
        1. Romanticism.   2. Literature, Modern—History and criticsm.
    3. Literature, Comparative.   I. Maertz, Gregory, 1958–
    II. Series.
    PN603.C85   1997
    809'.9145—dc21   97-7314
                                                              CIP
                                                               AC

10 9 8 7 6 5 4 3 2 1

809.9145
Cul

Contents

Vermitteln und Vermitteltwerden ist das ganze höhere Leben des Menschen, und jeder Künstler ist Mittler fur alle übrigen.

[To mediate and to receive mediation is the entire higher life of mankind, and every artist is a mediator for all others.]

—Friedrich Schlegel, *Athenäum Fragment No. 44*

Acknowledgments

*Our function as editor consists exclusively
in ordering and publishing the articles
that our colleagues have furnished us.*

—Jean d'Alembert,
from the Foreword to the
Encyclopédie, *Vol. III*

Collections of essays replicate the dialogic structure of academic discourse, and the design of *Cultural Interactions in the Romantic Age* reflects my own training in comparative literature, the best portion of which consisted of conversations with my teachers at Northwestern, Harvard, and Heidelberg. The idea for this book was conceived during more recent conversations with James Engell and Lilian R. Furst, and it evolved into its final form only after extensive dialogue with my contributors. Besides Engell and Furst, April Alliston, Fred Burwick, and John L. Mahoney were especially supportive as the project neared completion. I am indebted to my meticulous editors at State University of New York Press, David Ford, James Peltz, and Carola Sautter, and grateful to others who made helpful suggestions or offered encouragement as this project took shape: Leonard Barkan, James G. Basker, John Boening, Peter Brooks, Kevin L. Cope, Marilyn Gaull, Willard P. Gingerich, Peter W. Graham, Nancy Grayson Holmes, Naomi Lebowitz, John Lowney, Andrew McNeillie, David M. O'Connell, C.M., Derek Owens, Julie Stone Peters, Ruben Quintero, Stephen Sicari, Gordon Turnbull, Kevin Van Anglen, and Henry B. Wonham. Finally, for favors great and small, special thanks to Virginia Buccio, David L. Clark, Anthony Clemente, Jennifer Cortez, John DeSantis, Kevin DiCamillo,

Michelle Drago, Eliana Jaramillo, Michelle Liptak, and Eugenia Smilowitz. The cover illustration, "Heidelberg," School of Turner, appears courtesy of the Kurpfälzisches Museum, Heidelberg.

Gregory Maertz

Introduction

*"Think not of other worlds," the angel Raphael cautions
Adam in Milton's* Paradise Lost: *cultivate rather the
garden of this world and the company of Eve. Yet in
literature, as in science, there is a plurality of worlds.
We cannot take for granted that other cultures are like
ours; we must try to enter or understand them,
or else find a theory (and not just a prejudice)
that allows us to overlook their existence.*

—*Geoffrey Hartman,*
Criticism in the Wilderness

Comparative literature has always been a subversive discipline. Whether comparatists aligned themselves with the literary humanism of Ernst Robert Curtius, Erich Auerbach, René Wellek, and Harry Levin, or with Yale's theoreticians, they have always united in attacking the twin myths of the self-sufficiency of disciplines and the autonomy of literary works. Such myths are, of course, self-serving and arbitrary, more the product of academic politics and bureaucratic convenience than of scholarship. Applied to Romanticism they ring especially hollow, and never more so than in the immediate postwar period, when intense debate over the intercultural dimension of Romanticism erupted with the appearance in 1948 of A. O. Lovejoy's rationalization of disciplinary borders in "On the Discrimination of Romanticisms." Two years later Curtius offered a powerful rejoinder to Lovejoy's "plurality of Romanticisms." His *Kritische Essays zur europäischen Literatur* articulated a breathtaking vision of a common European cultural legacy that inspired scholars on both sides of the Atlantic to emulate his cosmopolitan humanism. Much of this work is remarkable for its enduring value, including Erich Heller's *The*

1

Disinherited Mind (1952), René Wellek's *Confrontations* (1964), the volume of essays edited by Helmut Prang, *Begriffsbestimmung der Romantik* (1968), Lilian R. Furst's *Romanticism in Perspective* (1969), and Paul de Man's *Blindness and Insight* (1971).

In the three decades since the heyday of literary humanism the comparative study of Romanticism has received fresh impetus for academic iconoclasm from critical theory. By emphasizing the philosophical, social, and material matrices of literary works, new generations of comparatists have transcended the narrow disciplinary boundaries of national literature departments. Among the works that played an influential role or served as important signposts in this process are de Man's *The Rhetoric of Romanticism* (1984), *Romanticism and Language* (1984), edited by Arden Reed, Jerome J. McGann's *Historical Studies and Literary Criticism* (1985), and *The Age of Wordsworth* (1987), edited by Kenneth R. Johnston and Gene W. Ruoff. This theoretical reorientation and contextual enrichment has also directed the interest of scholars and critics to the role of gender in writing and authorship, as in the anthology edited by Anne K. Mellor, *Romanticism and Feminism* (1988), and to the features of a work that may be traced to ethnic origins, such as those isolated and defined in *Romanticism and National Context* (1988), edited by Roy Porter and Mikuláš Teich, and *Romantic Revolutions* (1990), edited by Kenneth R. Johnston, Gilbert Chaitin, Karen Hanson, and Herbert Marks.

In recent years few books have appeared that exhibit the scope of the earlier work of Wellek, Furst, and de Man or the geographical and chronological breadth of the present collection. This is at least partly explained by a set of interlocking disciplinary, institutional, and social factors. Most prominent of these is the eclipse, by death and retirement, of the generation of émigré scholars, who had resurrected and reshaped comparative literature in the United States, and whose polycultural linguistic accomplishments it has proved difficult to restock with American-born scholars. Another significant cause may be the stunning success of theory: replacing the study of literary texts in original languages with courses in criticism not only has compensated for, but also may have abetted the decline of polylingualism. Ideological friction within the field, which has destroyed any consensus about disciplinary objectives, has exacerbated the threats to comparative literature arising from the larger crisis in the Academy: budget-slashing, the elimination of language requirements, the consolidation or outright cancellation of programs, and the collapse of the academic job market, which has been more drastic in comparative literature than in English. The shrinking presence of comparative literature has in turn encouraged rival departments to foster competing theory-oriented programs in cultural studies and literature in translation. At the same time, increasing concern for multiculturalism in the United States has led to the growth of interest in writers representing othernesses within the dominant culture rather than in mainstream European languages and literatures. Thus, the disciplinary raison d'être of comparative literature has become so eroded that the goods it offers on the intellectual marketplace are virtually indistinguishable from, and often considered less interesting than or inferior to, many others.

In response to the marginalization with which comparative literature is threatened, it seemed an appropriate time to publish a collection of new, previously unpublished critical essays by both established and younger writers that would reflect the continuing relevance of comparative approaches to Romanticism. Constituting a lively ecumenical dialogue between literary history and theory, and between critics based in comparative literature and national literature departments, the approaches represented here in various combinations include deconstruction, cultural studies, feminism, the history of ideas, intertextuality, literary history, and *Rezeptionsästhetik*. At a glance, the table of contents shows that the traditional chronological boundaries of Romanticism have been stretched slightly in order to embrace the diverse activity of writers, poets, and critics related through dialogue and appropriation, emulation and resistance, from the late eighteenth to the mid-nineteenth century. During this period interaction defined all cultural activity, whether it assumed the form of real or figurative pilgrimages, of imaginary or actual encounters between writers and their works. Just as European borders in the Romantic Age were fluid and permeable, cultural identity fostered through interaction was similarly elastic. To avoid the isolation of narrowly determined geographic and lingusitic identity, writers moved across cultural frontiers in search of stimulating and confidence-building cultural contacts. Contrary to the position taken by Porter and Teich, which is essentially a restatement of Lovejoy's position, that "different national Romanticisms coexisted in symbiotic relations to each other," the following essays suggest that national literary cultures in the Romantic Age did not simply "coexist" in "symbiotic relations," but drew their own specific identity from often multiple interactive relations with each other.[1] The catalytic forces of this process were not historical or ideological abstractions, such as the French Revolution or opposition to the Enlightenment, but concrete interactions with texts, places, and, in the case of Germaine de Staël and Rahel Varnhagen, living personalities. While not comprehensive in scope, the interactive cultural relations examined in the following essays—between Britain and Germany; Germany, Britain, and France;

Spain, France and Germany; France and Britain; France and Germany; Britain and America; and Denmark and Germany—are those in which some of the most interesting work is being done at the present time.

Essays by James Engell and Frederick Burwick have been placed together in the first of five sections, "Intertextual Interactions: Criticism and Poetry." Engell's "*Romantische Poesie*: Richard Hurd and Friedrich Schlegel" is an original study of intertextual dialogue between two literary and cultural traditions and the first systematic discussion of the connection between Hurd's writings and Schlegel's theory of "romantische Poesie" and the instrumental relationship "between English critical writing and the birth of German Romanticism." Comparing Hurd's *Letters on Chivalry and Romance* (1762) and "On the Idea of Universal Poetry" (1765) with Schlegel's influential "Athenäum-Fragment No. 116" and passages in *Gespräch über die Poesie* (1800), Engell demonstrates that any understanding of Schlegel or German Romanticism must include not only the contributions of Johann Gottfried Herder, Johann Wolfgang von Goethe, and Friedrich Schiller, but also the role played by Hurd and eighteenth-century British critics. In revealing the intertextual ligatures connecting Hurd and Schlegel, Engell reveals, for the first time, the source and inspiration for much of Schlegel's revolutionary critical agenda.

In "Romantic Madness: Hölderlin, Nerval, Clare" Frederick Burwick discusses three poets from different literary traditions whose collapse into mental illness is either prefigured or embedded in their work. Working from archival materials and employing a critical frame adapted from Shoshona Felman, Michel Foucault, and Jacques Derrida, Burwick presents Friedrich Hölderlin's "Patmos," Gérard de Nerval's "Christ on the Mount of Olives," and John Clare's "Child Harold" as "intriguing test cases for such a hermeneutic." Starting with Hölderlin, Burwick assesses the early, unprecedented efforts of the insane poet's contemporary, Achim von Arnim, to construct a hermeneutic based on the intertextual connections between Hölderlin's own poems. In parallel fashion, Burwick analyses Nerval's preoccupation, following his treatment at the clinic of Dr. Esprit Blanche, with classical myth and German Romanticism, and the means by which Clare "made 'Child Harold' the instrument of his own soul, the voice of his own troubled thought." Despite the daunting complexity of the interactions traced here, Burwick concludes that "poetry as poetry" in the work of Hölderlin, Nerval, and Clare is ultimately accessible, since it necessarily "escapes the solipsism of madness in the very act of communicating with other minds."

In section two, "Interactive Identities: Gender and the Novel," April Alliston and Roberta Johnson describe ways in which novels served as vehicles for the delineation of both feminine character and European national identity. Alliston argues in "Of Haunted Highlands: Mapping a Geography of Gender in the Margins of Europe" that "romantic national typecasting went alongside and in fact entailed the development of specific gender stereotypes that are still being invoked in the name of the nation." She asks why novels by women in three different countries all make Scotland the scene where a properly virtuous feminine character is staged as a spectacle of imprisonment, exile, and death; why narratives that literally traverse national boundaries consistently culminate there. In Sophie von La Roche's *Geschichte des Fräuleins von Sternheim*, Sophia Lee's *The Recess*, and Germaine de Staël's *Corinne* Scotland, like the ideal of domestic femininity, turns out to be a "state" of exile from national identity that is also contained within national boundaries, and secures them.

In "*La gaviota* and Romantic Irony" Roberta Johnson examines the struggle of displaced persons during the Carlist Wars, a period of extraordinary geographical and national fluidity in Spanish history. Her focus is on a novel by Cecilia Böhl von Faber, who wrote under the masculine pseudonymn Fernán Caballero. The offspring of a Spanish-Irish mother and a German father, Böhl was positioned between Spanish and German cultures, landscapes, and languages, and her novel, *La gaviota*, is similarly suspended between cultures, genres, and modes. Originally written in French for a Spanish audience, *La gaviota* occupies "that unclassifiable place between Romanticism and Realism, condemned to an eternal limbo of neither one nor the other." Until now critics have been unsure how properly to classify the novel, but Johnson suggestively links its structure and design to the influence of the author's interaction with the writings of the Schlegel brothers on romantic irony. By placing "the multigeneric context of *La gaviota* . . . within the sphere of romantic irony," we achieve a more complete understanding of *La gaviota* as the product of Böhl's interaction with the various national literary traditions that comprised her own cosmopolitan cultural identity.

In section three, "Institutional Interactions: *Salonières* and Schoolmasters," essays by Lilian R. Furst and John L. Mahoney examine the function of the literary *salon* and the private finishing school for girls as sites of cultural interaction. Furst's "The *Salons* of Germaine de Staël and Rahel Varnhagen" is the first comparative study of the two most prominent *salons* of the Romantic Age. Located in two such contrasting but immensely important cultural crossroads, cosmopolitan Berlin and Coppet in rustic Switzerland, the *salons* of Staël and Varnhagen differed not only as to their settings, but also in the social status of their habitués and in the social identity of their presiding spirits, a French aristocrat

and a member of the thoroughly assimilated German-Jewish bour-
geoisie. Despite the striking differences between these two *salons* and
their hostesses, Furst describes how each served as vehicles of "extreme,
quite unprecedented social heterogeneity, and became the seedbeds of
cultural interaction." Furst also identifies the particular contributions of
both *salons*: Coppet was the main source for the transmission of German
Romanticism to the French avant-garde at a time when the development
of French Romanticism was held in check by censorship and the
neoclassical bias associated with "official" revolutionary culture;
Varnhagen's Berlin *salon* was remarkable for its quiet transgression of
social codes through purely social interaction.

Drawing on archival research conducted at the Wordsworth Library
in Grasmere and in Boston-area archives, Mahoney's "The Rydal Mount
Ladies' Boarding School: A Wordsworthian Episode in America" relates
how the Rev. Henry K. Green and his wife, Sarah, served as agents of
cultural interaction between England and America in the mid-1840s.
Their short-lived educational experiment demonstrates how thoroughly
Wordsworthian precepts on human development had penetrated
American culture and, in this case, were appropriated for the instruction of middle-class schoolgirls in Charlestown, Massachusetts. In
Mahoney's discussion of Sarah Green's letters to William Wordsworth,
the reader sees how her "commitment to Wordsworthian principles" led
to an effort to apply a pedagogy based on thorough familiarity with
nature. The Greens' experience, which Mahoney traces in a meticulous
reconstruction of the available documentary evidence, suggests how
trans-Atlantic cultural interaction embraced contemporary social
history, church politics, and educational theory and praxis.

In section four, "Interactive Legacies: Rousseau and Staël in
England," essays by Annette Wheeler Cafarelli, "Rousseau and British
Romanticism: Women and the Legacy of Male Radicalism," and Kari
Lokke, "Sibylline Leaves: Mary Shelley's *Valperga* and the Legacy of
Corinne," examine the impact of French precursors—Jean-Jacques
Rousseau and Germaine de Staël—on the work of British women
novelists. As a corrective to the usual practice of emphasizing Rousseau's
influence on male writers, Cafarelli focusses on the female responses to
Rousseau's *La Nouvelle Héloïse* (1761) and *Émile, ou l'éducation* (1762). In
constructing a revisionist history of reception, she finds that the women
writers who were most opposed to Rousseau's influence in Britain were
not, as one might expect, conservatives aligned with Burke who opposed
the radical views generally associated with the French philosopher.
Instead, Rousseau's opponents among British women intellectuals were
radicals, like Mary Wollstonecraft, Mary Hays, and Catherine Macaulay,
who favored far-reaching social and political change. As Cafarelli

demonstrates, conservatives like Hannah More, Clara Reeve, and Sydney Owenson Morgan were actually more likely to appropriate Rousseau's prescriptions for women in their own work.

In her analysis of the intertextual and thematic correspondences of Staël's *Corinne* and Shelley's *Valperga*, Kari Lokke seeks to establish the instrumental relationship between Shelley and Staël and to assess their distinctive contributions to a "women's Romanticism" that corresponds to but also significantly differs from the variety of European Romanticism that has come to be associated with and nearly exclusively defined by the work of male writers. In contrast to Anne K. Mellor in *Romanticism and Gender* (1993), Lokke identifies the formative sources for this independent tradition in Shelley's interaction with Staël, a female writer working in a foreign tradition. Shelley's awareness of the necessity to establish a distinct and separate literary tradition for women is revealed in her efforts to bring "into focus Staël's role as an originary figure in the history of Western women's self-definition of poetic identity." Staël's *Corinne* is recognized as the foundation text on which Shelley builds her own literary independence, and *Valperga* reflects this search for literary predecessors.

The three essays in section five, "Ideological Interactions: Precursors and Epigones," trace the mediation of religious and aesthetic elements in the construction of romantic sensibility in Germany, Britain, and Denmark. David C. Hensley, in "Richardson, Rousseau, Kant: 'Mystics of Taste and Sentiment' and the Critical Philosophy," challenges the traditional understanding of *Clarissa*'s impact on the formation of German Romanticism. Hensley points out that in uncritically echoing the nineteenth-century perception of this process, which was overly dependent on Samuel Taylor Coleridge's well-known formulation in *Biographia Literaria*, twentieth-century scholarship has failed to notice Samuel Richardson's contribution to the "basic assumptions, preoccupations, attitudes, and patterns of thought and expression that define either British or German Romanticism." By tracing Richardson's spiritual and literary influence on the development of modern subjectivity, Hensley seeks to correct this error. He identifies the specific formal and ideological conditions in which Richardson's religious position was secularized and sent forth a myriad of influences in German as well as British culture. Hensley's analysis focuses on Immanuel Kant's reading of Richardson and Jean-Jacques Rousseau, which calls "attention to questions of historical mediation that still need to be explored and theorized before Coleridge's claim that *Clarissa* shaped German Romanticism can be turned into a basis for appropriately wide-ranging and detailed work in literary and cultural history."

Similarly revisionist in spirit, my essay, "Reviewing Kant's Early Reception in Britain: The Leading Role of Henry Crabb Robinson," examines the critiques of Kant that were published by several leading romantic writers. While my reading of Kant's critics includes a reevaluation of William Taylor, William Hazlitt, and Thomas De Quincey, my focus is on Robinson, whose writings on Kant predate the work of his more famous contemporaries. Robinson's views command our interest because he was genuinely qualified for his self-appointed task: besides speaking excellent German, he had studied with F. W. J. Schelling and had befriended other leading German cultural figures, including Johann Wolfgang von Goethe, August Wilhelm Schlegel, Clemens and Christian Brentano, and Carl August Böttiger, who considered Robinson a welcome addition to their circles. Robinson's "Letters on the Philosophy of Kant," which form the basis for my discussion, are a by-product of his early and intense interaction with German culture and embody the first British critique that is in broad sympathy with the project of transcendental idealism.

One of the most widely admired continental philosophers in the English-speaking world, Søren Kierkegaard may be truly appreciated only when placed in the context of late German Romanticism. In "Confessions of an Anti-Poet: Kierkegaard's *Either/Or* and the German Romantics," Marc Katz describes the literary and psychological dimensions of Kierkegaard's self-consciously epigonic relationship to Berlin and its writers during a sojourn there in 1841. Although Kierkegaard seems to embrace German Romanticism, his geographical and cultural immersion in German culture takes place at a moment in history when such an immersion in Romanticism was only possible as a deceptive figuration. *Either/Or* therefore represents the author's effort "to purge himself of the hermeticism of German theory, only this time on German soil," using all the conventions of German Romanticism to accomplish this exorcism. In Katz's essay, Kierkegaard is shown to have followed "through on the critical premises of two generations of German romantic fiction with a detachment and abandon beyond the reach of the most alienated of contemporary native writers."

"The reevaluation of Romanticism," Geoffrey Hartman has observed, "is a special feature of post-New Critical or revisionist criticism in America."[2] Whether affiliated with comparative literature or national literature departments, the contributors to this volume offer abundant proof that this process continues unabated. Their analyses of intercultural relations cut across national and linguistic boundaries, striking a blow against the tendency of literary studies to ossify into arbitrary enthnocentric categories. By promoting disciplinary dialogue, they defend difference against the imposition of static monolingual identities. The interactions examined in the ensuing essays suggest that Romanticism as a broad category of culture-creating activity from 1750 to 1850 is inseparable from international dialogue and appropriation.

NOTES

1. Roy Porter and Mikuláš Teich, ed., *Romanticism in National Context* (Cambridge: Cambridge University Press, 1988), p. 2.

2. Geoffrey H. Hartman, *Criticism in the Wilderness* (New Haven: Yale University Press, 1980), p. 44.

I

Intertextual Interactions

Criticism and Poetry

1

James Engell

Romantische Poesie

Richard Hurd and
Friedrich Schlegel

This essay presents and explores a profound relationship between Richard Hurd and Friedrich Schlegel, one essential to understanding Schlegel's theory of *romantische Poesie* and one essential to grasping the bond, recognized explicitly by Schlegel himself, between English critical writing and the birth of German Romanticism.

The only previous clue of this possibility, other than in Schlegel's own writings, is lodged in Raimund Belgardt's 1969 study, where, however, a footnote simply cites the connection between Richard Hurd, Bishop Percy, Thomas Warton, and Johann Gottfried Herder, rather than directly between Schlegel and any of the three English critics.[1] Belgardt notes that Herder lists this trio of Englishmen as sources for his 1778 *Preisschrift* "Über die Wirkung der Dichtkunst auf die Sitten der Völker in alten und neuen Zeiten" [Concerning the Impact of Poetry on National Customs in Antiquity and Recent Times]. Aside from quoting Herder's summary citation (Herder actually quotes and cites Hurd a number of times throughout his collected works), Belgardt does not follow the lead with regard either to Herder or Schlegel, who, of course, read Herder and drew part of his critical foundation from him.

Except for a juxtaposed reference to Hurd, Schlegel, and "romantische Poesie" in Herbert Mainusch's *Romantische Ästhetik* (1969), no link of Hurd to Schlegel has been posited or suggested—except, again, in Schlegel's own criticism. This is not so surprising, since no critic or scholar of Schlegel has evinced any direct or detailed knowledge of Hurd; and no scholar of Hurd—an endangered species, with Hoyt Trowbridge and one recent German study by Dieter A. Berger fending off extinction—has ever indicated interest in Hurd's connection with any German writer.[2]

But Hurd—and to a lesser extent, Warton and Percy—are instrumental to the development of German Romanticism. The relationship of two of Hurd's treatises to Schlegel's idea of *romantische Poesie* is deep, direct, and in ways as important, if not more so, than Schlegel's relationship to the critical writings of Friedrich Schiller and Herder, or to the philosophy of Johann Gottlieb Fichte. The two works of Hurd are "On the Idea of Universal Poetry" (1765) and *Letters on Chivalry and Romance* (1762).

A main point of Schlegel's theory is that *romantische Poesie* is confined to neither poetry (verse) or prose but comprehends and mixes the two and is related to the *Roman*. In his then well-known *Letters on Chivalry and Romance*, Hurd advances the claim that the romantic or Gothic literature he discusses is written in either prose or verse. So does Thomas Warton, in his dissertation "Of the Origin of Romantic Fiction in Europe," prefixed to his 1774 *History of English Literature*. A. O. Lovejoy separated Schlegel's use of *Roman* and *romantisch*, but Hans Eichner has shown how, for Schlegel, the two are used together and both described as *romantische*. This is precisely Hurd's point in discussing the "old romances," whatever genre or form they take.

From Schlegel's "Athenäum Fragment No. 116," we have the familiar statement: "Romantic poetry is a progressive, universal poetry. Its aim isn't merely to reunite all the separate species of poetry and put poetry in touch with philosophy and rhetoric. It tries to and should mix and fuse poetry and prose . . . the poetry of art and the poetry of nature. . . . It embraces everything that is purely poetic, from the greatest systems of art, containing within themselves still further systems, to the sigh, the kiss that the poetizing child breathes forth in artless song."[3]

In his essay "On the Idea of Universal Poetry" (1765), Hurd insists on much the same qualities in what he calls "universal poetry" or "poesie." As he notes about the quality of the poet's mind, "When the received system of manners or religion in any country, happens to be so constituted as to suit itself in some degree to this extravagant turn of the human mind, we may expect that poetry will seize it with avidity, will dilate upon it with pleasure, and take a pride to erect its specious wonders on so proper and convenient a ground." The "true poet," attracted in turn to "*pagan fable,* and *Gothic romance,*" will "ever adventure, in some sort, to supply their place with others of his own invention; that is, he will mould every system, and convert every subject, into the most amazing and miraculous form." Universal poetry "assembles, combines, or connects its ideas, at pleasure." It is progressive in that poetry first flatters our "restless and aspiring disposition," a striving anchored not in nature but "in the mind of man." Universal poetry is for Hurd always becoming, "restless and aspiring," and its power is located in a progressive—could we say transcendental?—power of the mind. It prefers "the agreeable, and the graceful, but, as occasion calls upon her, the vast, the incredible, I had almost said, the impossible, to the obvious truth and nature of things."[4]

In *Letters on Chivalry and Romance,* Hurd asks, "may there not be something in the Gothic Romance peculiarly suited to the views of a genius, and to the ends of poetry?"[5] In the *Works* of 1811, Hurd approvingly adds a passage quoted from a correspondent who read the first edition; that correspondent speaks of "the Romancers, whether in prose or verse."[6] Hurd in 1762 states that the "circumstances" in these fictions and manners uniquely "are proper to the ends of poetry," that is, they above all belong to the ends of poetry, they most truly characterize all poetry.[7] Here we have the true nature of all poetry, the poetry of poetry, whether in verse or prose, for Hurd speaks of verse, fairy tales, and old stories alike. In Schlegel's words, "The romantic kind of poetry is the only one that is more than a kind, that is, as it were, poetry itself: for in a certain sense all poetry is or should be romantic."[8]

Hurd takes a cue from Francis Bacon, that poetry is not strictly mimetic, but as "Lord Bacon should speak of *poesy as a part of learning,*" Bacon also says "that the essence of poetry consisted *in submitting the shews of things to the desires of the mind.*" And that "these *shews of things* could only be exhibited to the mind through the *medium of words.*" Here is recognition that the source of poetry resides in the interplay of the external world with the individual mind, and in putting to constant test "the shews of things" by submitting them "to the desires of the mind."[9] This bears on what Schlegel says: "It alone can become, like the epic, a mirror of the whole circumambient world, an image of the age. And it can also—more than any other form—hover at the midpoint between the portrayed and the portrayer, free of all real and ideal self-interest, on the wings of poetic reflection, and can raise that reflection again and again to a higher power, can multiply it in an endless succession."[10] For Hurd, this interface of the world and the mind is where poetic activity takes place endlessly also, and, borrowing Bacon's words, he describes it as "*submitting the shews of things to the desires of the mind . . .* through its power, or faculty of *imagination.*"[11]

Herder and, after him, Schlegel clearly note the historical origin of *romantische Poesie*; for Schlegel it comes from the age of adventures, from knights, the age of chivalry, from fairy tales; for Herder, it is characterized by adventures. As Herder states about the *Roman*: "the novel is defined by adventure and it is a combination of the most wonderful ingredients."[12] For Schlegel, "the source of the romantic is found among the moderns, in the writings of William Shakespeare, Miguel de

Cervantes, in Italian poetry, in the age of knights, of love and fairy tales. This is the origin of the concept and the term 'romantic' itself."[13]

These are familiar words about *romantische Poesie*. The following are less so, but equally explicit, though more than thirty years earlier: "What," asks Hurd, at the start of the *Letters*, "is more remarkable than the Gothic CHIVALRY? or than the spirit of ROMANCE, which took its rise from that singular institution?" Moreover, Hurd, like Schlegel later, identifies the historical origin as the older moderns, and that while chivalry as a practice itself faded, the spirit of romance lasted. "The spirit of Chivalry, was a fire which soon spent itself: But that of *Romance*, which was kindled at it, burnt long, and continued its light and heat even to the politer ages." The sense of historical origin and continuation are the same in Hurd and Schlegel. As Hurd says, "Don't you begin to favour this conjecture, as whimsical as it may seem, of *the rise and genius* of knight-errantry?"[14] "This . . . *feudal* service soon introduced," Hurd expands in his later edition, "what may be truly called *romantic*, the *going in quest of adventures*."[15]

What about fairy tales, as Schlegel claims? Consciously drawing on Dryden's notion of "*the Faery way of writing*," an important critical term revived and handed down by Joseph Addison, whom Hurd quotes, Hurd draws an explicit equation: "For *Faery Court* means the *reign of Chivalry*" and hence the source of the fictions in question. In fact, Hurd openly speaks of Edmund Spenser's "*Faery tales*," not perhaps the usage of "fairy tale" uppermost in our minds today, but the one we should keep in view when dealing with Hurd's and Schlegel's claim that romantic fictions or *romantische Poesie* originate in fairy tales from the age of chivalry.[16]

Hans Eichner, in his article on Schlegel's *romantische Poesie*, concentrates on three qualities that Schlegel, in his *Notebooks*, records as essential to that type of writing. It must be *fantastisch, sentimental*, and *mimisch*—that is, fantastical, sentimental with the theme of love, and yet—for all its fantasticalness—with something of the mimetic mixed in as well, some basis in truth or reality. It is these three qualities—the fantastic, the sentimental or love, and the mimetic—that are explicitly identified and repeatedly underscored by Hurd in his study of the romantic fictions.

Eichner states that probably in the fall of 1797 Schlegel's latest thinking about the romantic means a "new classification," which "implies therefore that the *Roman* should be *fantastisch, sentimental* and *mimisch*," and that Schlegel applied this tripartite formula not only to the *Roman* but also to romantic poetry and the ideal of all poetry. Eichner elucidates these three qualities, noting that at one point, "In the 'Brief über den Roman' [Letter on the Novel], Schlegel suggests that romantic poetry 'ruht ganz auf historischem Grunde'"; so, as

Eichner says, a work that is romantic would then "reflect real life to a certain extent."[17] But all three qualities—*fantastisch, sentimental, mimisch*—are to be co-present. Since his *Studiumaufsatz*, Schlegel recognized the *fantastisch* as a feature of postclassical poetry; and in the *Gespräch über die Poesie* [*Dialogue on Poetry*], he asks, "What then is the sentimental? That while it is dominated by feeling, it is not in fact a sensual, but a spiritual feeling that characterizes the sentimental. The source and soul of all of this stimulation is love, and the spirit of love must hover over romantic poetry in such a manner that it is invisibly visible."[18]

Putting aside for the moment that Schiller is a strong presence for Schlegel when it comes to the sentimental, what is the case for Hurd's *Letters on Chivalry and Romance*? The same triple characterization emerges. The passages that could be cited are numerous, so I select a sample. At the beginning of the *Letters*, speaking of the age of chivalry and its spirit of romance, Hurd addresses their fantastic yet also their mimetic qualities and says, "The modes and fashions of different times may appear, at first sight, fantastic and unaccountable. But they, who look nearly into them, discover some latent cause of their production." Part of Hurd's purpose is to show that however fantastic the romances seem, they are not fully so. At one time, he claims, the world was "familiarized to this Prodigy, which we now start at." He speaks of "all the excesses of military fanaticism, which are painted so strongly, but scarcely exaggerated in the old Romances." And so Spenser, argues Hurd, considers ways to seek the mimetic, that is "to give an air of probability to his *Faery tales*." The romancers "think it enough if they can but bring you to imagine the possibility of them."[19] Hurd in a later edition warns those skeptics who would not see and balance the mimetic with the fantastical by saying, "the *extravagance* of these fictions . . . is frequently, I believe, much less than these laughers apprehend." After a specific example, he then states, "But if the profane will not be kept within this decent reserve, we may give them to understand, that this fancy, as wild as it appears, had some foundation in *truth*."[20] These statements emphasize claims made in the first edition of 1762.

For the category of the sentimental, Hurd provides ample emphasis also. At one level he traces "The free commerce of the ladies," and says, "We are even told, that *the love of God and of the ladies* went hand in hand, in the duties and ritual of Chivalry"; or, more specifically, while the classical writings keep alive the "boisterous passions," the romantic does not ignore those, but "together with these, the gentler and more humane affections are awakened in us by the most interesting displays of love and friendship; of love, elevated to its noblest heights."[21] This mixing of all passions with its ultimate emphasis on the gentler sentiments and on love that is elevated to its noblest—love that is spiritual and not sensual—says Hurd, gives the romantic "a vast advantage" over the classical. The romantic poet seeks generosity and gallantry. The knight is devoted to the other sex far more than was the classical hero.[22] Romantic fictions, he notes in a letter inserted in a later edition, display "the courtesy of elegant love, but of a wild and fanatic species."[23]

Hurd's parallels with Schlegel's *fantastisch, sentimental,* and *mimisch* are evident—they saturate the *Letters*—and, without stretching a point, clearly anticipate these salient features of *romantische Poesie.*

Schlegel considers William Shakespeare the true center and kernel of the romantic imagination.[24] Herder had already identified Shakespeare as the great postclassical writer whose plays themselves are *Romane.* Eichner carries out this focus on Shakespeare from Herder through Schlegel, connecting it with the "tendency" of Shakespeare toward *romantische Poesie,* even though he wrote plays. Eichner speaks in this context of such Shakespearean art being open to the "divinatory criticism" of which Schlegel speaks in "Athenäum Fragment No. 116": "It can be exhausted by no theory and only a divinatory criticism would dare try to characterize its ideal."[25]

Hurd sees Shakespeare—even though he wrote plays, not old romances as such—as the greatest example of romance and romantic poetry. In "On the Idea of Universal Poetry," Hurd quotes the lines from *A Midsummer Nights Dream* to characterize "the magic virtue of poetry."[26]

> The poet's eye, in a fine frenzy rolling,
> Doth glance from heaven to earth, from earth to heaven;
> And, as imagination bodies forth
> The forms of things unknown, the poet's pen
> Turns them to shapes, and gives to airy nothing
> A local habitation and a name.
>   (Act V, Scene I, ll. 12–17.)

And of this kind of poetry, requiring for Schlegel a "divinatory criticism," Hurd closes one of his *Letters* this way: "I say nothing of Shakespeare, because the sublimity (the divinity, let it be, if nothing else will serve) of his genius kept no certain rout." Hurd laments at the end of his book that *"Earth-born* critics" blaspheme the charmed spirit of fairy Spenser, but that the gods are "ravish'd with delight."[27]

There is something more unusual and specific in Schlegel's and Hurd's assessment of Shakespeare. In Schlegel's emphasis on *romantische Poesie* as a *mischgedicht,* as a type of poetry that mixes genres and modes, he sees Shakespeare as a prime example. Shakespeare mixes, melds, and fuses all. As Eichner points out, for Schlegel, the plays of Shakespeare

are for this reason "*romantisch* rather than *dramatisch.*" From Schlegel's *Notebooks*: "Shakespeare's tragedies are synthesized from classical tragedy and the novel." And: "In Shakespeare everything is synthesized romantically; we can discern no definite tendency apart from this."[28]

Now, according to Hurd, "Shakespeare . . . kept no certain rout, but rambled at hazard into all the regions of human life and manners. So that we can hardly say what he preferred, or what he rejected, on full deliberation. Yet, one thing is clear, that even he is greater when he uses Gothic manners and machinery, than when he employs classical."[29] "But, if you require a comparison," adds Hurd after the first edition, "I can tell you where it is to be made, with much ease, and to great advantage. I mean, in Shakespeare's *Macbeth*, where you will find (as his best critic observes [William Warburton?]) 'the *Danish* or *Northern*, intermixed with the *Greek* and *Roman* enchantments; and all these worked up together with a sufficient quantity of our own country's superstitions . . . where the ingredients are gathered from every thing shocking in the *natural* world; as here, from every thing absurd in the *moral.*'" The Gothic or romantic "system" is for Hurd a mixed "aggregate" and not a "single system."[30] So, for Schlegel, "One of the essential functions of the novel is the synthesis and interweaving of heterogenous components, including the combination of all mythologies. Only in the novel can an obsolete or antiquated mythology receive adequate treatment. Also, the synthesis or connection of several mythologies is possible only in the novel."[31]

We can recall that *romantische Poesie*, as a progressive universal poetry that has not yet achieved its end, mixes and unifies all kinds of genres.[32] And, not dissimilarly for Hurd, in discussing his ideal of universal poetry, while recognizing that kinds of literature do exist, he states, "We may, indeed, mix and confound them, if we will (for there is a sort of literary luxury, which would engross all pleasures at once, even such as are contradictory to each other)."[33] Throughout their respective discussions, Hurd and then Schlegel use the same terms—*Poesie*/poesie or poetry; *Geist*/spirit; *Genius*/genius—to describe the universalizing spirit of genius that effects the romantic mandate of mixing and fusing all materials and kinds of writing.

Both Hurd and Schlegel differentiate how an author represents wonders in romantic fiction and how an author represents them on the romantic stage; that is, Hurd and Schlegel both contrast romantic narrative and romantic drama: "The drama should also be romantic, like all poesie; but a novel is such, except under certain restrictions."[34] Now, Hurd previously makes a similar distinction, where "That, which passes in *representation* [on the stage], and challenges, as it were, the scrutiny of the eye, must be truth itself, or something very nearly approaching to it. But what passes in *narration*, even on the stage, is admitted without much difficulty." That is, as long as you tell about something in the drama, it can be as fantastical as anything in narrative, but if you act it out on the stage, restrictions apply. The dramatic mode is more circumscribed, while the pure narrator can enlarge "his impostures at pleasure, in proportion to the easiness and comprehension" of the imagination.[35]

Schlegel posits a difference between the classical and the romantic, but sees the *romantische* in the classical. *Romantische poesie* is an element of all poetry, it is "the poetry of poetry." Hurd could not be clearer in this conviction, too. For Schlegel, "The romantic poetic genre is the only one that is more than a genre or category, that is, as it were, poetry itself: for in a certain sense all poetry is or should be romantic." It is "Poesie der Poesie."[36] Or, in the *Gespräch über die Poesie*, "only with this difference, that the romantic is both a genre and an element of poesie, which is alternately strongly present or recedes into the background, but is never completely absent."[37] Later, in the *Geschichte der alten und neuen Literatur* [*The History of Ancient and Modern Literature*], Schlegel makes a similar statement and cites a specific case: "Indeed the romantic is not in conflict with antiquity in its most authentic form. The legend of Troy and the Homeric songs are thoroughly romantic."[38] Schlegel is extrapolating Herder's statement, "Homers Gedichte selbst sind Romane in ihrer Art" [Homer's poems are themselves novels in their way].[39]

For Hurd, the same is true, as he explains at length, with some help from a treatise in the *Memoirs of the Academy of Inscriptions and Belles Lettres* (vol. 20). First, he notes, "That there is a remarkable correspondency between the manners of the old heroic times, as painted by their great romancer, Homer, and those which are represented to us in books of modern knight-errantry." Hurd says, "the resemblance between the heroic and Gothic ages is very great."[40] In the collected works he adds, "so great it did not escape the old Romancers themselves, with whom, as an ingenious critic observes, *the siege of* THEBES *and* TROJAN *war were favourite stories; the characters and incidents of which they were mixing perpetually with their Romances.*"[41] But, like Schlegel, from the first he has no doubt about which mode, the ancient or the romantic, is superior and found everywhere: Spenser affords Hurd "the point, I principally insist upon, I mean, *The preeminence of the Gothic manners and fictions, as adopted to the ends of poetry, above the classic.*"[42]

Schlegel distinguishes the *Romantische* from the *Moderne* as well as from the classical or ancient: "However, I implore you not to assume that the romantic and the modern are identical."[43] Hurd, too, distinguishes the romantic not only from the classical, as we have seen, but from the "modern." Several places in the *Letters* he alludes to the current spirit of the "modern." Hurd objects to "the philosophic moderns" who may "have gone too far, in their perpetual ridicule and contempt" of the Gothic and romantic fictions. He identifies the "fastidious modern" as one too bound by a sense of definite reality and verisimilitude.[44]

Another way to see that Schlegel and Hurd share views here is to recall their attitude toward the contemporary novel exemplified by Samuel Richardson and others. For Schlegel, this kind of novel centers on *Wirklichkeit* (reality) and what is *alltäglich* (ordinary).[45] As Eichner notes, Schlegel speaks of this kind of novel with a certain irony and lack of full-blooded enthusiasm: "The prose narratives in the manner of the English novelists—'der Roman . . . , insofern er eine besondre Gattung seyn will' [the novel . . . , insofar as it is a special genre] or 'die sogenannten Romane' [the so-called novels] of Richardson and his imitators—are but minor and undesirable variants."[46] In "On the Ideal of Universal Poetry," Hurd asks, "what are we to think of those *novels* or *romances,* as they are called, that is, fables constructed on some private and familiar subject?" Hurd speaks of some of these novels as appealing to a "sickly imagination," "a sure prognostic of expiring Letters."[47] There are other passing but interesting similarities on topics of mutual interest to Hurd and Schlegel: on gardening in the romantic style, and on Spanish romances.[48]

What are the specific authors and examples of *romantische Poesie,* aside from Shakespeare, that both Hurd and Schlegel are fond of citing? Camillo Guarini, Cervantes, Ludovico Ariosto, Torquato Tasso, Spanish romances and, above all, the Italian poets, especially the ones mentioned here, and *Gerusalemme liberata.*[49] Hurd's greatest example, however, is Spenser. We do not find Spenser mentioned by Schlegel until we look ahead to the *Geschichte der alten und neuen Literatur* in the early nineteenth century. There Schlegel praises the *Faerie Queene*—as "*lyrisch*" (lyrical) and "*idyllisch*" (idyllic)—in terms almost precisely those of Hurd's, down to the remark that Spenser's poem, otherwise so excellent, contains a flaw in design.[50] We can also observe that Hurd sees an affinity between the romantic tendencies of Britain and of Germany. He says that feudal institutions spread to these two areas at the same time; and that the refined gallantry of romantic fiction was "laid in the ancient manners of the German nations."[51] For Schlegel, the connection is stronger yet. In his *Geschichte der alten und neuen Literatur,* he says about Hurd's favorite poet, "Spenser is, as far as his use of the language goes, the most German or Germanic of all English poets." And, for Hurd's other great examplar, "Shakespeare's poetry is more closely related to the German spirit than the work of any other foreigner, so much so that he will be accepted by the Germans just like a poet writing in their native tongue."[52]

Many elements of Friedrich Schlegel's famous theory of *romantische Poesie*—as well as many of its specific exemplifications and characteristics—Richard Hurd states some thirty years earlier in *Letters on Chivalry and Romance* and in his essay "On the Idea of Universal Poetry." Did Schlegel find any of them there? Three specific things indicate Schlegel's knowledge and valuation of Hurd.

First, Herder cites Hurd explicity, as we have noted, and Schlegel read Herder's citation, which also includes Warton and Percy. Hurd's work is chronologically first.

Second, during years vital for the evolution of his theory of *romantische Poesie*, 1795–1797, Schlegel actually quotes Hurd in his *Über das Studium der griechischen Poesie* [On the Study of Greek Poetry].[53] Here he disagrees with Hurd, but the disagreement is itself instructive. What he quotes from Hurd's work on the ancient Greek poets is this: "The ancients were masters of composition; it is therefore the case that in their writings we find this quality developed to the highest degree." To this direct quotation from Hurd, Schlegel adds, "Nothing less! The Greek taste was already completely decadent, even as the theory was in its infancy."[54] The quoted material is, incidentally, not dissimilar to Hurd's comment in the *Letters on Chivalry and Romance* about "the ablest writers of *Greece*," that their works were "master-pieces of composition" (104). But here, Schlegel, still in his classical period, cannot agree and in fact violently disagrees. What are we to make of this? Oskar Walzel shrewdly remarks that soon after this point in Schlegel's career, his "mania for objectivity vanished immediately and, after the publication of his treatise *Über das Studium der griechischen Poesie*, he joined at once and unreservedly the ranks of . . . the Romanticists." Walzel continues to explain: "The bitter words which Friedrich Schlegel heaped upon the moderns in his study grew merely out of disguised affection. He treated them so badly because spiritually they were so close to him."[55] And so, too, with this violent spat with Hurd— it comes out of Schlegel's disguised affection, which he later articulates, as we shall now examine.

Third, in 1812 (published in 1814), in his *Geschichte der alten und neuen Literatur*, Schlegel specifically cites a short list of the criticism of the English, and a few of their writings on poetry, "Die Kritik der Engländer und einige ihrer Schriften über Poesie," the influence of which on German literature has been singularly strong and positive: "Actually, only under the influence of English critics such as James Harris, Hurd, and Warton did German critics themselves develop in a thoroughly independent direction, more perhaps than any other branch of our literature." These critics, says Schlegel, were more learned and acute than the French, and thus the English critics, "entsprachen daher dem deutschen Geiste mehr" [correspond more closely to the German mind].[56] Perhaps Schlegel first ran across Hurd through Herder's citation; at any rate, he later quotes Hurd's work and lists him as one of a select few English critics exerting unprecedented impact on the development of German literature.

We could interject that ideas of romance and chivalry became common enough. But Hurd, however descriptive rather than theoretical his work, remains a first and major impetus for those ideas in German and European literature and literary criticism. With regard to *romantische Poesie*, the confluence of qualities and examples—and the direct correspondences—between Hurd and Schlegel are unmatched by other English or German critics. Furthermore, the idea of universal poetry or *Universalpoesie*—and the existence of that particular term, probably by analogy with universal history—was not common in English or German criticism. It was rare and, as far as I can tell, Hurd presents it first.

Any mention or invocation of Schlegel's theory of *romantische Poesie* should now recognize the importance of Hurd, whose work provides an original and recurring touchstone. Any grasp of Schlegel or of German Romanticism may reach out to include not only the role played by Herder and of course Schiller, but also the role played by Hurd and the English critics. Comparative studies involving Schlegel's *romantische Poesie* should embrace this connection. It is part of a larger comparative map of English criticism and German Romanticism, a map whose intricate territories remain relatively uncharted by Germanists and virtual *terra incognita* for readers of English literature who, if acquainted with German developments, consider Warton, Percy, and especially—and ironically—Hurd to be minor or merely antiquarian. Fritz Strich, in his *Deutsche Klassik und Romantik*, makes this keen remark: "In England the German Romantics found an entirely different situation. In this Germanic nation the first romantic feeling for nature and a romantic affinity for the historical past were first felt in Europe, and this was not without influence over the origin of German Romanticism."[57]

What did Schlegel think of the English? His verdict is clear: "In the eighteenth century the English surpassed all other Europeans and were the dominant nation in the literary world." The French story, he says, points to other issues, so that "Germany, by contrast, received the first intimation of the new literary movement in the middle of the eighteenth century through contact with English poetry and criticism."[58] In this regard, Richard Hurd, as Friedrich Schlegel himself recognizes and acknowledges, is of primary importance.

NOTES

Unless otherwise indicated, all translations are by Gregory Maertz.

1. Raimund Belgardt, *Romantische Poesie: Begriff und Bedeutung bei Friedrich Schlegel* (The Hague and Paris: Mouton, 1969), p. 39n.

2. Dieter A. Berger, *Imitationstheorie und Gattungsdenken in der Literaturkritik Richard Hurds* (Frankfurt: Athenäum Verlag, 1972).

3. Friedrich Schlegel, "Athenäum Fragment No. 116," *Kritische Ausgabe*, II: 182–83: "Die romantische Poesie is eine progressive Universalpoesie. Ihre Bestimmung ist nicht bloß, alle getrennte Gattungen der Poesie wieder zu vereinigen, und die Poesie mit der Philosophie und Rhetorik in Berührung zu setzen. Sie will, und soll auch Poesie und Prosa . . . Kunstpoesie und Naturpoesie bald mischen, bald verschmelzen. . . . Sie umfaßt alles, was nur poetisch ist, von größten wieder mehrere Systeme in sich entfaltenden Systeme der Kunst, bis zu dem Seufzer, dem Kuß, den das dichtende Kind aushaucht in kunstlosen Gesang." English translation: Friedrich Schlegel, *Philosophical Fragments*, translated by Peter Firchow (Minneapolis: University of Minnesota Press, 1991), p. 31.

4. Richard Hurd, "On the Idea of Universal Poetry," *The Works of Richard Hurd, D. D.*, 8 vols. (London: T. Cadell and W. Davies, 1811), I: 10, 9, 8.

5. Richard Hurd, *Letters on Chivalry and Romance* (London and Cambridge: A. Millar and W. Thurlbourn and J. Woodyer, 1762), p. 4.

6. Hurd, *The Works of Richard Hurd*, 1811, IV: 259. Cited hereafter as 1811.

7. Hurd, *Letters on Chivalry and Romance*, p. 5.

8. Schlegel, "Athenäum Fragment No. 116": "Die romantische Dichtart ist die einzige, die mehr als Art, und gleichsam die Dichtkunst selbst ist: denn in einem gewissen Sinn ist oder soll alle Poesie romantisch sein." Translation by Firchow, *Philosophical Fragments*, p. 32.

9. Hurd, "On the Idea of Universal Poetry," p. 17.

10. Schlegel, "Athenäum Fragment No. 116": "Nur sie kann gleich dem Epos ein Spiegel der ganzen umgebenden Welt, ein Bild des Zeitalters werden. Und doch kann auch sie am meisten zwischen dem Dargestellten und dem Darstellenden, frei von allem realen und idealen Interesse auf den Flügeln der poetischen Reflexion in der Mitte schweben, diese Reflexion immer wieder potenzieren und wie in einer endlosen Reihe von Spiegeln vervielfachen." Translation by Firchow, *Philosophical Fragments*, p. 32.

11. Hurd, "On the Idea of Universal Poetry," p. 17.

12. Quoted by Hans Eichner, "Schlegel's Theory of Romantic Poetry," *PMLA* 71, 5 (December 1956): 1020. From Johann Gottfried Herder, *Sämtliche Werke*, edited by B. Suphan, 18, 59f: "Er heißt *Abentheuer, Roman*; ein Inbegriff des wunderbarsten, vermischtesten Stoffs . . ."

13. Friedrich Schlegel, *Gespräch über die Poesie, Kritische Ausgabe*, II: 335: "Da suche und finde ich das Romantische, bei den alten Modernen, bei Shakespeare, Cervantes, in der italiänische Poesie, in jenem Zeitalter der Ritter, der Liebe und der Märchen, aus welchem die Sache und das Wort selbst herstammt."

14. Hurd, *Letters on Chivalry and Romance*, pp. 3–4, 23.

15. Hurd, *The Works of Richard Hurd*, 1811, IV: 246.

16. Hurd, *Letters on Chivalry and Romance*, pp. 91, 17, 31.

17. Hans Eichner, "Schlegel's Theory of Romantic Poetry," 1024, 1025n, 1034.

18. Quoted in Eichner, 1025: "Was ist denn nun dieses Sentimentale? Das was uns anspricht, wo das Gefühl herrscht, und zwar nicht ein sinnliches, sondern das geistige. Die Quelle und Seele aller dieser Regungen ist die Liebe, und der Geist der Liebe muß in der romantischen Poesie überall unsichtbar sichtbar schweben."

19. Hurd, *Letters on Chivalry and Romance*, pp. 2, 3, 12, 31, 89.

20. Hurd, *The Works of Richard Hurd*, 1811, IV: 317, 320.

21. Hurd, *Letters on Chivalry and Romance*, pp. 17, 19, 47.

22. Ibid., pp. 47, 22–23, 40.

23. Hurd, *The Works of Richard Hurd*, 1811, IV: 256.

24. Schlegel, *Gesprach über die Poesie, Kritische Ausgabe*, II: 335: " . . . und erinnern sich dann an Shakespeare, in den ich das eigentliche Zentrum, den Kern der romantische Fantasie setzen möchte."

25. Quoted in Eichner, 1020: "Sie kann durch keine Theorie erschöpft werden, und nur eine divinatorische Kritik dürfte es wagen, ihr Ideal charakterisieren zu wollen." Translation by Firchow, *Philosophical Fragments*, p. 32.

26. Hurd, "On the Idea of Universal Poetry," pp. 9–10. There may be a connection here, too, with Schlegel's *Magie*; in the *Letters on Chivalry and Romance* Hurd says, "Shakspear [*sic*] . . . gives us another idea of the *rough magic*, as he calls it, of fairy enchantment" (50).

27. Hurd, *Letters on Chivalry and Romance*, pp. 60, 120. For a thorough discussion of *Magie*, of the religious implications of Schlegel's theory of *Universalpoesie*, and its intimate ties with German idealism, see Ernst Behler, "Friedrich Schlegels Theorie der Universalpoesie," in *Jahrbuch der Deutschen Schillergesellschaft*, edited by Fritz Martini, Herbert Stubenrauch, and Bernhard Zeller (Stuttgart: Alfred Kroner Verlag, 1957), pp. 211–52.

28. Quoted in Eichner, 1030: "Shakespeares Trauerspiele sind gemischt aus der classischen Tragödie und dem Roman." And "Im Shakespeare ist *alles* Romantische gemischt . . . er hat gar keine bestimmte Tendenz."

29. Hurd, *Letters on Chivalry and Romance*, p. 60.

30. Hurd, *The Works of Richard Hurd*, 1811, IV: 286–87.

31. From the *Notebooks*, quoted by Eichner, 1027: "Die Vermischung und Verflechtung sehr heterogener Bestandtheile und selbst *aller* Mythologien ist eine nothwendige Aufgabe des Romans. Eine *antiquirte* Mythologie kann nur im Roman behandelt werden.—Auch die Verbindung *mehrere* Mythologien ist nur im Roman möglich."

32. Schlegel, "Athenäum Fragment No. 116": "Ihre Bestimmung ist nicht bloß, alle getrennte Gattungen der Poesie wieder zu vereinigen . . ."

33. Hurd, "On the Idea of Universal Poetry," p. 19.

34. From the *Jugendschriften*, II: 373, quoted by Eichner, 1029n: "Das hauspiel soll auch romantisch seyn, wie alle Dichtkunst; aber ein Roman ist unter gewissen Einschränkungen, ein angewandter Roman."

35. Hurd, *Letters on Chivalry and Romance*, pp. 96, 96–97.

36. Schlegel, "Athenäum Fragment No. 116," 238: "Die romantische Dichtart ist die einzige, die mehr als Art, und gleichsam die Dichtkunst selbst ist: denn in einem gewissen Sinn ist oder soll alle Poesie romantisch sein."

37. Schlegel, *Kritische Ausgabe*, II: 335: "Nur mit dem Unterschiede, daß das Romantische nicht sowohl eine Gattung ist als ein Element der Poesie, daß mehr oder minder herrschen und zurücktreten, aber nie ganz fehlen darf."

38. Schlegel, *Kritische Ausgabe*, VI: 285: "In der Tat streitet auch das Romantische an sich mit dem Alten und wahrhaft Antiken nicht. Die Sage von Troja und die Homerischen Gesänge sind durchaus romantisch . . ."

39. Herder, *Sämtliche Werke*, 19, p. 110.

40. Hurd, *Letters on Chivalry and Romance*, pp. 26, 38.

41. Hurd, *The Works of Richard Hurd*, 1811, IV: 272.

42. Hurd, *Letters on Chivalry and Romance*, p. 76.

43. Schlegel, *Gespräch über die Poesie, Kritische Ausgabe*, II: 335: "Indessen bitte ich Sie doch, nun nicht sogleich anzunehmen, daß mir das Romantische und das Moderne völlig gleich gelte." For this distinction and its evolution in Schlegel's thought, see Eichner, 1040.

44. Hurd, *Letters on Chivalry and Romance*, pp. 4, 2–3.

45. See Schlegel, *Kritische Ausgabe*, VI: 277, 331.

46. Eichner, 1034, quoting *Jugendschriften*, II, 374f; see also Eichner, 1025n.

47. Hurd, "On the Idea of Universal Poetry," pp. 19, 20.

48. Belgardt, *Romantische Poesie: Begriff und Bedeutung bei Friedrich Schlegel*, pp. 35–39; *The Works of Richard Hurd*, 1811, IV: 300–1; *Kritische Ausgabe*, VI: 285; *The Works of Richard Hurd*, 1811, IV: 252.

49. Eichner, 1024; *Gespräch über die Poesie, Kritische Ausgabe*, II: 335; *The Works of Richard Hurd*, 1811, IV: 315, 239, 279, 280, 309, 328, 328; sections devoted to Italian poetry in Letter X.

50. Schlegel, *Kritische Ausgabe*, VI: 290–94; *The Works of Richard Hurd*, 1811, Vol. IV, Letter 12.

51. Hurd, *Letters on Chivalry and Romance*, pp. 10, 19; see also p. 34.

52. Schlegel, *Kritische Ausgabe*, VI: 291: "Spenser ist in der Sprache unter allen englischen Dichtern am meisten deutsch oder germanisch . . ." And p. 293: "Shakespeares Poesie ist dem deutschen Geiste sehr verwandt, und er wird von den Deutschen mehr, als jeder andere fremde und ganz wie ein einheimischer Dichter empfunden."

53. Eichner, 1039.

54. Both quotations are from Schlegel, *Kritische Ausgabe*, I: 350: "Die Alten sind Meister in der Komposition; es müßen daher diejenigen unter ihren Schriften, welche zur Ausübung dieser Kunst Anleitung geben, von dem höchsten Werte sein." And: "Nichts weniger! Die Griechische Geschmack war schon völlig entartet, als die Theorie noch in der Wiege lag."

55. Oskar Walzel, *German Romanticism*, translated by Alma Elise Lussky (New York: G. P. Putnam's Sons, 1932; Reprint, Capricorn Books, 1940), p. 40.

56. Schlegel, *Kritische Ausgabe*, VI, 336: "Doch hat die deutsche Kritik nur die erste Veranlassung von den Engländern Harris, Hurd, Warton genommen,

und sich bald durchaus selbständig entwickelt, mehr vielleicht als irgendein anderer Zweig unsrer Literatur."

57. Fritz Strich, *Deutsche Klassik und Romantik*, Fünfte Auflage (Bern and Munich: Francke Verlag, 1962), p. 354: "In England fand die deutsche Romantik eine andere Situation vor. In diesem germanischen Volk war ein romantisches Naturgefühl und ein romantischer Drang in die historische Vergangenheit ja zuerst in Europa erwacht und war nicht ohne Einfluß auf den Ursprung der deutschen Romantik geblieben."

58. Schlegel, *Kritische Ausgabe*, VI: 319: "Im achtzehnten Jahrhundert waren die Engländer überhaupt vor allen andern Europäern, das herrschende Volk auch in der literarische Welt." And "in Deutschland dagegen hat der neue Aufschwung der Literatur in der Mitte des achtzehnten Jahrhunderts zunächst durch die Poesie und Kritik der Engländer den ersten Anstoß und seine herrschende Richtung erhalten."

2

Frederick Burwick

Romantic Madness
Hölderlin, Nerval, Clare

Attributing rapture and irrationality to poetic inspiration has a venerable tradition. "In vain does one knock at the gates of poetry with a sane mind," wrote Plato in the *Phaedrus* (§245a).[1] "Poetry demands a man with a special gift," Aristotle affirmed, "or a touch of madness" (*Poetics*, ch. 17).[2] And from Democritus, Cicero quotes the pronouncement: "no sane-minded poet could ever enter Hélicon."[3] None of the classical enunciations of poetic madness presume, however, to account for the nature of the mental aberration.

When such Renaissance critics as Marsilio Ficino (*De Furore Divino*, passim; *Problemata*, XXX, 954a) describe the divine inspiration of poets, the assumption is that the fantastic constructs are not engendered within the poet's own mind. Inspiration, to be sure, requires the receptivity and mediating skills of the poet: the images may be the poet's, but the ideas have a higher provenance. While such a doctrine renders a pathology of derangement irrelevant to the *furor poeticus* or *furor divinus*, occasionally the wild visions were accompanied as well by unbridled actions. When a court poet grew disruptive, as happened in the court of Ferrara with Torquato Tasso, speculations on the causes of the apparent delusions fed the fires of gossip. Frustrated desires and an unbridled imagination were blamed for instances in which the poet failed to recover from a fit of inspiration. Although the return trip was seemingly but a short distance, daring to trespass beyond the boundaries of reason might well leave genius stranded in uncharted territory. The dangerous proximity prompted John Dryden's well-known couplet on the Earl of Shaftesbury: "Great wits are sure to madness near allied, / And thin partitions do their bounds divide" (*Absalom and Achitophel*, 163–64).

Prior to the eighteenth century, the *furor poeticus* was posited in literary criticism much as the *lasus naturae* was the resort of natural scientists who, as Jonathan Swift observes, "disdaining the old evasion of occult causes, whereby the followers of Aristotle endeavor in vain to disguise their ignorance, have invented this wonderful solution to all difficulties, in the unspeakable advancement of human knowledge" (*Gulliver's Travels*, part 2, ch. 3). Swift and his readers were alert to the obfuscation of empty terms. The *furor poeticus* had been historically just such "a wonderful solution" to the mystery of the creative imagination. When the concept was revived in the very midst of the Age of Reason, principally as a means of escaping the rigorous dictates of rationalism, it was caught up in a vicious cycle of defining the reason of unreason. The very attempt to grant the poet freedom from the dictates of reason required a philosophical or scientific rationale.

In order to explain how inspiration enabled the poet or artist to reach beyond the limits of logic and experience, such critics as Edward Young ("Conjectures on Original Composition," 1759) and William Duff ("Essay on Original Genius," 1767), Johann Georg Hamann (*Sokratische Denkwürdigkeiten*, 1759; "Aesthetica in nuce," 1762) and Johann Gottfried Herder ("Über die Neuere deutsche Literatur," 1767) sought to locate "original genius" within "the native and radical power which the mind possesses." The arguments on the peculiarities of artistic sensibility and the special mental powers of inspiration and imagination were not only contemporary with works on the nervous system (Albrecht von Haller or David Hartley) and on the treatment of insanity (John Monro or Thomas Arnold), but they also shared basic assumptions about the links between brain and mind, physical experience and the processes of thought.

These assumptions, of course, are still with us, and still baffled by the riddles of the "black box." While the consequences of traumatic head injury and brain damage are tragic in themselves, it is some consolation that cracks in the "black box" have enabled neurophysiologists to map areas of memory and sensory response (Hunt, 44, 100, 149). Just as observing the operation of the damaged brain has led to understanding the functions of the healthy organ, part of the fascination with the poetry of irrational excess has been for the revelation it might provide into the creative process per se. When one traces the developments in hermeneutics through Wilhelm Dilthey, Martin Heidegger, and Hans-Georg Gadamer, it is notable that they all turn to the poetry of Friedrich Hölderlin to put their theories to the test in elucidating the "dark passages."

Whatever idiosyncracies in language might distinguish insanity from sanity, irrationality from rationality, the one no less than the other bears the imprint of a human mind. The first to propose that a hermeneutic might be constructed from the study of Hölderlin's works was his contemporary, Achim von Arnim. Hölderlin had engaged his own hermeneutic in the commentary to his translation of the *Oedipus* and

Antigone by Sophocles, in his poetic drama on Empedocles, and in the hymn on the vision of St. John at Patmos. From the very intertextuality of Hölderlin's works, Arnim intended to find leverage to interpret the obscurity in the poet's often peculiar syntax and imagery. For much the same reason, critics of Gérard de Nerval and John Clare have given special scrutiny to the intertextuality of the late poety. Nerval, following his treatment at the clinic of Dr. Esprit Blanche in Montmartre, plunged ever deeper into the psychic realms of classical myth and German Romanticism. Clare discovered in Byron's *Childe Harold* the "soul" of thought which emerged from a brain "In its own eddy boiling and o'erwrought, / A whirling gulf of fantasy and flame" (III: 51, 55–58). As a patient in the private asylum of Dr. Matthew Allen in Epping Forest, Clare made *Childe Harold* the instrument of his own soul, the voice of his own troubled thought. Hölderlin's "Patmos," Nerval's "Christ on the Mount of Olives," and Clare's "Child Harold" are all intriguing test cases for such a hermeneutic endeavor.

Impressed by the wisdom and practicality of the earlier writings, especially *Hyperion,* Arnim believed that Hölderlin, much in the manner of his own Empedocles, had commenced a journey of exploration. Empedocles justified his leap into the volcano as a search for the quintessence of mind. Hölderlin, similarly, fell into madness in order to chart that subjective *terra incognita* beyond the reach of rationality. Still penning his poetry, even while totally dependent on the care of Ernst Zimmer's family, Hölderlin kept sending his messages from the realm of madness. Some day he might return, Arnim wrote, to tell us what he had seen in the "lonely abyss."[4] In the meantime, these poetic messages required an interpreter.

"Patmos" is the poem which for Arnim best illustrates Hölderlin's bold exploration into the realm beyond rationality. Shame, Arnim declares, "inhibited most poets from tracing the origin of their being" [die Wurzelkeime ihres Daseins"].[5] They feared the risks, he explains, in trying to rediscover the primal ground in the unconscious. Hölderlin was too earnest in his art to be confused by such an investigation. But even he, at the beginning of "Patmos," asks for aid "to cross over and return" ["Hinüberzugehn und wiederzukehren"]. It was to be regretted, then, that Hölderlin had not charted the way. The only recourse is to follow Hölderlin on his journey.

As Arnim saw it, Hölderlin's distress over the Napoleonic intervention, combined with his "most unfortunate attraction" to Susette Gontard, precipitated his mental breakdown. In "Excursions with Hölderlin," Arnim builds upon a series of quotations to document the historical and biographical circumstances. The story he tells is intended to anticipate and elucidate the narrative in "Patmos." Grounding his hermeneutic on Hölderlin's own earlier works, Arnim defined the conditions for rendering Hölderlin's later poetry accessible to the rational mind. In Hölderlin's commentary to Sophocles, Arnim thinks he has discovered an apt link to "Patmos."[6] The poet is not escaping into the past, he is resurrecting from the past a vision of apocalypse and salvation for the present. Although he confesses that he has only an "unclear transcription" [undeutliche Abschrift],[7] his emendation addresses not a faulty text but an obscure meaning. The poet, "with beating pulse and echoing words has ascended the mountain peak," and has peered beyond mortal bounds. "Is it different," Arnim asks, "in that mental realm?" [Ist es im Geistigen anders?] The answer must be yes, for Hölderlin's language became strange and perplexing.

> Many a word was uncertain, some fully veiled in highest contemplation, some had to be omitted or a couple of explanatory words added. No effort was spared. What need is there to excuse how I made clear to him who is far remote as well as to myself, we who scarcely perceived a whisper in the air, this wonderful mirage, which revealed for a moment all wisdom and glory of the world to the prophet in the desert, to the others, however, who threw themselves down, seemed only a suffocating desert wind.[8]

Thus, Arnim defines himself as mediator as well as interpreter. His task is to render the vision clear and accessible. Even though the poet may have stepped beyond the bourn of rationality in order to experience it, the vision itself may bear meaning to the rational world.

Arnim entitled one of his drafts "Aesthetic Excursions with Hölderlin" (Äesthetische Ausflüge mit Hölderlin) and another, with his reading of "Patmos," has the heading "First Excursion." Recollecting his earlier plan for "Lectures on a Practical Aesthetic based on Hyperion" (Vorlesungen über praktische Ästhetik nach Hölderlins Hyperion),[9] Arnim seems ready to write a series of "Aesthetic Excursions" in which he will travel to the very brink with the poet and endeavor to interpret the strange language from beyond:

> Once I had a plan very dear to me to construct a so-called Aesthetic upon a poet such as Hölderlin, who plunged so magnificently into a crater in order to experience something that not even he could communicate.[10]

What might lie beyond the threshold of his Hyperionic farewell or his Empedoclesian *salto mortale* the poet left concealed in silence. In his "Patmos," however, he continued to sing even as he entered into the prophetic vision of St. John. If Arnim is to satisfy the hermeneutic task of his practical aesthetic, he will have to follow the poet even "to the lofty heights of mind."

> This is the stuff which penetrates him in Hyperion. Then he sings praises to the sun and earth in their magnificence. Thus the spirit leads him through loneliness to salvation. Already in departing from mankind, dazzled by magnificence, he beholds Patmos; expression becomes infinitely difficult for him, and his thoughts are confused even retrospectively. Breathless, with pounding pulse, with fading words the mortal approaches the peak of the mountain. How shall he reach the lofty heights of mind without similar danger? Painful destiny, the most unfortunate love had broken his strength. The poem excites in every moment, but it wraps itself in obscurity as it approaches the highest intuitions.[11]

Arnim admits his limited access to this dangerous realm, and confesses "that much that was incomprehensible had to be left out." Conscious of the constraints on his own hermeneutic endeavor, he recognizes that Hölderlin, too, had assumed a very similar hermeneutic mission.

"Patmos" begins with the poet feeling the "nearness of the Divine in its incomprehensibility." Arnim provides a seven-point outline which reconstructs the steps in Hölderlin's visionary hermeneutic of Johannine vision: (1) To penetrate and elucidate that "incomprehensibility"; (2) the poet undertakes his mental journey to Patmos; (3) when he enters "into the view of St. John, the stories of the New Testament surround him, especially the introduction of the Lord's Supper"; (4) the mystery of the Crucifixion and the confusion of the Apostles is resolved through the diffusion of the Holy Ghost; (5) with heightened awareness the poet is able to perceive from the vantage of the biblical past the course of corruption in the present; he interprets this as the chaff to be purged by the Sower who casts the grain (Matt. 3:12); (6) he understands the paradox of death and resurrection: "the spirit if resurrected as it feels itself reanimated, as it comprehends the world" (7); commending his divine revelation, "he delivers his Song as offering."

As Hölderlin's poem is a visionary hermeneutic of Johannine vision,[12] Arnim's essay is a hermeneutic of that hermeneutic. The love of God requires, Hölderlin declares at the end of his poem, that the biblical text should be cherished and its enduring truth rightly interpreted,

> that we keep the letter
> Fast in our care and well interpret
> What endures. Which German song obeys. (224–26)[13]

Although Arnim seeks to interpret Hölderlin's interpretation, "to make clear to the far removed and to me," he fails to elucidate several passages of the poem: "some parts veiled themselves fully in highest intuition, some had to be omitted." Among the forty-nine "veiled" lines which Arnim omits, the major lacunae are lines 106–15, 130–40, 142–46, and 162–82 (briefer omissions are 70–71 and 190). Not Hölderlin's "holy madness," but his biblical exegesis baffles Arnim's comprehension. His difficulties occur at the fifth point in his outline of the poem. He has not understood how "the outpouring of the spirit" has given the poet "heightened insight." He has presumed a "Luftspiegelung," an airy vision of spendid images. Hölderlin's poetic argument, however, is that the divine truth is imageless.

The passages that Arnim omits are precisely the passages in which Hölderlin insists upon the invisible manifestation of spirit. Although he might well have informed his interpretation with Hölderlin's account of the "boundless division" as the necessary complement to the "boundless union," he does not seem to comprehend Hölderlin's affirmation of that division. The "boundless union" with Christ is followed by the "boundless division" of the Holy Ghost. In strophe 8, Arnim omits the passage that tells us of division and darkness:

> Now that he appeared to them
> Once again in farewell.
> And how the kingly sun's
> Light went out and broke
> His sceptered beams
> In godly pain, due
> To return when times
> Were right. Far worse, had it
> Happened later, brutally tearing men
> From their work (106–15)[14]

In the presence of Christ, John could directly behold the face of God. Now that the divine light is eclipsed, its beams, as a divine scepter, no longer touch mortal eyes. It will be restored with the Resurrection. In the meantime the efforts of men are vain and "untreu." Arnim does quote the lines which immediately follow:

> so from now on
> It was a joy
> To live in loving night, to keep
> Abysses of wisdom

> Fixed in clear eyes. And living images
> Grow green in depths of mountains. (115–20)[15]

These lines affirm the joy of dwelling "in loving night." Even for simple eyes there is wisdom in the dark abyss. With the death of Christ, the realm of the spirit becomes an imageless darkness. The sensory images of the material world cannot supplant the imageless abyss of the spirit. That Arnim failed to comprehend Hölderlin's distinction between the spiritual and material is evident in his altering "living images" to "living woods."

The poetry of vision, Arnim no doubt thought, would be characterized by strong visual imagery. The symptoms of madness, should they be present, would most likely be exhibited in hallucinations and visual delusions. His reading of "Patmos" goes awry when the inspired "Seer" denies vision. The passages which he omitted were not unintelligible, but given his set of expectations it is not surprising that he found them obscured "in highest intuition." The longest passage which he deleted is the one in which the poet most vigorously refuted the temptation of images. The poet describes that temptation at the close of strophe 11:

> Just as mines yield ore
> And Etna glows with resins,
> I would have enough in my possession
> To shape an image of him and
> Contemplate Christ as he was (162–66)[16]

Building materials abound for the artist to create an image of Christ. The material image, "as he was," would necessarily be bound in time, a static icon rather than a dynamic truth. In strophe 12 the poet goes on to reject the error of worshiping the material image instead of remaining open to spiritual revelation:

> as if a slave
> Could imitate the image of God—
> I once saw the lords of heaven
> Visibly furious that I wanted to be something
> Rather than learn. (169–73)[17]

Hölderlin's lyrical language, of course, is never without an image. The unmined "ore" and the volcanic "resin" from which he might sculpt an image are images against image-making. The rich appeal to material imagery celebrates God's creation. The "heaven's triumphal march" [himmlischer Triumphgang] may be "like the sun" [der Sonne gleich], but no physical similitude can suffice as an adequate image of God. Thus, the poet offers a paradoxical "sign of deliverance" [Losungszeichen]— the signless sign of poetic song (179–82).

Although Arnim could not follow the poet's appropriation of the biblical warning against worshiping images,[18] he certainly understood the argument that the song is a hymn of praise. His sixth and seventh points appropriately interpret the concluding section of the poem, and his transcription omits only the reference to the bridle of gold [der goldene Zaum] as image of imageless of faith:

> Yet many timid
> Eyes await a glimpse
> Of the light, reluctant
> To flower in the glare,
> Their courage bridled by the gold. (185–90)[19]

Because Arnim has read "Patmos" as visionary hermeneutic, he has emphasized how the poet has assimilated the Johannine vision. Strophe 15 he interprets as the poet's offering for divine revelation: "He praises the Heavenly for what has been revealed to him; he presents his Song as an offering, while he discloses the source of German song."[20] The final strophe commences with the lament,

> Too long, too long now
> The honor of the Heavenly has been invisible (211–12)[21]

Arnim has apparently understood that this imageless condition already has been alleviated by the poetic vision. He is right, of course, yet not because the poet has retrieved the invisible into visionary perception, rather because the poet has relied on faith and the bible without turning away from the visible and palpable glories of God's material creation.

We have been reading Arnim reading Hölderlin reading John. The constellation is no less complex when we turn to Nerval's reading of Christ on the Mount of Olives. He adapts his biblical narrative from the Gospels (Matt. chapters 24–26; Mark chapters 13–14; Luke chapters 19, 21; John chapters 8, 13). In the first three of the five sonnets, however, Nerval is reading Germaine de Staël reading Jean Paul Richter reading the Gospels. Nerval, perhaps with less constraint than most writers, immersed himself personally into his texts. His friend, Théophile Gautier, and his physician, Dr. Emil Blanche, both recognized in his writing a rewriting of the self, a repetition and a displacement of the very agonies of his own identity. Dr. Blanche thus saw Nerval's writing as therapeutic.[22] Gautier, however, feared the consequences of his friend's autobiographical self-projection. Should his fictive self become inextricably entangled in the web of narrative displacement, the fragile hold on his own identity might well be jeopardized (a fear also expressed by other friends at the time of Gautier's first bout of madness).[23]

With a structural effect not unlike that achieved by Percy Bysshe Shelley in weaving five sonnets into an "Ode to the West Wind" (1819), Nerval developed the symbolic action of "Christ on the Mount of Olives" (1844) in a five-sonnet sequence. His motto is from Jean Paul: "God is dead! The heavens are empty . . . / Weep, children, you no longer have a father!" [Dieu est mort! le ciel est vide . . . / Pleurez! enfants, vous n'avez plus de père!].[24] The "Speech of the dead Christ" from Jean Paul's *Siebenkäs* (1796–1797) had been introduced to French readers in Staël's *De l'Allemagne* (1810). From his nightmare of the immortal soul abandoned in a godless universe, Jean Paul turns to a reaffirmation of divine immanence. His English imitators—Samuel Taylor Coleridge in "Limbo" and "Ne Plus Ultra" (1811), Thomas Carlyle in "The Everlasting No" and "The Everlasting Yea" of *Sartor Resartus* (1833), Thomas De Quincey in the vision of the eyeless face in the Orion nebula and the "Dream upon the Universe" from "System of the Heavens" (1846)—all followed Jean Paul in reaffirming divine presence after conjuring the possibility of an utterly moribund deity. Nerval's "Christ on the Mount of Olives," much like Alfred de Vigny's "Mount of Olives" (also inspired by the "Speech of the dead Christ" and published three months after Nerval's poem), offers no such happy resolution.

Abandoned isolation is the motif that dominates the "Speech of the dead Christ." Jean Paul makes no mention of betrayal, the motif that defines and directs the agonies of Nerval's "Christ on the Mount of Olives." Christ's torment, Nerval's poem, results from the betrayal of his closest friends: "Long lost in speechless agonies, and knew / Himself betrayed by thankless friends" (I: 3–4).[25] Elaborating the motif of betrayal, Nerval adapts from the Gospels Christ's prophecy that brother shall betray brother (Mark 13:12), that his followers will be betrayed by friends and relatives (Luke 21:16), will betray one another (Matt. 24:10), and will betray him (Matt. 26:21, Mark 14:18, John 13:21). In Nerval's reading of the Gospels, there are more subtle and insidious models of betrayal than the overt greed and deceit in Judas's kiss. Betrayal is also in Peter's self-protective denial that he is a friend of Christ. And, specifically pertinent to that night Christ spent on the Mount of Olives, betrayal is in the failure of his friends to see his need. They slumber while he holds his lonely vigil (Matt. 26:40).

Jean Paul's text, then, informs and is informed by Nerval's reading of the biblical text. As mediator of the poet's torment, Nerval's Christ raises his arms to the skies "as poets do" [comme font les poètes], feels keenly the hurt of isolation and betrayal, and cries out in desperation to the sleeping apostles. God, he shouts, has ceased to exist [Dieu n'est plus!]:

> They slept. "The change, friends—can you see it now?
> I've touched the eternal firmament with my brow;
> I've suffered many days, bleeding, broken!
>
> Brothers, I cheated you: Abyss, abyss!
> God's missing from my altar of sacrifice . . .
> There is no God! No God now!" They slept on. (I: 9–14)[26]

When the biblical Christ calls out from the cross, "Eloi, Eloi, lama sabachthani," the fear of abandonment and betrayal is brought to a sublime climax: "My God, my God, why hast thou forsaken me?" Since this is the only instance in the Greek Testament in which Christ's words are recorded in Aramaic (Mark 15:34; Matt. 27:46 gives them in Hebrew), the act of quotation is boldly proclaimed. In repeating the words of Ps. 22, Christ speaks not of mere personal fear, but of the human agony he shares in putting on the flesh and surrendering his miraculous powers. Precisely this human agony is crucial to Nerval. It is not the threat of a godless universe [Dieu n'est past! Dieu n'est plus!] that produces the empty pain and sad desolation of being betrayed by thankless friends. Rather, the causality works the other way around. It is the betrayal of friends that leaves the world godless, the self a martyr.

In the second sonnet, Nerval's Christ-persona, ignored by his friends, discovers not just God, but the world, the entire universe is dead: "'*Tout est mort! J'ai parcouru les mondes; / Et j'ai perdu mon vol dans leurs chemins lactés*'" (II: 1–2). The spheres move, "'*Mais nul esprit n'existe en ces immensités*'" (7–8). Nerval's Christ journeys through the same bleak desolation and beholds the same bottomless socket described by Jean Paul's Christ.[27]

> I looked for God's eye, only saw a black
> Bottomless socket pouring out its dark
> Night on the world in ever thickening rays. (II: 9–11)[28]

In the third sonnet, again echoing Jean Paul,[29] the familiar oppositions of mechanist and vitalist thought are revoked. Is the world governed by destiny, by cold necessity, or by chance? Or is there a mindless "*puissance originelle*" capable of animating, perhaps even reanimating the cycle of things and beings? Or is there some kindred creative mind truly deserving to be called *"mon père"*? Nerval's Christ has no sooner called forth the human image of a divine Father than he reasserts the motif of betrayal. Impossible in a universe of mechanical necessity or haphazard chance, betrayal, as Nerval knows, asserts itself in the Judeo-Christian doctrine of the Fall. While Jean Paul himself avoids any reference to Satan or a Manichean power of darkness, his image of the "Angel of Death" [Würgengel] (see note 29) may have given Nerval a hint for the *"ange des nuits"* in the sestet. Nerval reasserts the crisis of betrayal by evoking the primal strife when the fallen angel in jealous rivalry commences the rebellion against the Father. Perhaps the outcast renegade has won. What then?

> Father! Within me, is it you I feel?
> Have you the strength to live and conquer death?
> Or will the outcast angel of the night
>
> Have overturned you with his final thrust?
> I am alone in suffering and grief,
> And if I die, it's death to everything! (III: 9–14)[30]

Bereft even of the Father who has betrayed him, Christ is left in abject solitude, sole survivor and last vestige of life.

Sonnet-stanzas II and III are given over completely to the mono-logue of the Nerval-Christ. In stanza IV, Nerval returns to the opening scene with the sleeping apostles so preoccupied with their selfish dreams of power (as kings, or sages, or prophets) that they cannot be roused even by Christ's urgent cries. Christ now perceives that one apostle remains awake—the traitor Judas. Nerval's collation of Jean Paul's vision and the biblical account of Christ's lonely vigil results in his emendation of both texts: the one because it has omitted the power of evil and betrayal, the other because it represents the deceit of Judas as the worst of the multiple acts of betrayal. For Nerval, the overt double-cross is far less an evil than the hidden duplicity. Thus, Nerval's Christ welcomes the forthright crime of Judas:

> "Judas!" he shouted, "Sell me, don't waste time
> Getting the deal done; you know what I'm worth:
> I suffer here, friend, lying on the earth,
> Come! For at least you have the strength of crime." (IV: 5–8)[31]

Sonnet-stanza III merely guesses whether the dark angel has the power to succeed in his rebellion. In stanza IV, the power is acted upon. The act, however, leaves Judas guilt-ridden. Chance, the prevailing element in the mechanist universe at the opening of stanza III is joined by pity at the close of stanza IV in Pilate's summons to seek out the madman Christ: "'Go, find this lunatic!'" [Allez chercher ce fou!].

In Nerval's concluding stanza, Christ is exalted as the sublime madman, "*ce fou, cet insensé sublime.*" If not dead or overthrown, the Father of the Gospels has Himself been abandoned. Nerval lingers no longer as an exegete interpreting and glossing the texts of Jean Paul or Matthew or Mark. He turns instead to the world of classical myth, where the forgotten Icarus again dons his wings, Phaeton again rides Apollo's chariot, and Cybele again resurrects the slain Attis (V: 1–4). The biblical text has been relinquished, but its narrative of the Fall and Resurrection continue to resonate in Icarus, Phaeton, and Attis, whose mythic fate makes them fitting fellows of the sublime madman Christ.

Unlike Hölderlin, Nerval has penetrated into his texts to find at the core no meaning at all. His Christianity is set alongside mythology, and the whole cast of characters are reduced to reading the entrails of the sacrificial victim to interpret the meaning of life and death. Caesar himself demands to know whether a god or a devil now rules the world. The answer, if there is an answer, it is not forthcoming: the oracle is silent, and the possible creator, "He who gave a soul to the sons of clay" [Celui que donna l'âme aux enfants du limon] (V: 14), remains enshrouded in mystery.

In Clare's "Child Harold" the sense of Clare reading Byron is subordinate to Clare adopting and transforming Childe Harold as his own *alter ego*. Clare, to be sure, was fully aware that Byron's poetic strategy involved a subtle in-and-out relationship of narrator and character. If this is parody, it is desperately earnest. As in Hölderlin's "Patmos" and Nerval's "Le Christ aux Oliviers," Clare writes his text by reading himself into another text. An outcast from the society of the London beau monde where he had been fêted for a season, Clare no doubt felt a certain sympathy with the poet who left England amidst scandal. He recognized, too, and appropriated the ironic displacement of self which Byron accomplished in engendering his poetic persona.

Most critical commentary on Clare's "Don Juan" and "Child Harold" has been preoccupied with the mimicking of Byron. In line with the preceding investigation of Hölderlin and Nerval, I stress instead Clare's hermeneutic penetration into Byron's text where he recovers the "wandering outlaw of his own dark mind" and engenders his own "being more intense" (Canto III, stanzas 3 and 6). This is Clare's poem, not Byron's. Clare's Spenserian stanza is more roughshod, and his "Child Harold" is the form of his own fancy, the image of his own life.

> Many are the poets—though they use no pen
> To show their labours to the shuffling age
> Real poets must be truly honest men
> Tied to no mongrel laws on flatterys page
> No zeal have they for wrong or party rage
> —The life of labour is a rural song
> That hurts no cause—nor warfare tries to wage
> Toil like the brook in music wears along—
> Great little minds claim right to act the wrong (1–9)

Clare's opening stanza stubbornly insists upon his right to be a poet. Reared among the hovels of itinerant farm laborers, he is an "honest" man who has heard a song amidst the sweat and toil. During the 1820s he won acclaim, but soon discovered that he had been received as little more than a curiosity and a freak, a minstrel ploughboy. His early poems are notable for their keen observation of nature; his asylum poems are introspective and tinged with irony and defiance. With this shift from a Wordsworthian to a Byronic mode, Clare denies the ideological contests of the established parties. He champions the voice of the marginalized working class: "Great little minds claim right to act the wrong."

Undercutting the posturing of his poetic self-projection, Clare's "honest" persona does not conceal the squalor of his existence and the sad confrontation with the futility of his ideals and ambitions:

> My life hath been one of love—no blot it out
> My life hath been one chain of contradictions
> Madhouses Prisons wh-reshops—never doubt
> But that my life hath had some strong convictions
> That such was wrong—religion makes restrictions
> I would have followed—but life turned a bubble (145–50)

Clare's Child Harold does not range across the nations of Europe; he travels the lonely backroads, a man abandoned and betrayed.

> Life is to me a dream that never wakes
> Night finds me on this lengthening road alone
> Love is to me a thought that never aches
> A frost bound thought that freezes life to stone (255–58)

The cause of Clare's debilitation has been variously attributed to epilepsy or alcoholism. The Child-Harold self, in the stanzas just quoted, hints at venereal infection. The anguish of which he sings, however, is not of physical suffering, but of blighted hope.

Fame blazed upon me like a comets glare
Fame waned and left me like a fallen star
Because I told the evil of what they are (426–28)

More than either Hölderlin or Nerval, Clare turns within the precincts of his hermit-crab text to shake his fist at the society that rejected and incarcerated him.

The first draft of "Patmos" was completed late in the fall of 1802, following Hölderlin's return from France in a distraught and confused condition. Because of recurring periods of derangment, he was taken to Dr. Autenrieth's clinic in 1806; in 1807 he was placed in private care. The late poetry, signed Scardanelli and dated variously from 1648, 1748, 1849, and 1940, were the last messages that Hölderlin sent forth from his tower in the home of Ernst Zimmer, where he died after forty years of progressive mental debility in 1843. Nerval suffered his first mental collapse in 1841. "Le Christ aux Oliviers," the sonnet-ode that Nerval published in March 1844, may well echo the betrayal he felt following his release from the asylum at Montmarte. The poem effectively established the style for the ensuing collection of *Les Chimères*, completed during his later confinement at Passy in 1853 and 1854. Nerval hanged himself from a lamppost in January 1855. Clare, after several attacks of nervous debility, began to suffer delusions and lapses of memory in 1836. From 1838 to 1841, he was in the asylum of Dr. Matthew Allen. Here he wrote "Don Juan" and "Child Harold." He escaped from Forest Epping in 1841, but was soon brought to Northampton Asylum where he spent the next twenty-two years until his death in 1864.

There can be no doubt that these poems, with their visions into the imageless abyss, with their themes of isolation and betrayal, are powerfully evocative in communicating dialogic and hermeneutic intertextuality. In exploring other texts, they thematize the activity of seeking out meaning in poetic language, a quest which they transform into their own poetic expression. As a response to the age-old argument about the *furor poeticus*, the key word here is communication. These poems are not babblings or ravings. Foucault may well be right that poetry is twin-born with madness in the dark undercurrents of the mind (285–89). But poetry as poetry escapes the solipsism of madness in the very act of communicating with other minds. In the midst of their private torment, Hölderlin, Nerval, and Clare grasp—indeed, thematically command—that communicative act.

NOTES

1. Plato, *Phaedrus* 492. See also: *Republic*, Book 10, 604–605; *Ion*, § 535–36; 221–22, 827, 830.

2. Aristotle, *Poetics*, 1472. See also: *Rhetoric*, iii. 7, 199.

3. Democritus, quoted in Cicero, *De Divinatione*, I: 80; and in Horace, *Ars Poetica*, 295 (cf. 402). See also: Seneca, "De Tranquillitate," *Moral Essays*, 17.10; Aristotle, *Problemata*, 30.1.

4. Achim von Arnim "Ausflüge mit Hölderlin," *Berliner Conversationsblatt*, 2. Jg. (1828), no. 2. Heft, Nr: 31–35; *Schriften*, 6: 862–68; "Literatur-Notizen," *Der Gesellschafter oder Blätter für Geist und Herz*, 2. Jg. (1818), Nr. 199; *Schriften*, 6: 636–40.

5. FDH ms 7212; in the published version of "Ausflüge," the phrase is altered to *Wurzelkeime ihres Wirkens*.

6. Achim von Arnim, "Ausflüge mit Hölderlin": "Die tragische Darstellung beruhet, wie in den 'Anmerkungen zum Oedipus' angedeutet ist, darauf, daß der unmittelbare Gott ganz eines mit dem Menschen (denn der Gott eines Apostles ist mittelbarer, ist höchster Verstand in höchsten Geiste), daß die *unendliche* Begeisterung *unendlich*, das heißt in Gegensätzen, im Bewußtsein, welches das Bewußtsein aufhebt, heilig sich scheidend, sich faßt, und der Gott in der Gestalt des Todes gegenwärtig ist."

7. Of the nine "Nachtgesänge" ("Chiron," "Thränen," "An die Hoffnung," "Vulkan," "Blödigkeit," "Ganymed," "Hälfte des Lebens," "Lebens-alter," "Der Winkel von Hart"), which had appeared in Wilman's *Taschenbuch* (1805), copies of the first seven are in the Arnim-Nachlaß (Nr. 452), Goethe-und Schiller-Archiv, Weimar; this ms. file also contains Arnim's copies of Hölderlin's poems from Vermehren's *Musenalmanach* (1803) and Seckendorf's *Musenalmanach* (1807 and 1808).

8. Achim von Arnim, "Ausflüge mit Hölderlin": "Manches Wort war ungewiß, einiges verhüllte sich völlig in höchster Anschauung, einiges mußte weggelassen, ein Paar Worte erklärend zugefügt werden. Mühe ist nicht gespart, was bedarfs der Entschuldigung, wie ich diese wunderbare Luftspiegelung, die dem Seher in der Wüste alle Weisheit und Herrlichkeit der Welt für einige Augenblicke nahte, den andern aber, die sich nieder warfen, wie die erstickende Wind der Wüste erscheinen mochte, hier den Weitentfernten und mir verdeutliche, die wir kaum ein Sausen in der Luft vernahmen."

9. ———. "Vorlesungen über praktische Ästhetik nach Hölderlins Hyperion," in Arnim's "Taschenbuch": ms. B44, 185: Freies Deutsches Hochstift, Frankfurt. A transcription of the "Taschenbücher" (mss. B44 and B69) is currently being prepared for publication by Jürgen Knaack and Ulfert Ricklefs. See also: *Arnims Briefe an Savigny*, 96; also his letter to Brentano (3 Aug. 1813): "Außer dem Hyperion sind mir in dieser Zeit keine andern <Bücher> als meine eignen treu geblieben" Steig I: 316–17; and to the Brothers Grimm (21 Sept. 1817): "schon vor ein paar Jahren machte ich mir einen Plan, eine Aesthetik nach Hölderlins Hyperion auszuarbeiten, denn elegisch wird sie ihrer Natur

nach, und diese herrlichsten aller Elegieen giebt dazu den mannigfaltigsten Anlaß." Steig III: 402.

10. Because of errors in Thomasberger's transcriptions in "Der gedichtete Dichter," 292–300, I have relied on Roswitha Burwick's transcriptions of FDH mss. 20128 and 7212; the brackets indicate Roswitha Burwick's conjectural reading; the word "ebenfalls" in Thomasberger's transcription is an incorrect reading. FDH ms. 20128: "Es war einmal ein Plan, der mir scheint <ausgestrichen: sei es> <darüber: ? ordentlich> lieb wurde, die sogenannte Aesthetik an einem Dichter wie Hölderlin abzuhandeln, der sich so großartig in den Krater stürtzt um etwas zu erfahren, was er doch nicht mittheilen kann."

11. Roswitha Burwick corrects Thomasberger's reading "Ziel" and "verhallenden" to "Heil <?> and "verschallenden." FDH ms. 7212: "Dieser Stoff ist es der ihm im Hyperion durchdringt. Dann besingt er Sonne und Erde in ihrer Herrlichkeit. So führt ihn der Geist durch Einsamkeit zum Heil <?> und schon im Abscheiden von den Menschen, geblendet von Herrlichkeit, erblickt er Pathmos, der Ausdruck wird ihm unendlich schwer, er verwirrt sogar seine Gedanken rückwirkend, athemlos, mit schlagenden Pulsen, mit verschallenden Worten naht sich der Sterbliche den Gipfel der Berge, wie soll er zur Höhe des Geistigen ohne ähnliche Gefahr gelangen? Schmerzliche Schicksale, die unglücklichste Liebe hatten seine Kraft gebrochen. Das Gedicht regt an in jeden Momente, aber es verhüllt sich nahe den höchsten Anschauungen . . ."

12. Jochen Schmidt, *Hölderlins geschichts-philosophische Hymnen,* (Darmstadt: Wissenschaftliche Buchgesellschaft, 1990), 185–97, documents Hölderlin's hermeneutic task in "Patmos" as a response to the request of the Landgrave of Homburg, who wanted a poem which would effectively refute the biblical exegesis of Deism and the Higher Criticism.

13. With one exception, the English rendering of "Patmos" is from Hölderlin, *Hymns and Fragments,* translated by Richard Sieburth (Princeton, N.J.: Princeton University Press, 1966). The exception (lines 212–13) is quoted from Hölderlin, *Poems and Fragments,* translated by Michael Hamburger (Cambridge: Cambridge University Press, 1966). The latter is more literal and endeavors to retain the often convoluted syntax. The German text is quoted from Hölderlin, *Bevestiger Gesang:*

> *daß gepfleget werde*
> *Der feste Buchstab, und Bestehendes gut*
> *Gedeutet. Dem folgt deutscher Gesang* (224–26)

14. Hölderlin, "Patmos":

> *Itzt, da er scheidend*
> *Noch einmal ihnen erschien.*
> *Denn erlosch der Sonne Tag,*
> *Der Königliche, und zerbrach*
> *Den geradestrahlenden,*

> *Den Zepter, göttlichleidend, von selbst,*
> *Denn wiederkommen sollt es,*
> *Zu rechter Zeit. Nicht wär es gut*
> *Gewesen, später, und schroffabbrechend, untreu,*
> *Der Menschen Werk* (106–15)

15. Hölderlin, "Patmos":

> *und Freude war es*
> *Von nun an,*
> *Zu wohnen in liebender Nacht, und bewahren*
> *In einfältigen Augen, unverwandt*
> *Abgründe der Weisheit. Und es grünen*
> *Tief an den Bergen auch lebendige Bilder.* (115–20)

16. Hölderlin, "Patmos":

> *Zwar Eisen träget der Schacht,*
> *Und glühende Harze der Ätna,*
> *So hätt ich Reichtum,*
> *Ein Bild zu bilden, und ähnlich*
> *Zu schaun, wie er gewesen, den Christ* (162–66)

17. Hölderlin, "Patmos":

> *und von dem Gotte*
> *Das Bild nachahmen möcht ein Knecht —*
> *Im Zorne sichtbar sah ich einmal*
> *Das Himmels Herrn, nicht, das ich sein sollte etwas, sondern*
> *Zu lernen.* (169–73)

18. Exod. 20:4–; Lev. 26:1; Deut. 4:16–, 5:8–, 27:15: Isa. 40:18–; in the New Testament, see especially Acts 17:22–.

19. Hölderlin, "Patmos":

> *Es warten aber*
> *Der scheuen Augen viele,*
> *Zu schauen das Licht. Nicht wollen*
> *Am scharfen Strahle sie blühn,*
> *Wiewohl den Mut der goldene Zaum hält.* (185–90)

20. FDH ms 7212: "Er preiset das Himmlische, was sich ihm offenbart hat, er bringt seinen Gesang als Opfer dar, indem er die Quelle des deutschen Gesanges entdeckt." In the published version of "Ausflüge," Arnim states only: "Er bringt seinen Gesang als Opfer dar."

21. Hölderlin, "Patmos":

Zu lang, zu lang schon ist
Die Ehre der Himmlischen unsichtbar (211–12)

22. Paul Youngquist makes a similar case in *Madness and Blake's Myth* (University Park: Pennsylvania State University Press, 1989); see also Dr. Martin T. Orne's records on Anne Sexton, in Diane Middlebrook, *Anne Sexton: A Biography* (Boston: Houghton and Mifflin, 1991).

23. Jean Richer, *Naval par les témoins de savie*, provides an excellent collection of contemporary documents. Nos. 1 and 2 are accounts of Nerval by Gautier and George Bell. In no. 9, sections II and III, Alphonse Karr recollects a hashish party with Nerval and a conversation during Nerval's first bout of madness in 1841. No. 13, sec. IV, is Alexander Weil's record of his visit with Nerval in the sanitarium in Montmarte. No. 30 is an essay by Charles Asselineau from the *Revue fantaisiste* (Sept. 1861), recording a conversation with Nerval during his confinement at Passy, and speculating on the relation between the poet's insanity and his interests in mythology and mysticism. No. 40 is Alexander Dumas's well-known account of Nerval's chronic melancholy which accompanied the publication of "El desdichado" (subsequently first in the sequence of *Les Chimèras*) in *Le Mosquetaire* (10 Dec. 1953). For additional contemporary accounts of Nerval's madness, see: Jules Janin, *Critique portraits et caractéres contemporains* (Paris: Hachette, 1841), pp. 305–7, avoids the usual variations on the *furor poeticus* and tells instead of the hardships that come with living a literary life; Eugène Mirecourt, *Gérard de Nerval* (Paris: Rouet, 1854), which Nerval regarded as his obituary, insists that Nerval's madness was no more than the consequence of inspiration and imagination which the poet could only control and overcome through writing; Maxime du Camp, *Souvenirs Littèraires*, vol. 2 (Paris: Hachette, 1883), p. 159–78, recalls conversations with Nerval during his madness, emphasizing the intermittent periods of lucidity, describing the hallucinations about Jenny Colon, and noting how Nerval's interest in hermeticism emerged amidst his deranged thoughts.

24. Nerval does not quote his epigram from Staël's translation: "Jésus, n'avonnous pas de père?—et il résponit, avec un torrent de larmes: —Nou sommed tous ophelins, moi et vous nous n'avons point de père. — A ces mots, le temple et les enfants s'abîmèrent, et tout l'édiice du monde s'écroula devant moi dans son immensité." Jean Paul: "Da kamen, schrecklich für das Herz, die gestorbenen Kinder, die im Gottesacker erwacht waren, in den Tempel und warfen sich vor die hohe Gestalt am Altare und sagten: 'Jesus! haben wir keinen Vater?' — Und er antwortet mit strömenden Tränen: 'Wir sind alle Waisen, ich und ihr, wir sind ohne Vater.' Da krieschten die Mißtöne heftiger — die zitternden Tempelmauern rückten auseinander — und der Tempel und die Kinder sanken unter— und die ganze Erde und die Sonne sanken nach — und das ganze Weltgebäude sank mit seiner Unermeßlichkeit vor uns vorbei." (II: 269)

25. Translations are from Nerval, *Chimeras*, translated by Peter Jay with essays by Richard Holmes and Peter Jay (Redding Ridge, Conn.: Swann Books,

1984); for the original text, I use Norma Rinsler's edition of *Les Chimères* (London: Athalone Press, 1973). "*Se fut longtemps perdu dans ses douleurs muettes, / Et se jugea trahi par des amis ingrats*" (I: 3–4).

26. Nerval, "Le Christ aux Oliviers":

> *Ills dormaient. "Mes mais, savez-vous les nouvelle?*
> *J'ai touché de mon front à la voûte éternelle;*
> *Je suis sanglant, brisé, souffrant pour bien des jours!*
> *Frères, je vous trompais: Abîme! abîme! abîme!*
> *Le dieu manque à l'autel, où je suis la victime . . .*
> *Dieu n'est pas! Dieu n'est plus!" Mais ils dormaient toujours!*

27. Nerval's second sonnet appropriates but visually enhances the imagery of Jean Paul: "Christus fuhr fort: 'Ich ging durch die Welten, ich stieg in die Sonnen und flog mit den Milchstraßen durch die Wüsten des Himmels; aber es ist kein Gott. Ich stieg herab soweit das Sein seine Schatten wirft, und schauete in den Abgrund und rief: 'Vater, wo bist du?' aber ich hörte nur den ewigen Sturm, den niemand regiert, und der schimmernde Regenbogen aus Wesen stand ohne eine Sonne, die ihn schurf, über dem Abgrunde und tropfte hinunter. Und als ich aufblickte zur unermeßlichen Welt nach dem göttlichen Auge, starrte sie mich mit einer leeren bodenlosen Augenhöhle an; und die Ewigkeit lag auf dem Chaos und zernagte es und wiederkäute sich'." (II: 269)

28. Nerval, "Le Christ aux Oliviers":

> *"En cherchant l'œil de Dieu, je n'ai qu'un orbite*
> *Vaste, noir et sans fond; d'où la nuit qui l'habite*
> *Rayonne sur le monde et s'épaissit toujours."* (II: 9–11)

29. Jean Paul: "Starres, stummes Nichts! Kalte, ewige Notwendigkeit! Wahnsinniger Zufall! Kennt ihr das unter euch? Wann Zerschlagt ihr das Gebäude und mich? —Zufall, weißt du selber, wenn du mit Orkanen durch das Sternen-Schneegestöber schreitest und eine Sonne um die andere auswehest, und wenn der funkelnde Tau der Gestirne ausblinkt, indem du vorübergehest? —Wie ist jeder so allein in der weiten Leichengruft des Alles! Ich bin nur neben mir—O Vater! o Vater! wo ist deine unendliche Brust, daß ich an ihr ruhe? — Ach wenn jedes Ich sein eigner Vater und Schöpfer ist, warum kann es nicht auch sein eigner Würgengel sein?'" (II: 270)

30. Nerval, "Le Christ aux Oliviers":

> *"O mon père! est-ce toi que je sens en moi-même?*
> *As-tu pouvoir de vivre et de vaincre la mort?*
> *Aurais-tu succomé sous un dernier effort*
>
> *De cet ange de nuits que frappa l'anathème . . .*
> *Car je me sens tout seul à pleurer et souffrir,*
> *Hélas! et si je meurs, c'est que tout va mourir!"* (III: 9–14)

31. Nerval, "Le Christ aux Oliviers":

> "*Judas! lui cria-t-il, tu sais ce qu'on m'estime,*
> *Hâte-toi de mi vendre, et finis ce marché:*
> *Je suis souffrant, ami! sur la terre couché . . .*
> *Viens! ô toi qui, du moins, as la force du crime!*" (IV: 5–8)

REFERENCES

Aristotle. *The Basic Works of Aristotle.* Edited by Richard McKeon. New York: Random House, 1941.

Aristotle. *The Rhetoric of Aristotle.* Edited by Lane Cooper. iii: 7, p. 109. New York: Apple, Century, Crofts, 1932.

Achim von Arnim und die ihm nahestanden. Edited by Reinhold Steig and Herman Grimm. 3 Vols., Stuttgart and Berlin: Cotta, 1894–1913; Reprint. Bern: Herbert Lang, 1970.

Arnim, Achim. *Achim von Arnim. Werke.* Edited by Roswitha Burwick, Jürgen Knaack, Paul Michael Lützeler, Renate Moering, Ulfert Ricklefs, and Hermann Weiss. 6 Vols., Munich: Deutsche Klassiker Verlag, 1989; *Schriften,* 6 (1992): 622–25.

Arnims Briefe an Savigny, 1803–1831, mit weiteren Quellen als Anhang. Edited by Heinz Härtl. Weimar: Herman Böhlaus Nachfolger, 1982.

Arnim, Archim. "Ausflüge mit Hölderlin." *Berliner Conversationsblatt* 2. Jg. (1828): 2. Heft, Nr. 31–35; *Schriften,* 6 (1992): 862–68.

———. "Autobiographische Auszeichungen." Goethe- und Schiller-Archiv Weimar, Arnim-Nachlaß 226, U8 and U11. In Dorothea Streller, "Arnim und das Drama." Ph.D. diss. (masch.) Göttingen, 1956, pp. 110–12.

———. "Literatur-Notizen." *Der Gesellschafter oder Blätter für Geist und Herz* 2 Jg. (1818): Nr. 199; *Schriften,* 6 (1992): 636–40.

———. Tagebuch, Handschrift B44. Freies Deutsches Hochstift, Frankfurt.

———. "Theoretische Untersuchung." In *Achim von Arnim und die ihm nahestanden.* Edited by Reinhold Steig und Herman Grimm Vol. 3 (Stuttgart, 1894–1913), pp. 242–44.

———. "Vorrede zum Stoff des Empedokles." (ms 1826?; GSA, Arnim-Nachlaß 92/12).

Arnim, Achim and Clemens Brentano. Eds. *Zeitung für Einsiedler.* Heidelberg: Mohr und Zimmer, 1808. Facsimile Reprint. Edited by Hans Jessen. Darmstadt: Wissenschaftliche Buchgesellschaft, 1962.

Arnold, Thomas. *Observations on the Nature, Kinds, Causes and Prevention of Insanity.* 2 Vols. Leicester: Robinson and Cadell, 1782–86; 2nd ed. London: Phillips, 1806.

Battie, William. *A Treatise on Madness* (1758). Reprinted with John Monro, *Remarks on Dr. Battie's Treatise on Madness* (1758), and an introduction by Richard Hunter and Ida Macalpline. London: Dawsons, 1962.

Bertaux, Pierre. *Friedrich Hölderlin.* Frankfurt: Suhrkamp, 1978.

Böschenstein, Bernhard. "Hölderlins späteste Gedichte," *Hölderlin-Jahrbuch* 14 (1965–1966): 35–56.

Burwick, Roswitha. "Exzerpte Achim von Arnim zu unveröffentlichen Briefen." *Jahrbuch des Freien Deutschen Hochstifts* (1978): 298–395.

———. *Dichtung und Malerie bei Achim von Arnim.* Berlin: De Gruyter, 1989.

———. "Achim von Arnims Ästhetik. Die Wechselwirkung von Kunst und Wissenschaft, Poesie und Leben, Dichtung und Malerie." *Neue Tendenzen*, 98–119.

Burwick, Roswitha and Berndt Fischer. *Neue Tendenzen der Arnimforschung.* Bern: Peter Lang, 1990.

Clare, John. *The Poems of John Clare's Madness.* Edited by Geoffrey Grigson. London: Routledge and Kegan Paul, 1949.

———. *John Clare.* Edited by Eric Robinson and David Powell. Oxford: Oxford University Press, 1984.

Derrida, Jacques. "Cogito et histoire de la folie." In *L'écriture et la différence.* Paris: Seuil, 1967.

du Camp, Maxime. *Souvenirs Littéraires.* Vol. 2. Paris: Hachette, 1883.

Duff, William. *An Essay on Original Genius.* Edited by John L. Mahoney. London: Edward and Charles Dilly, 1767; Gainesville, Fla.: Scholar's Facsimiles and Reprints, 1964.

Felman, Shoshona. *La folie et la chose littéraire.* Paris: Seuil, 1978.

Ficino, Marsilio. *De Furore Divino.* 1457.

Foucault, Michel. *Folie et déraison: Histoire de la folie à l'âge classique.* Paris: Plon, 1961.

Hamann, Johann Georg. *Sokratische Denkwürdigkeiten.* 1759; "Aesthetica in nuce." 1762.

Hamlin, Cyrus. "'Stimmen des Geschiks': The Hermeneutics of Unreadibility (Thoughts on Hölderlin's 'Griechenland')," *Jenseits des Idealismus. Hölderlins letzte Homburger Jahre* (1804–1806). Edited by Christoph Jamme and Otto Pöggeler (Bonn: Bouvier Verlag, 1988), pp. 252–72.

Herder, Johann Gottfried. "Über die Neuere deutsche Literatur" (1767). In *Werke*, Vol. I: 547–94. Ed. Karl-Gustav Garold. Munich: Hanser Verlag, 1953.

Hölderlin, Friedrich. *"Bevestiger Gesang": Die neu zu entdeckende hymnische Spätdichtung bis 1806.* Edited by Dietrich Uffhausen. Stuttgart: J. B. Metzler, 1989.

———. *Gedichte.* Edited by Gustav Schwab, Ludwig Uhland, Justinus Kerner. Stuttgart and Tübingen: Cotta, 1826.

———. *Hymns and Fragments.* Translated by Richard Sieburth. Princeton, N.J.: Princeton University Press, 1984.

———. *Poems and Fragments.* Translated by Michael Hamburger. Cambridge: Cambridge University Press, 1966.

———. *Sämtliche Werke.* Edited by Friedrich Beißner and Adolf Beck. 7 Vols., Stuttgart: Kohlhammer, Cotta, 1943–1977.

Hunt, Morton. *The Universe Within. A New Science Explores the Human Mind.* New York: Simon and Schuster, 1982.

Jamme, Christoph. "'ein kranker oder gesunder Geist'? Berichte über Hölderlins Krankheit in den Jahren 1804–1806." *Jenseits des Idealismus.*

Hölderlins letzte Homburger Jahre (1804–1806). Edited by Christoph Jamme and Otto Pöggeler, 279–90. Bonn: Bouvier Verlag, 1988.

Janin, Jules. *Critique portraits et caractéres contemporains.* Paris: Hachette, 1841.

Jeanneret, Michel. *La Lettre Perdue. Écriture et Folie dans l'oeuvre de Nerval.* Paris: Flammarion, 1978.

Jean Paul. *Sämtliche Werke.* 10 Vols. Edited by Walter Höllerer, Gustav Lohmann, Norbert Miller. Abteilung II. Edited by N. Miller and Wilhelm Schmidt-Biggeman. Munich: Hanser Verlag, 1959–1985.

Kristeva, Julia. *La révolution du langage poétique.* Paris: Seuil, 1974.

Lokke, Kari. *Gérard de Nerval. The Poet as Social Visionary.* Lexington, Ky.: French Forum, 1987.

Middlebrook, Diane. *Anne Sexton: A Biography.* Boston: Houghton and Mifflin, 1991.

Mirecourt, Eugène. *Gérard de Nerval.* Paris: Rouet, 1854.

Monro, John. *Remarks on Dr. Battie's Treatise on Madness.* London: Clarke, 1758.

Müller-Seidel, Walter. "Hölderlin in Homburg. Sein Spätwerk im Kontext seiner Krankheit." In *Homburg vor der Höhe in der deutschen Geistesgeschichte. Studien zum Freundeskreis um Hegel und Hölderlin.* Edited by Christoph Jamme and Otto Pöggeler, 161–88. Stuttgart: Klett-Cotta, 1981.

Nägele, Rainer. *Literatur und Utopie. Versuche zu Hölderlin.* Heidelberg: Lothar Stiehm Verlag, 1978.

Nerval, Gérard de. *Chimeras.* Translated by Peter Jay, with essays by Richard Holmes and Peter Jay. Redding Ridge, Conn.: Black Swann Books, 1984.

———. *Les Chimères.* Edited by Norma Rinsler. London: Athalone Press, 1973.

Plato. *The Collected Dialogues of Plato.* Edited by Edith Hamilton and Huntington Cairns. Princeton, N.J.: Princeton University Press, 1961.

Richer, Jean. *Nerval par les témoins de sa vie.* Paris: Menard, 1970.

Ricklefs, Ulfert. "Arnims poetologische Theorie." *Magie und Grenze. Arnims 'Päpstin Johanna'-Dichtung,* 19–58. Göttingen: Vandenhoeck and Ruprecht, 1990.

Röllecke, Heinz. "Achim von Arnim und Friedrich Hölderlin. Ein neuentdecktes Fragment Arnims über 'Empedokles'," *Hölderlin-Jahrbuch* 18 (1973/74): 149–58.

Ryan, Thomas E. *Hölderlin's Silence.* New York, Bern, Frankfurt, Paris: Peter Lang Verlag, 1988.

Schmidt, Jochen, ed. *Dichter über Hölderlin.* Frankfurt: Insel Verlag, 1969.

———. *Hölderlins später Widerruf in den Oden "Chiron," "Blödigkeit," und "Ganymed."* Tübingen: Max Niemeyer Verlag, 1978.

———. *Hölderlins geschichts-philosophische Hymnen "Friedensfeier," "Der Einzige," "Patmos."* Darmstadt: Wissenschaftliche Buchgesellschaft, 1990.

Streller, Dorothea. *Achim von Arnim und das Drama.* Ph.D. diss. Göttingen, 1956.

Thomasberger, Andreas. "Der gedichtete Dichter. Zum metaphorasischen Charakter der 'Ausflüge mit Hölderlin' von Ludwig Achim von Arnim." *Aurora* 45 (1985): 283–300.

Young, Edward. *Conjectures on Original Composition.* London: Printed for A. Millar and R. and J. Dodsley, 1759.

Youngquist, Paul. *Madness and Blake's Myth.* University Park: Pennsylvania State University Press, 1989.

II

Interactive Identities

Gender and the Novel

3

April Alliston

Of Haunted Highlands
Mapping a Geography of Gender
in the Margins of Europe

The map of Europe during the period of transition from the Enlightenment to Romanticism is a map of sensibility, in that it involves a gradual plotting of geographical boundaries in accordance with conceptions of national character that precede, in many cases, the existence of corresponding states. Political boundaries may be contested, fluid, or permeable and unpoliced by their very topographical impassability.[1] The entities they delineate may be centralized nation states or occupied territories; they may be principalities, communes, or republics, with or without loose cultural and political association. Much more stable are the boundaries of discourse defining the various national characters that compose the cultural idea of Europe being institutionalized in our own historical moment. Enlightenment national typecasting went alongside and in fact entailed the development of the specific gender stereotypes that are still being invoked in the name of the nation, integral as they are to notions like "family values."[2]

Femininity, in the post-Enlightenment era, is domesticated by its exile to that private realm on the separation from which the idea of the nation state is founded. On the map of national character, Scotland is likewise a wild margin, surely yet uneasily domesticated, since the early eighteenth century, within the boundaries of one of Europe's strongest nation states. A series of later eighteenth-century plots marks off Scotland's boundaries around the proof of the domestication of femininity: the spectacle of suffering feminine virtue. This essay will survey an international insistence upon locating that scene in Scotland, and upon making it the intersection of a heroine's plot as destiny (*destinée*, Providence, *Schicksal*) with her "plot" of ground, a destination marked off for her.[3] Pursuing this "Scottish plot" through German, French, and English novels written by women—Sophie von La Roche,

Sophia Lee, and Germaine de Staël—I shall attempt to show what kind of boundary lines plot the borders of Scotland as a heroine's "plot" in these fictions, and where those lines situate the feminine in late eighteenth-century Europe.[4]

Exile from the public sphere entails exile from legal (i.e. public) identity, and hence from the possession and transmission of property.[5] Women's novels of the period therefore tend to express exile from the public sphere as exile from real estate as well, and from the lines of inheritance through which it is transmitted. Thus, exile from the public sphere is in fact exile from the domestic space itself, or exile to it *and* from its proper possession. The state of exile from the patriline plot that describes both public and private spheres is not in fact a state, but an itinerary.[6] Its "dynamic logic," to misapply a phrase from Peter Brooks, is created here not out of a hero's desire, but out of the torsion of several "vectors" of desire: that of the heroine's desire, that of paternal will, and that of the maternal figure's educating direction.[7] The heroine's desire cannot be specified any more than as a desire to trace out the boundaries of her own plot; but this inevitably entails crossing the intertwined plot-lines of patrilineal will and of the borderlines that are gradually dividing Europe into nation states roughly corresponding to the earlier ideas of national character.

If the trajectory of female desire has a geographical destination, it might be called "the mother country," a place whose "national character" was described by Sandra Gilbert and Susan Gubar in the terms of the nineteenth-century writers whose works they were interpreting—and who inherited their ideas in large part from earlier writers, notably Germaine de Staël, whose work will be considered here. In those terms, the mother country is one whose social and historical borders are not defined patrilineally, where power, agency, identity are heritable through female lines.[8] The "mother country" is, of course, a utopia, and this makes it a false destination. Its unstable borders, the boundaries of a state of exile, can only be plotted through the trajectory of the heroine's sentimental journey. A heroine cannot dwell in this state: being always neither here nor there, she can only haunt it.

The tie that binds, or twists together the heroine's desire for self-destination together with the paternal will to determine all destinations through the transmission of property (the children's sexual desire shall conform itself to paternal real estate transactions), is the third vector of desire: the maternal education in virtue.[9] For the inheritor of feminine virtue, any active expression of desire is proscribed by definition. The demand of a reader—of one who would know the truth of the heroine's virtue—both authorizes and compels the narrative which alone can establish it. The plots that are generated in response to that narrative demand are various, but the crossing of national boundaries is common to many, and more than one of these narrative roads leads to Scotland.

I

National character is as heritable as real estate in Sophie von La Roche's *Geschichte des Fräuleins von Sternheim* (1771), but the novel questions the sense in which any "property" (in both senses, that of "possession" and that of "quality") is transmissible through blood lines. Sophie von Sternheim inherits an estate from her father, the middle-class son of a professor ennobled through his own masculine virtues, as developed through a proper education.[10] This inheritance is from the outset unusual in terms of the conventions of contemporary sentimental novels: here the estate is not hereditary to the father but purchased by him, just as his title is acquired through education, not received. Moreover, the father has spent his life improving the estate according to enlightened liberal principles of educating and assisting the poor.[11] Sophie inherits the land with the propensity to "improvement" in all its senses, but she is simultaneously the inheritor of a complex maternal legacy.

From her mother—another Sophie whose own mother had been an English aristocrat—our Sophie receives some distinctly un-German sensibilities. We are told that "in addition to all the gentle amiability of an Englishwoman, [Sophie's mother] seemed to have inherited from her mother the melancholy which distinguishes that nation. . . . She loved solitude, which she put to use in diligently reading the best books, without, however, neglecting any opportunity of sequestering herself with the members of her family without outside company" (52 [20–21]). Throughout her own life, the younger Sophie demonstrates that she is truly heir to her maternal legacy (e. g. 70–71 [51–52]). Transmission by inheritance and transmission by education are conflated, as both the paternal, German propensity to "improvement" and a sensibility characterized as at once feminine and foreign (English), are inherited along with the improved real estate.

As an inheritance, feminine virtue resembles both character traits and real estate. It is associated with the English nation and the feminine gender, and is "inherited" through education. As a "property" it is unlocatable, and yet it provides the necessary grounds for any possession of real property. The important difference between feminine virtue and either national character or patrimony is its peculiar status as a "property" of the heroine, or more specifically the problem of verifying her possession of it. We already know, for example, that no female can be more virtuous than Sophie's mother, when we see her giving vent to her English melancholy over her own secret but virtuous desire for the social inferior who is to become our heroine's father. Yet because of the fundamental unverifiability of virtue as a property or possession, her own brother is able to misinterpret that melancholy as evidence of her failure to have inherited virtue (56 [28]). Unrepresentable as plot (solid ground, heritable real estate), feminine virtue must respond to the demand for evidence from an inscribed reader (here, the brother), whose interpretive authority alone is capable of conferring reality on the "estate" of virtue. This virtue must inscribe itself through a *narrative* plot that continually insists upon its own status as the staging of a visible spectacle.[12]

The process of education through which Sophie "inherits" her parents' character traits is also that which transmits the instability of virtue as a property. We only begin to see this, however, after the necessity of representing virtue as narrative in response to a reader's demand has propelled the heroine off of her inherited plot of ground. That narrative must traverse national boundaries in order to establish, stage, and locate the truth of her virtue, the property which alone can characterize her as a proper heroine. Indeed, Sophie's own character as one that crosses the boundaries of national character is stressed throughout the book (e.g. 70–71, 74 [51–52, 57]). Only once Sophie has left her inherited plot of ground for the court of D.—in response to the demand of a bad substitute mother—is it established that this necessity of staging the narrative of her virtue was always already a determining quality of that virtue.

The court of D. is, like the French court in *La Princesse de Clèves*, a stage upon which all is spectacle and feminine virtue is unrepresentable because nothing is what it appears to be. Sophie's first *appearance* at court is as an *apparition* (*Erscheinung* has both meanings); no sooner has she costumed herself for her first court appearance and stepped into her first ballroom, than she is taken for a ghost. The first courtier she meets jokes that Sophie looks like a house-haunting ghost (*Hausgespenst*).[13] Lame as this is as *galanterie*, the pun makes it clear to Sophie that in truth she is "a kind of ghost [*Gespenst*], not only in this house, but also in town and at court" (78–79 [64–65]). In thus defining and locating herself as ghost, Sophie succinctly delineates the foreignness of D. in relation to her home at P. By replacing place names with initials, La Roche renders unrecognizable any political boundary Sophie may have crossed in her journey, in order to emphasize instead the crossing of a boundary between the rural retirement of private life, as valued by Sophie's English sensibilities, and the public life of town and court as spectacle, where, again as in Marie de Lafayette's novel, the private and the public are intertwined. If D. is foreign, it is not because it may be in a different

German principality from P., but rather because it is not "English" enough.

The princess of Clèves continues to haunt Sophie's text when the latter characterizes herself as a ghost. Sophie is not surprised by anything she sees in a place she describes as "according to all my sensibilities an entirely new world," because pictures of it were painted for her by her father, just as "pictures of love" were painted for the princess by her mother.[14] This *Bildung*—both education and painting—makes it possible for Sophie to draw solemn comparisons disadvantageous to the frivolous world she now haunts. One of the principle subjects of her disapproval is the participation of women in public affairs (which notably characterized Lafayette's descriptions of French court life). She admits a certain unavoidable astonishment, however, at seeing what for her had always been a still picture, although a very familiar one ("painted" for her by her father), suddenly come into motion "through a *foreign* power" (*fremde Kraft*) (76–80).[15] The court is thus as ghostly for Sophie as she is to it. It is as much a foreign power to her as her sensibility is foreign to it: "Oh, my dear, what a stranger (*wie fremd*) my heart is in this place" (99).[16]

The relation of the foreign to the familiar in this passage has the character of possession. The "foreign power" that uncannily animates the court for Sophie already haunts Sophie herself, by means of a combination of maternal inheritance and paternal education (the latter itself modeled on maternal education in a foreign text—*La Princesse de Clèves*). This haunted foreignness, or "possessed" quality in Sophie explains the otherwise puzzling remark on her appearance as apparition by the courtiers at D. (who are themselves ghostly). For Sophie already has an educational history as a specter. On being shown a portrait of her recently dead mother, the "excessive sensibilities" inherited from that mother cause her, as a child, to "fall on her knees dissolved in tears, and ardently wish to die, that she might be with her [mother]" (70 [51]). Her father's educational corrective for this sympathetic desire to become as dead as the picture: to make his daughter dress up in her mother's plain English-style clothing, thus transforming her into the mother's "lively image." This is done to such effect that the father, on seeing her transformed into her mother's image, feels the same astonishment at seeing a picture come to life as that ~~~~~ ~~ ~~ on her arrival at court (72–73, 80 [55, 68]).

In this first stage of Sophie's itinerary, she transports with her from the paternal home to D. both aspects of her "possession." Portraits of father and mother, set in a locket that conceals earth from their graves beneath the miniatures, stand both metaphorically and metonymically for the inheritance she leaves behind in the patrimonial ground that was the scene of her upbringing, and to which she fears her parents' ghosts are bound. A glimpse of her mother's image, rendered disturbingly *unlike* her own when she makes her first court *toilette*, immediately precedes Sophie's "apparition" at court. She reassures herself that this unlikeness can go no further than dress, since the essential element of the resemblance, what makes her both the ghost of her mother and a ghost at court, haunting it despite her own moral disapproval and displacement, is her willingness to defer to the demands of others. Such deferral is a characteristic of feminine sensibility and virtue, but it can also compromise both qualities in the eyes of others, as the mother's and the daughter's story both demonstrate (e.g. 54–56, 89–90, 144, 217 [24–28, 83, 175, 305]).

If a picture suddenly come to life is possessed, it is also dramatized: the stage-like quality of the court has already been noted. D. becomes the scene where several competing plots are staged, and at stake in the competition is the public establishment of Sophie's virtue. Her kin manipulate her English-feminine-virtuous quality, willingness to please, in their efforts to make her the Prince's mistress as part of an exchange of their property in her feminine virtue for his real property. Mylord Seymour, the typically feminized sentimental hero, who possesses the same excessive English sensibilities as Sophie, intends marriage in accordance with both his desire and his honor. The rake, Mylord Derby, devises a "plan for a German novel" around his own seduction of Sophie and consequent triumph over his two rivals.[17] The problem for Seymour and Sophie, for the plot of virtuous desire culminating in marriage, is that before he possesses her he must *know* that she truly possesses virtue.[18] That is why, knowing of the Prince's plot, he waits to see how Sophie will perform in the spectacle concerted to achieve her downfall instead of warning her of it. But since virtue is unrepresentable on and at this stage, he misinterprets her performance and leaves her to seek protection from the pressure of the court plot in the clutches of the rake.

The demand for a spectacular narrative or theater of virtue thus fails initially in its overt aim: that of establishing the heroine's possession of virtue (or rather her possession *by* virtue as the form of ghostly *Bildung* that made her a foreigner at the aristocratic court). Instead that demand generates a kind of traveling show in which each repetition is only a rehearsal, never attended by the proper audience, the one who might legitimate her at last. Whisked off to a sham marriage and abandoned shortly thereafter by the rake, Sophie crosses her first national border alone, and adopts her own stage or pen name, Madame Leidens (Mrs. Suffering). She sets up her "Seminary for Domestics" in Belgium, and her orphaned pupils take on her name along with her education. Although at this point she creates her own identity, writes her own history and will, and establishes both a successful business and a matrilineal "separatist" society, it is nevertheless ominous that the name she passes on is that of Leidens (183 [244]). The "German novel" of female desire, while plotting its own destination through matrilineality, education, and escape from the court's coercive demand for a spectacle, either of virtue or of a fall from it, still continues to be staged for its inscribed audience (the reader of Sophie's epistolary narration) in terms of the very plot and spectacle from which she would escape: the proof by ordeal of her entitlement to the inheritance of feminine virtue.[19]

To return to Scotland—where Sophie's narrative, after further extending itself over time and geography, carries its heroine onto virtue's ultimate stage:

> I question whether there be, on the whole surface of the earth, a spot (Winkel) more wild and frightful than that which encompasses this wretched cottage (Zirkel um diese Hütte), destined for the melancholy prison of the lovely SOPHIA; and everything (das Schicksal) has concurred to promote the barbarous design of tormenting the most sensible of human souls.[20]

The rhetoric of this passage not only conveys a strong sense of the Gothic sensibilities that delineate the borders of Scotland on the eighteenth-century map of national character, but also precisely identifies the intersecting lines of signification with which they are drawn. The use of words from geometry, *Winkel* (angle) and *Zirkel* (both the circle and the compasses that describe it), implies the drawing of lines upon the earth: geographic lines frame the landscape in which destiny (*Schicksal*) plots the spectacle of suffering virtue, and locate that Gothic scene upon the map of Europe. These terms also inscribe the domestic reading audience, notably absent from the depicted scene, in the *Winkel* (corner) and *Zirkel* (social circle, gathering), that frame the spectacle for its view.[21]

Within the magic circle of the Scottish landscape, Sophie again appears as a ghost, condemned by the rake to "exile" from her "native country" (*Vaterland*; 226 [319]). Exile from the "fatherland" seems to mean exile from Germany, but Derby's "German novel" has now doubly exiled its heroine, this time from England too. Having found England haunted by the comforting presence of her mother's ghost, the heroine as "Mrs. Suffering" has pursued a plot to "view the land [England] as that of my fathers" (202 [dieses Land für mein väterliches Land ansehe[n], 278]; also 209 [291]). The mother's country, then, becomes the ghostly double of the fatherland, its displaced shadow, as the mother herself is the mere double of the father in terms of contemporary legal and economic definitions of parenthood.[22]

Returned to the ghostly character that was already inscribed in her early education, Sophie haunts the highlands as a "dead image" (*totes Bild*) because she has been from birth a "lively image" of her dead mother, with all her excessive sensibility, her willingness to lend herself to others' plots, and her unverifiable, because unrepresentable, feminine virtue.[23] Derby's and Seymour's plots for Sophie are in fact the same—and the same as her father's educational plot—in that all three men desire to construct her history as a narrative unfolding towards a static endpoint that would reveal the heroine to them as the "moving" picture of feminine virtue, capable of "moving" *them* only insofar as it no longer moves itself. Thus, even Lord Derby, insensible when he watched her perform, capable of deceiving, raping, and abandoning, then abducting and imprisoning Sophie in the flesh, is moved by her image: "her picture made a stronger impression on me than all the attributes of her character" (215 [301]). All these masculine plots end in and point to Scotland, where Sophie's imaginary death transforms her into a pure exemplary image that haunts only their minds. Her own plot, however, of fictionalizing that death and surviving her own exemplarity (unlike Clarissa or Julie, and unlike the heroines of the other two novels read here) gives the change to all her male counterplotters.

Scotland is no more distinguished from England politically in the novel than P. is from D. within Germany. It is a corner (*Winkel*) of the English "mother country," where Madame Leidens can be exiled from England while still imprisoned within its boundaries—that is, haunting it. Described in the Gothic terms associated throughout with the mother and England, Scotland as "plot" (the whole country is restricted for the heroine to "a small plot of ground near an old ruinous castle") is the scene of a paradoxical exile that is also a paradoxical haunting: a haunting by a ghost who is not dead, but has been subjected to a form of live burial. Only from within the tomb (she is at one point literally left for dead in the ruined castle) can Sophie write the last in a succession of histories and wills—"The Journal of Madame Leidens in the Highlands of Scotland," ghostwritten in madness for no earthly reader, and containing the text of her own epitaph. This text will stand at last as documentary evidence of her virtue. She does of course manage to transmit this evidence to an audience within the text, once more by educational means. By teaching her poor keepers' daughter to do fancy needlework, she is able indirectly to attract a countess's curiosity to know where the girl learned it. With the aristocrat's help, she stages a further plot of her own to escape her Scottish imprisonment.

The *Zirkel* of Scotland seems to be the proper scene for the staging of the narrative of virtue, just as the court had earlier been described, despite its evils, as "the most proper stage" (*Kreis*—another word, like *Zirkel*, for "circle") for the exhibition of certain qualities (107 [113]). Scotland is the Gothic stage required by the convergence of masculine plots for the transformation of a living woman into a ghostly image, a *totes Bild* that evidences virtuous education (*Bildung*). Its "barren mountains," furthermore, set the necessary scene for the new education that actually *produces*, rather than merely evidencing, the heroine's virtue by allowing her scope for the display of charitable virtues independent of masculine financial means (e.g. 229 [325]). Virtue itself has taken on new moral value as staged within the Scottish plot, and so has the heroine's own plotting. Sophie has viewed her trajectory from D. to Scotland as punishment for the fault of having engaged in "secret cunning" (173 [227]). The Highlands as *Zirkel*, however, a picturesque panopticon prison that creates by enclosing and renders knowable what it creates, afford a new perspective on the relation between feminine virtue and female plotting. Thus, Sophie concludes of her final scheme to escape: "I should be culpable indeed if I did not use every opportunity to achieve my freedom" (224 [316]). In Scotland, the narrative demand that had drawn the heroine from the circle of her own property across the map of Europe has at last become her own active appeal. Plotting and feigning finally become "honest means," that is, the means of establishing the heroine's honesty, with an appeal to a powerful maternal figure (the countess) through the education of a substitute daughter (the keeper's daughter). The narrative of virtue, always subject to skeptical demands for unproducible evidence, becomes in Scotland a ghost story of self-determining female desire.

Ghostliness becomes identified in the circle of the Highlands as knowledge of virtue's truth, of the meaning of its own plot as completed by Providence. Sophie expects that this knowledge (*die Endzwecke*) will be revealed there to her soul after death. This is a knowledge more complete than the higher moral understanding, the perspective with a view to the end, that previously made her ghostly at court (224 [316]). Her final plot is her own burial plot, in which she stages her burial in and exhumation from Scotland's "maternal earth." Her plot to determine the signification of her own virtue through the text of her last will calls for multiple monuments in the absence of remains, a strategy that will allow her to haunt various places simultaneously. (She has already enabled her parents to do this by making part of their grave portable, in the locket she wears.) Because her burial plot is fictional (unlike Clarissa's), it thwarts the new united plot of Seymour, Derby, and Seymour's fatherly but lovestruck brother to assuage their own guilt by disturbing her remains in order to bury them with pomp beneath an inscription that would reinsert her into their own plot: "where the description of her virtues and sufferings is to be engraved beside the evidence of his eternal repentance" (230 [326]). Instead, Sophie's triumphant plot of return from the grave kills off the rake, transforms the paternal suitor into a living tombstone on which her virtues are eternally graven, and puts her in possession not only of her own virtue, but of her new husband, Seymour, and his property. This possession will make possible not only the continued display of charitable virtue on a grand scale, but even the removal, by replication, of her own paternal estate to English soil (242 [346]; cf. the removal of earth from the paternal grave).[24] Marrying Seymour does mean not retiring to her own inherited estate, to which she had always wanted to return. Instead she remains in the "mother country" where, she has learned, her heart is as foreign as it had been at D. (235 [334]). But now that the expression of her virtue is "bounded only by Seymour's vast possessions," she possesses the "honest means" to map the foreign as familiar, that is, to possess the other, to haunt. At the end of her plot, Sophie can haunt all the places and all the men her narrative has traversed; she possesses them, finally, as she possesses the plot of virtue and of her double estate.

II

In Sophia Lee's *The Recess* (1783–1785), Scotland is no longer the circle within which a heroine can stage her own narrative of virtue and self-destination, and thereby constitute herself as reader of her own virtue, in possession of all the elements of her inheritance. Lee's Scotland is instead the ghostly estate promised by maternal inheritance, which turns out to be only the dead-end plot of return to the "mother country." Differently than in *Sternheim*, it is the grave-plot of maternal origin.

The twin orphaned heroines of *The Recess* grow up literally in a tomb, reared by a substitute mother who lives in it with them, and by a religious "father" who comes and goes mysteriously through a concealed passage. When they come of age, their dying foster mother at last reveals the secret of their identity: they are the clandestine heirs of Mary, Queen of Scots, hidden away so as not to endanger their own lives or their mother's. This bequest of substantiatable identity does not provide them with the longed-for means of escape from the Recess, however, because the Queen of Scots still lives, like them, in a death-in-life of imprisonment in England. As long as she survives, her daughters are condemned to mirror her destiny, under threat of precipitating their mother's death. Yet at the same time their mother's state of imprison-ment and exile, unrecognized "in the midst of a kingdom to which she is the lawful heir," is what authorizes all plots to escape their own "live burial" in order to restore their mother to freedom and kingdom.[25] The source of the tension that drives the plot of the novel is the double bind of the demand that, on the one hand, the heroines follow the educative example of their foster mother and "walk willingly into the tomb" in order to save the true mother from the axe to which she is already historically doomed, while, on the other hand, they expose their inherited proofs of identity to readers carefully chosen as sympathetic and empowered to help make good the line of transmission those proofs represent. That double bind constitutes, finally, the only actual or possible legacy of the Queen of Scots.

Propelled by their narrative double bind from one concealment to another, the heroines describe a wide geography. The flight of one sister from England separates the twins and splits their narrative into a doubled memoir-letter.[26] Each twin travels a different route, but both heroines die of a failure, ultimately, to determine their own plots.

The heroines and their journeys are each associated with an inher-itance from one of their parents. Matilda is her mother's "perfect image"; she becomes a mother herself, and she never commits an action not strictly conformable to the feminine virtue inherited from her mother and learned from her sustitute mother (I: 57). Her journey through two false destinations delineates a paradoxical border that locates the impossibility of the mother country in relation to the nation of England. England may be ruled over by a queen, indeed (Elizabeth I), but it is characterized by that queen's "unfeminine use of power" (I: 214). Matilda first looks to France as an equally powerful, independent nation in which she may find enough residual maternal influence to help her regain the inheritance of Mary, who was once a queen there. The problem with her conception of the French nation state as potential mother country is that the maternal power she seeks there depends on unreliable others: these others turn out to be a dead king and a substitute mother figure dominated by what English Gothic fiction characteristically paints as a negative trait of French national character: "superstition" (Catholicism).

As in *Geschichte des Fräuleins von Sternheim*, the heroine's plot always depends here on the hand of Providence lent through another; thus, her plot is inextricably intertwined with the paternal plot of Providence working through others' competing plots. But since others do have their own competing plots, they tend to be unreliable aids. A man who offers escape from Matilda's new prison (a French convent) takes her captive to Jamaica, which, like France, is a mother country *manqué*. There

Matilda, pregnant by her murdered husband (the earl of Leicester), becomes the mother of a new female heir to the throne of Scotland. Condemned in turn to mirror maternal destiny, this daughter is raised within prison walls. A tower—phallic prison—with a commanding view of the colony, replaces the ambiguous fissure within the English state, at once protective and restrictive, at once enclosing and open, that is the Recess. The imprisoning tower proves to be an equally ambiguous structure whose prospect makes escape possible through a necessary communication with an outside power capable of penetrating its enclosure.

The lent hand here is that of an African slave woman whose queenly power derives from her illicit relations with the Jamaican governor. She becomes a substitute mother to Matilda's daughter, passing on to her the means of escape much as Matilda's own substitute mother did to her at the beginning of the novel. But as Matilda's inheritance of knowledge (knowledge, that is, of her own identity and the secret springs that open the Recess) was transmitted through the double bind of female virtue that kept her returning alive to the tomb, her daughter's inheritance is also doubly valent. When the slave on her deathbed hands to Matilda's daughter the casket containing her legacy, just as Mrs. Marlow did to Matilda and Ellinor, Matilda worries that the "horrible distemper" of which the slave is actually dying will be transmitted to her daughter along with the treasure (II: 148–49). The "dis-temper" indeed proves more dangerous than any fleeting fever: the daughter ultimately ruins Matilda's last plot to regain the Scottish throne and dies a fallen woman, all the result of following her own plot of desire for the wrong man instead of obediently marrying her cousin, the Stuart heir to the English crown, according to her mother's desire.

Thus, Jamaica turns out to be a false "mother country." It is not the low road that would lead, any faster than the high road of France, back to a Scotland that could be reconstructed as the mother's kingdom. Jamaica as mother country remains a colony, despite its slave rebellion and a demonstrated degree of female sexual freedom unthinkable within the nation proper. It is a colony where female desire is free but not unfettered, a country controlled through a system of slavery for the sole use and profit of the nation state. While it remains imprisoned within the boundaries of the European "mother country," it also remains untranslatably free of European definitions of the proper lady. The maternal inheritance that is transmitted there fails to liberate because it cannot locate a woman in any proper place within the borders of the European nation that ineluctably contain both woman and colony as other. The daughter's Jamaican desire refuses to follow the patrilineal trajectory of her mother's plot, and once again the borders of the utopian mother country disappear as the Stuart succession brings Scotland, by Lee's own time, as surely and as uneasily within the boundaries of the English nation state as is its counterpart, the Jamaican colony.

The heroine's twin, Ellinor, is by contrast her father's daughter. Matilda remarks at the outset her sister's uncanny resemblance to the full-length portrait of the nobleman that hangs next to that of an equally imposing woman, concealing the exit to their tomb. Unlike Matilda, Ellinor does not become a mother, nor does her feminine virtue remain equally unquestioned (e.g. II: 152). This difference comes about because for Ellinor the threat of fault for the mother's death, which fastens the double bind of feminine virtue, becomes reality: unlike Matilda, she learns of Mary's death when it happens, and is tricked by Elizabeth into considering herself responsible for it. Asking herself how she can have "survived her innocence," Ellinor proceeds to stage the plot of her own ghostliness, refusing a perfectly gallant offer of rescue by her swain in order to conceive and carry through her own plot of escape by staging, like Sophie von Sternheim, the spectacle of her own death and burial (II: 55). From this point, where Ellinor's travels begin, she is characterized by an unfeminine insistence on actively "framing fictions," a quality represented as highly ambiguous by the standards of Matilda's unerringly feminine virtue. This property in Ellinor only passes the standards of authorial and readerly virtue because of Ellinor's status as double of her sister, who remains the primary heroine (II, 164). Upon a double the burden of action can be safely placed without compromising the novel's main heroine.[27]

Just as Matilda's journey plots an impossible geography of the "mother country," Ellinor's traverses a series of "fatherlands." After stubbornly following her lover (the earl of Essex) on his disastrous Irish campaign, straight into the forbidden masculine world of warfare, she is captured by Tyrone's forces but escapes on her own by dressing as a man. It is thus as man *and* ghost (she is still generally believed dead) that Ellinor steers her own boat towards the north of England (Norfolk, the domain of the fourth duke, her father), but is shipwrecked instead at a castle on the rocky coast of Scotland at Dornock. Providence's plot thus intervenes in her self-steered course to bring her away from the place that bears the paternal name, and instead into a place whose name inscribes the Christian imperative of petitioning for divine assistance ("*Knock*, and the *door* shall be opened"). The door of a Gothic castle is opened to her call for help after the shipwreck, but it opens into a prison without walls, where assistants without means are just as circumscribed by it as she is: "a scanty library, a lute, some rustic airs, and a pedigree as old as the creation, bounded the possessions, and the knowledge of our young friends, and could not add any thing to our own" (III: 104). Trapped by the desolate landscape itself, and by the "bounded possessions" of its inhabitants, Ellinor finds in Scotland a dead-end for female agency. Still, in her masculine disguise, she attracts the young chatelaine, but the latter and her young brother are completely powerless under the patriarchal despotism of a boorish elder brother, whose very isolation in the Scottish landscape makes him truly a king in his own castle. Ellinor cannot help them directly because her masculinity is only a fiction, but, like the fiction of her death, it does help her elude the permanent imprisonment to which she would have been vulnerable in feminine guise.

Ellinor's version of crossing gender boundaries is represented more positively in this novel than Queen Elizabeth's, but that is because it lacks the latter's *"unfeminine use of power"*; thus, the heroine finally finds herself entrapped, like her mother, "in the midst of a kingdom to which she is the lawful heir" (I: 181; III: 101–3). Having "interred her name" by framing her first boundary-crossing fiction—that of her own death— she had hoped "to emerge again with unfaltering reason, and a temper superior to the shocks of misfortune" (III: 43). But she can only emerge from Scotland by relying at last on her lover's rescue, and her subsequent death in madness proves that the plotted rebirth was only fantasy. Ellinor raised from the tomb remains a foreign ghost, haunting "the country of all her ancestors," where the inhabitants speak "a language unknown to her." Scotland's foreignness within the nation state renders it the location of an impotent and unlegitimizable, unverifiable female inheritance. Negative gender conventions are reinforced, so that the crossing of their boundaries renders the heroine a nonpresence, an impotent specter whose forcible re-feminization conjures her away into England, madness, and death.

III

Scotland is no "mother country," by contrast, in Germaine de Staël's *Corinne* (1807). It is the location neither of an inheritance of maternal character nor of any maternal rights to authority, however illegitimate. It is, however, the site of transmission of both patrimonial real estate and a substitute mother's education in feminine virtue—which alone, as in the other novels, can authorize a heroine's possession of real property. Corinne's rejection of that education (which this novel, like *Sternheim*, attributes to English national character) therefore entails as well her forfeit of her English patrimony. She becomes at first an exile from the site of her own patrimony. Returning across its boundary, towards the end of the novel, she finds that the only kind of presence she can maintain within it is that of a ghost—a haunting presence.

The property itself, the alienated Scottish patrimony, is real estate in the Gothic taste: the dead fathers of both Corinne and her lover Oswald have left adjoining estates, sharing a common boundary line, the focal points of which are the tombs where their spirits hover. (Like Sophie von Sternheim, Oswald leaves his patrimonial ground with the guilty sense of abandoning his father, expressed as a similar anxiety that the spirits of the dead are confined to the burial place.)

In her Italian exile Corinne, unlike the earlier heroines, actually seems to have found that utopia, the "mother country." What breaks the magic circle of its border is another version of the same force that penetrates the boundaries of Sophie von Sternheim's patrimonial estate and the *Zirkel* of her Scottish landscape, or the apparently exitless Recess and the series of enclosed spaces that substitute for it. That force is the tension of narrative energy generated when the female desire to possess a plot of one's own meets with the inscribed reader's desire to possess the narrative that alone can represent feminine virtue. Here the providential plot of God the Father is thinly disguised as the will of ghostly fathers. In *The Recess* and *Geschichte des Fräuleins von Sternheim*, the providential plot ambiguously represents the paternally authorized demand for a closed narrative of virtue, while also masking (and thus authorizing) the plot generated by the heroine's own desire. Here, paternal will directs that it be virtuous Lucile, and not self-willed Corinne, whom his son Oswald shall marry. The fact that this is the will of a *dead* father not only apotheosizes it, but also provides for its literal mapping onto Corinne's own inherited plot of land. For Oswald's father has a second tomb, a memorial erected by Corinne's half-sister Lucile on their own dead father's adjacent land: a book in which Oswald's dead father has inscribed his appreciation of the unsullied feminine virtue of Lucile, the perfect product of a maternal education.[28]

Oswald's straying into Corinne's mother country for his health and "the southern air" represents a feminized tergiversation against paternal plot, a resistance through delay rather than a direct opposition to the paternal destination.[29] When he arrives in Italy, she recognizes that her utopian, self-plotted life there has remained unsatisfying in its international relations. The perversity of Corinne's desire is that it cannot disentangle itself from the plot of the father: what makes Oswald uniquely desirable to her is precisely his having inherited that melancholy, haunted English character most fully expressed in the Scottish landscapes, and represented by the haunted paternal estate. As in the other two novels, the narrative torsion that twists the plot of female desire together with that of the paternal will generates the heroine's narrative and moves her out of her initial stasis, carrying her through and back out of that liminal country, the non-nation of Scotland.

The problem with Italy as mother country lends a different expression to the similar problems of Jamaica or Scotland as mother countries in *The Recess*. All three places, in their different ways, are inscribed within the margins of a Europe that is beginning to define itself on a map drawn of shared but mutually exclusive boundaries. Inscribed within the margins of that map, Italy, like Jamaica and Scotland, is denied the clear borderlines of property that would make it recognizable as a cohesive and independent state. It is at once too divided internally and too indistinct from the nation states that seek, like Napoleon's France, to incorporate it within the expanding boundaries of the nation as new Roman Empire.[30] Because of the mother country's problematic status as a recognizable plot of ground, presence in the mother country—be it a fluid collection of city-states on the border of Europe, an ancient kingdom become the "Celtic fringe" of one of its strongest states, or the distant colony at once absorbed by and excluded from that nation—is never fully presence. It is never a stable stasis, that is, in a proper place. Presence there always also signifies absence, exile, and death within the borders of the *patrie*.

Italy is a plot, then, that resembles the plot of feminine virtue: lacking a stable ground that would allow it to be recognized as property, its borders can only be plotted through history, in narrative time. Thus, most of the novel's length is a presentation of Italy as travelogue, as place-become-narrative, the only kind of ground where the heroine's own plot can begin and end. Corinne, as travel guide and *improviste*, creates Italy as the ground of her own mother country, region by region and ruin by ruin, out of her narration of its history. Already possessed by the same paternal muse who returns to haunt her in the melancholy Scottish character of Oswald, she finally constructs, or rather recollects, the free, sunny Italy of the maternal utopia as one enormous Gothic ruin, abandoned by a long history of dead fathers who have littered the landscape with the traces of their empire: "O memory, noble power, your empire is here!"[31] This empire of memory occupies the site of the mother country, the place where women like Corinne can live—for a while. Even there, however, they live in irrevocable exile from the land of dead fathers, wandering the ruins like exiled ghosts: "our soul seems to yearn for an ancient fatherland, towards which the past leads us."[32] Thus Corinne sings of the Roman women whose heroism consists in surviving the republican heroes, their husbands and lovers, all of whom died for the *patrie*: "Wandering like ghosts on the ravaged shores of the eternal river, these unfortunate creatures yearn to cross to the other side" (244).[33] When Oswald returns to England/Scotland, Corinne left behind in Italy can only sigh, like the Roman widows, with an exile's desire for that other shore. Her desire, intertwined as it is with the providential plot of the dead father's will, is strong enough to return her there. But Corinne's epic journey to the "underworld" or ghostly realm of Scotland remains where it begins, its beginning, like its endpoint, contained within the "empire of death," or of dead fathers.[34]

Even by the waters of Acheron, Corinne will not find rest. If ancient Italy is portrayed as a land of dead men that was haunted by living women, modern England is the burial plot, not only of the fathers, but of the daughter as well. Her return to it is that of a *revenant*, a ghost come back to haunt her survivors.[35] Corinne has abandoned her patronym at the demand of the substitute mother who unsuccessfully tried to force upon her the English model of feminine virtue, and who framed the fiction of Corinne's death in order to protect the virtue of her own daughter, Lucile, from taint by association. The grounds of Corinne's alienated patrimony now enclose, therefore, the tombstone upon which her own name, including her abandoned patronymic, is inscribed. Proscribed by the dead father's will (here mediated by a stepmother), Corinne first arrives in London to find herself a nearly invisible cipher, a faceless foreigner in this "country that should have been my fatherland."[36] Unrecognizable in England, she invisibly shadows Oswald to Scotland. Corinne's situation in Scotland turns out to be precisely that of the Roman widows:

> That unhappy woman wandered aimlessly along the dark paths of an estate she had the right to deem her own in days gone by, for she felt a stranger [étrangère, foreigner] now—though on paternal soil, a person isolated—though near the man she had hoped to marry. The ground gave way under her feet, and there was only the ferment of grief to give her strength (354).[37]

At this fatal moment of her encounter with Lucile on the grounds of their joint patrimonial estate, Corinne has become a ghost hovering over the tomb of their father. Lucile sees her, but recognizes in her only an apparition, a spectral Madonna whose only desire is to intercede for Lucile with their ghostly father to make good his will. Corinne understands and complicitously mediates his plot for the transmission of the plot of ground on which Corinne herself can no longer properly stand, through his other, properly feminized (and Anglicized) daughter (II: 217–18).

Scotland is here, as in the other two novels, politically indistinguishable from England, and is sometimes referred to as *Angleterre*. The boundary between the two countries, as that between P. and D. in *Geschichte des Fräuleins von Sternheim*, is really the boundary between the public and private spheres, and is as permeable. In London, the center of that political activity which Corinne admires as the most positive quality of the English character, she is seen as a living woman, but an invisible one, recognizable, if at all, only as Italian and female, excluded from participation in England's public life. In Scotland, the realm of the private world to which English women are banished, Corinne is exiled one step further, since the paternal will and the substitute mother's education leave not even a domestic space as the real inheritance of a woman who, like Corinne, attempts to oppose their "domestic plot." By "domestic plot," I mean the definition of the "domestic," with woman as its center, in opposition to both the "public" and the "foreign." The result of the heroine's resistance is her triple exile in Scotland—exile from her Italian mother country, from the public life of England, and from the Scottish patrimonial estate itself—where she becomes permanently both foreign and a ghost.

Once in Scotland, always a ghost. Even upon her return to Italy, all there is left for Corinne to do is haunt. She can and does haunt Oswald and Lucile, not only in memory, but ultimately by "possessing" their daughter. If the plot of patriline will forces her into the position of ghostly substitute mother in spite of her own rejection of the substitute mother's education in feminine virtue, her most effective form of haunting will be to educate Lucile's daughter according to her own plot, the plot of female desire, the plot of the mother country.[38] Little Juliette will speak with the same Italian accent as Corinne. She will learn to sing, not only the "*air écossais*" that rends Oswald with memories of his time with Corinne, but also, like the young girl in white who appears on the last pages of the novel to supply the voice that the shade-like Corinne has lost forever, to sing the fragmentary and fugitive songs of the mother country with which Corinne will inspire her (II: 293, 298 [411, 415]). By possessing the daughter her properly feminine sister bears to Oswald, Corinne as ghost still threatens to disrupt the transmission of the domestic plot.

IV

On the map of Europe plotted through the histories, or sentimental journeys, of later eighteenth-century heroines, Scotland's unstable borders are delineated through the intersections of the several vectors of female plot: the heroine's desire for self-destination, the providential plot of patriline transmission, and the maternal plot of education as reproduction of feminine virtue. Their torsion describes Scotland as a plot of ground circumscribed by the same borders of empire that define the European nation state, but simultaneously mark it as a state of exile *from within* it. These paradoxical boundaries render Scotland a state of haunting rather than a state of being on the map of national character. Its landscape represents a displacement of stereotypical English sensibility to its Gothic extreme of spectacular suffering. As a "mother country" without recognized political or public boundaries, its "domestic" identity is always foreign: its national character is a displaced English one, or a geographically placed feminine one that has dislocated itself from the domestic sphere in opposition to which the English nation state (and by extension others) is defined. It has thus become foreign without possessing a territory or a national character distinctly its own.[39] Its boundaries are restrictive because of their very lack of definition. Limited only by the horizon of a picturesque landscape lacking real estate,—without, that is, the manor house necessary to focus or frame such a landscape, to domesticate it enough to make it picturesque—it closes in on the heroine, becoming an imprisoning place of transmission represented as stage and as burial plot. As such Scotland is never a true destination, but always a crisis in the trajectory of a narrative that can find no final resting place.[40]

In such a state, no desiring subject can either dwell or die; she can exist only as a self-reduplicating plot, as revenant. That plot reduplicates the reader as its ghostly possessor, who both identifies with the heroine and desires to fix, to grasp the truth of her exemplary virtue. The narrative projects onto its reader the desire to reduplicate the heroine's virtue outside the text (by imitating it), yet also forces her to recognize the impossibility of that virtue as a real state. It can be embodied only in the fictional heroine, whom the reader must inhabit. The narrative leads the reader to expect firm possession of virtue's truth as the promised end of a providential plot, but diverts that plot via the detour of Scotland, where female virtue, or the feminine "national character," must be staged but can never be fixed, because the stage lacks proper boundaries. Scotland is doubly suited to become a stage for the portrayal of later eighteenth-century feminine character: first, because the kingdom of Scotland had lost its political independence from England at the beginning of the century; and secondly, because the Highlands were invented in the second half of the century as the site of a romantic "national character" without a nation, the Gothic margin and foil to the enlightened state of England.[41]

NOTES

1. On the permeability of real geographical boundaries during the period, see Peter Sahlins, *Boundaries: The Making of France and Spain in the Pyrenees* (Berkeley: University of California Press, 1989).

2. National character and gender characteristics are often considered as belonging to the same type of category during the period. See, for example, Julia V. Douthwaite, *Exotic Women: Literary Heroines and Cultural Strategies in Ancien Régime France* (Philadelphia: University of Pennsylvania Press, 1992), p. 9 n. 22: "In the name of protecting French literature from any possible impropriety, the critic Mesnardière presented a list of 'implausible' cultural types, including the courageous girl, the learned woman, the loyal Persian, the truthful Greek, and the uncivil Frenchman."

3. For a different approach to the relations among narrative plots, plots of ground, and problems of transmission, see Peter Brooks, *Reading for the Plot: Design and Intention in Narrative* (New York: Alfred A. Knopf, 1984), pp. 11–12, 26–28.

4. The peculiar position of Scotland described in this essay extends beyond the three works upon which I concentrate here. See also the earlier *Histoire de Miss Jenny Revel* of Mme Riccoboni (Paris, 1763), and, a century later, Wilkie Collins, *No Name* (New York: Dover Publications, 1978; [Harper and Brothers, 1873]), in which he rewrites this and other plots of the female Gothic, again making Scotland the ultimate scene of the heroine's plotting. Indeed, in what I would consider a good candidate for the first Gothic novel, *Clarissa*, domestic incarceration on the brother's Scottish estate already looms even more darkly than imprisonment in the uncle's moated mansion.

5. William Blackstone, *Commentaries on the Laws of England*, vol. I (New York: Dyckink, Long, Collins and Hannay, 1827), p. 343. The principal of "couverture" or the "feme-covert" was current in one form or another throughout the nations of eighteenth-century Europe discussed here. Blackstone's famous formulation is, "the husband and wife are one person in law." Johann Gottlieb Fichte "deduced" a natural philosophy of the sexes on the basis of similar laws in Germany. See Johann Gottlieb Fichte, "Deduktion der Ehe," in *Grundlage des Naturrechts*, vol. I, 4, pp. 95–106, *Gesamtausgabe der Bayerischen Akademie der Wissenschaften*, edited by Reinhard Lauth and Hans Gliwitzky (Stuttgart: Friedrich Frommann Verlag, 1970).

6. See also Julia V. Douthwaite, who writes of the "journey model" of socialization for heroines as well as for women writers: "Whether identified primarily by their sexuality or cultural background, the heroines of early modern novels must all negotiate their passage through a marginal space on the borders of society to gain membership in the known (French) world" (184). Novels that locate heroines in Scotland in order to represent their relation to Europe and to the "foreign," instead of in Persia, Tahiti, or Peru, demonstrate how European women are already defined as "exotic women" *within* Europe.

7. Cf. Brooks, *Reading for the Plot*, p. 39.

8. Sandra Gilbert and Susan Gubar, *The Madwoman in the Attic: The Woman Writer and the Nineteenth-Century Literary Imagination* (New Haven: Yale University Press, 1979), pp. 99–101.

9. The conflict between the increasing sentimentalization of marriage and the increasingly anxious desire of parents to control the economic contract that marriage had always been culminated, in England, in the passage of the Hardwicke Act, more strictly defining the criteria for valid marriages (including parental consent for minors). Scotland instantly became famous as the place where amorous young couples—or rakish schemers—could evade the new law designed to protect the "virtue"—and with it the property value—of young heiresses. See Lawrence Stone, *The Family, Sex, and Marriage in England, 1500–1800* (New York: Harper and Row, 1977), p. 35.

10. Sophie von La Roche, *The History of Lady Sophia Sternheim*, translated by Christina Baguss Britt (Albany: State University of New York Press, 1991), p. 51; *Geschichte des Fräuleins von Sternheim* (Stuttgart: Philipp Reclaim Jun., 1983), p. 19. Further references to the text will be to these editions, the English first, followed by the German in square brackets.

11. For a similar English utopian community, see Sarah Scott, *Millenium Hall* (London: Printed for J. Newbery, 1762).

12. A similar relation of the narrative of virtue to spectacle can be observed in *La Princesse de Clèves* Marie de Lafayette, edited by Antoine Adam (Paris: Garnier Flammarion, 1966), and in the novels of Samuel Richardson.

13. Christina Baguss Britt translates: "The first sight of her figure, dress, and light, sylphlike walk, made me think she might be the apparition of an amiable spirit of the house" (78); however, "spirit" here stands in not for the usual equivalent (*Geist*), but for a word with much more overtly spooky connotations (*Gespenst*).

14. Lafayette, La *Princesse de Clèves*, p. 41.

15. Christina Baguss Britt translates "through a strange power" (80), which is certainly better English, but cannot express the other meaning of *fremd* in the original, "durch eine fremde Kraft" [61–68].

16. Again the word is *fremd*, foreign: "wie fremd ist mein Herz in diesem Lande!" [99]

17. Anonymous English translation, 1776, 99 (Britt, 99). The German is "Entwurf einer deutsch-galanten Historie" (99–100). Part of the German national character as it is identified in this novel is a less-than-English delicacy about sexual matters. For example, the German "free and indecent" country dances are contrasted with the more modest English ones (137); yet it is a more serious character than the French. Mylord Derby both echoes Richardson's Lovelace (the eighteenth-century English translator expresses this in the choice of the name "Loveill" for him), and anticipates Laclos' Valmont.

18. This sense of a wife as possession in the sense of "property" (*Eigentum*) is evoked by Seymour himself when referring to Sophie's marriage to Derby (163 [210]).

19. See also Sally Winkle, "Innovation and Convention in Sophie La Roche's *The Story of Miss Von Sternheim* and *Rosalia's Letters*," in *Writing the Female*

Voice: Essays on Epistolary Literature, edited by Elizabeth C. Goldsmith (Boston: Northeastern University Press, 1989), p. 80: "The reader of the novel is forced to take a more active role, as the reader adopts the position of the absent addressee."

20. Anonymous English translation (London, 1776), II: 162–62. I have used the eighteenth-century English translation of *Sophie von Sternheim* for this passage because it translates contemporary ideas about the picturesque, the Gothic, national character, sympathy, and plots of female virtue more perfectly than any more literal or modern translation could (see Britt, 230). The German text reads: "Die ganze Erde hat keinen Winkel mehr, der so elend, so rauh sein kann wie der Zirkel um diese Hütte. Mit Grausamkeit hat das Schicksal in dieser Landschaft dem böshaftesten unter allen Menschen die Hand geboten, die emfindsamste Seele zu martern" (326).

21. See also Andrew Parker, Mary Russo, Doris Sommer, and Patricia Yeager, eds., *Nationalisms and Sexualities* (New York: Routledge, 1992), p. 12: "Newspapers, film, novels, and theater all create sexed bodies as public spectacles, thereby helping to instill through representational practices an erotic investment in the national romance. But these same media can be deployed as well for other kinds of civic education, counter-narratives that reveal the dangers implicit in such castings of national history."

22. See April Alliston, "The Value of a Literary Legacy," in *The Yale Journal of Criticism* 4, no. 1 (October 1990): 115–18.

23. *Sophie von Sternheim,* 214 [300]). Britt translates "image of death."

24. Compare Pamela after her marriage to Mr. B.

25. Sophia Lee, *The Recess; or, a Tale of Other Times,* vol. 1 (Dublin, 1785 [London, 1783–85]), p. 181. The idea of live burial pervades the book; it is used to describe the heroines' situation in "the Recess" in vol. I: pp. 9, 23, 97, for example.

26. See Janet Gurkin Altman, *Epistolarity: Approaches to a Form* (Columbus: Ohio State University Press, 1982), p. 204: "We note, for example, that the 'type Marianne' exists but there seem to be no novels composed by two or more correspondents removed [in time] from the action." *The Recess* is that, perhaps unique, novel.

27. This is a frequent authorial strategy of women novelists of the period; see also Mme de Boisgiron, *Lettres de Mademoiselle de Boismiran* (Paris and Amsterdam: Changuion, 1777), for example.

28. See April Alliston, "*Corinne* and Female Transmission: Rewriting *La Princesse de Clèves* through the English Gothic," forthcoming in *The Novel's Seductions:* Corinne, or Italy *in Critical Interpretations,* edited by Karyna Szmurlo (Bucknell University Press).

29. Germaine de Staël-Holstein, *Corinne, ou l'Italie,* edited by Claudine Herrmann, vol. 1 (Paris: des femmes, 1979), p. I: 21, and *Corinne, or Italy,* translated by Avriel Goldberger (New Brunswick: Rutgers University Press, 1987), p. 3. All further references will be to these editions. The pattern of feminine tergiversation is repeated in the earlier sojourn in France that Oswald narrates to Corinne (II: 30–53 [Goldberger 209–28]).

30. "Déjà Rome et Florence étoient occupées par les Français" (Herrmann II: 257).

31. "O souvenir, noble puissance, ton empire est dans ces lieux!" (II: 73). Goldberger translates: "Oh memory, noble power, thou art sovereign in these places!" (242). Note also that Corinne alters the tone of her first improvisation on catching sight of Oswald's melancholy expression (Herrmann I: 56–57); during the lovers' last tour of Rome together, St. Peter's is described as proleptically in ruins (II: 131).

32. "Notre âme semble regretter une ancienne patrie dont le passé la rapproche" (II: 73). Goldberger translates, "our souls seem to long for a former homeland that the past brings closer" (242).

33. "Ces créatures infortunées, errant comme des ombres sur les plages dévastes du fleuve éternel, soupirent pour aborder à l'autre rive" (II: 75).

34. See also Parker, et. al., *Nationalism and Sexualities*, p. 5: "Nations are forever haunted by their various definitional others"; here, Woman. Carla L. Peterson in *The Determined Reader: Gender and Culture in the Novel from Napoleon to Victoria* (New Brunswick, N.J.: Rutgers University Press, 1987 [1986], pp. 55–58, and Nancy Miller, *Subject to Change: Reading Feminist Writing* (New York: Columbia University Press, 1988), pp. 189–90, 192, discuss Corinne in terms of its epic revisions.

35. The lack of correspondence from Oswald in Scotland makes Corinne begin to read the features of Italy instead, and to read them as ghosts, horrifying signs of her own fears of separation and death. This spectral act of reading effectively transforms the reader into a ghost through a pun on the verb of coming and going, of communication: "elle avoit pris une sorte d'horreur pour tous les objets qu'elle voyoit en allant et *en revenant* ils étoient tous comme les *spectres* des ses pensées, et les retraçoient á ses yeux sous d'horribles traits" (II: 191). Her transformation is complete when this act of reading propels her to go back to Scotland.

36. "Respectable pays, qui deviez être ma patrie" (II: 206). Goldberger translates, "estimable country who should have been my country" (346).

37. "L'infortunée, qui se sentoit étrangère sur le sol paternel, isolée près de celui qu'elle avoit espéré pour époux, parcouroit au hasard les sombres allées d'une demeure qu'elle pouvoit autrefois considérer comme la sienne. La terre manquoit sous ses pas, et l'agitation de la douleur lui tenoit seule lieu de force" (II: 215).

38. Corinne's education of Juliette is indeed felt as a haunting, a disturbing, ineradicable presence: "Rien de tout ce qui s'étoit passé n'avoit fait autant de peine à Lucile, que cette influence donnée à Corinne sur l'éducation de sa fille" (II: 292) ["Nothing that had gone before had distressed Lucile as much as the influence given Corinne over her daughter's education"; Goldberger 411].

39. See also Parker, et. al., *Nationalisms and Sexualities*, p. 6: "This trope of the nation-as-woman of course depends for its representational efficacy on a particular image of woman as chaste, dutiful, daughterly or maternal. . . . [W]omen are predictably enshrined as . . . a trope of ideal femininity, a fantasmatic female that secures male-male arrangements and an all male history."

40. See also Douthwaite, *Exotic Women,* p. 18:"The imaginary communities of women's fiction evidence a preference for more provisional domestic solutions to potentially political conflicts."

41. Scotland was united to England under the name of Great Britain on May 1, 1707. On the artificial and romantic invention of the fiction of Highland culture and history in the second half of the eighteenth century, see Hugh Trevor-Roper, "The Invention of Tradition: The Highland Tradition of Scotland," in *The Invention of Tradition,* edited by E. J. Hobsbawm and Terence Ranger (Cambridge: Cambridge University Press), 1983. In a paper presented at the 1996 MLA Convention in Washington, D.C., Deborah White made a related argument that William Collins is able to construct himself as an Enlightenment poet by constructing Scotland as "fancy's land," the site of superstition in opposition to England and the Enlightenment.

4

Roberta Johnson

La gaviota *and* Romantic Irony

Cecilia Böhl von Faber, whose literary pseudonym was Fernán Caballero, once wrote to Juan Eugenio Hartzenbusch "so Fernán has dared to strike out at you? That is an infamy and insolence of which Cecilia was unaware; she will in future call that blockhead Fernán *no caballero* [pun on the last name which means gentleman]."[1] Böhl, who often spoke of her pseudonym in the third person, was schizophrenic on numerous counts, of which switching her literary personality to the masculine gender was a dramatic manifestation. She sharply divided herself between the public and private spheres, asserting a strong repugnance for the notion of a woman seeking attention in the public arena; "Cecilia" was the feminine domestic self, while "Fernán," her masculine mask, was charged with facing the public.[2]

Born of a Spanish-Irish mother and a German father, from her earliest childhood she was caught between the Spanish and German, cultures, and the French, German, and Spanish languages; she wrote in all three, but controlled none of them completely (her manuscripts were translated and/or edited by [male] Spanish-speakers).[3] Her earliest years were spent in Spain where her father had business interests, but from age nine to sixteen (1805–1813), she resided in Germany with her father, while her mother remained in Spain (significantly, there was during these years a small, but important number of women in Germany who made their living by writing—Caroline Auguste Fischer, Anna Luisa Karsch, Sophie von La Roche, Sophie Mereau—models, Böhl would eventually follow, albeit with trepidation). During her residence in Germany she was educated at a French school, but in 1813 she returned to Spain where she was reintegrated into Spanish society and culture. Her father had aristocratic pretensions and preferred reading, writing, and holding forth with friends at intellectual gatherings to the demands of his business. In Spain he held *salon*-like *tertulias*

79

with his wife, through which they introduced German Romanticism into Spain. Complicating Cecilia Böhl's confusion over gender and culture roles was the peculiarity that her mother was a feminist with intellectual pretensions, a fact that much vexed her father. Her mother was responsible for getting Böhl's first story into print, an event that occasioned a chagrined letter to the editor of the journal from the young author; Böhl's father on the other hand, discouraged her literary efforts.

Like Cecilia Böhl's life, which fit no traditional models, her first published novel *La gaviota* is suspended in that unclassifiable place between Romanticism and Realism, condemned to an eternal limbo of neither one nor the other. José Montesino's summary of Fernán Caballero's generic allegiances is characteristic: "historicism and folklorism are two poles between which Fernán Caballero's realism is stretched and beneath all there beats a romantic heart."[4] The work has suffered nearly a century and a half of classification and reclassification: romantic, realist, *costumbrista* (customs sketch), or most often a hybrid of all three. By bringing *La gaviota* into the sphere of romantic irony, a quality or tendency of some romantic works, we can allow it to be what it is, a heterogeneous mixture of a number of things: romantic sentimentality, humorous buffoonery, realistic sketch, moral tale, tragedy, and comedy. Such a denomination also permits us to overcome the persistent received wisdom that Fernán Caballero's works rather monolithically uphold ultraconservative moral values, a fairly universal claim for *La gaviota* that has recently been convincingly challenged by Paul Olson.[5]

Friedrich Schlegel is still our authority on romantic irony, and while I do not want to insist too stridently on Schlegel's direct influence on Fernán Caballero's artistic vision, I will just note that her father wrote to her mother in 1807 during their separation that he was reading both Friedrich and August Wilhelm Schlegel (Carnero, 81). Of course, the Schlegel's writings were an important source of the romantic ideology that Böhl introduced into Spain after 1813. Schlegel's most important works defining romantic irony, specifically the aphorisms, were published shortly before this date. In those seminal thoughts, he defined irony as a thesis and antithesis with no resolution or synthesis, a dialectical movement between destruction and creation, creation and destruction that remained true to the contradictions of life. Anne K. Mellor, quoting Schlegel's "On Incomprehensibility," in her book *English Romantic Irony*, points out that philosophical irony denies the possibility of absolute order in natural events: "isn't this entire, unending world constructed by the understanding out of incomprehensibility or chaos?"(7).

Schlegel also believed, anticipating contemporary dialogic theories of the novel, that the novel with its arbitrary mixture of poetry, song, prose, dramatic exchanges, epic, pastoral, satire, and the mock heroic, was the best way to express romantic irony artistically. In the novel, the ironic artist can portray his or her beliefs and then reflect critically upon them. It is significant that Caballero, when she finally decided to publish, chose the novel form, which for Schlegel was the romantic genre par excellence. (Dialogue occupies at least two-thirds of *La gaviota* as compared to the narrator's one-third, a highly dialogic situation that allows for a large infusion of divergent voices.) Javier Herrero in *Fernán Caballero: Un Nuevo Planteamiento* has demonstrated that much of Caballero's early writing was in the form of *costumbrista* sketches of local scenes and customs she encountered in her native Andalusia. These could perhaps have been published as they stood, but she preferred to weave them into novelistic plots, and by 1829 she had completed a novel *La familia de Alvareda* written in German. The material was intended at first only for private consumption; for example, Washington Irving saw *La familia de Alvareda* when he visited the Böhl family in Andalusia in the late 1820s. Cecilia Böhl's writerly vocation was contradicted by her sense that women should remain out of the public eye.

By the time she was composing *La gaviota*, economic considerations had come into play (and it has been well established that economic necessity was foremost in Böhl's decision to burst into print in the late 1840s). The novel form also gave her the license to hide behind the characters voices and to be ironic (in the Schlegelian sense of generically ambivalent) and to present the conservative values inherited from her parents, as well as male romantic literary models, and simultaneously to mock them. Caballero's ironic stance in *La gaviota* is a response to the vicissitudes of her own life, beginning with her mixed heritage and early separation from her mother, whom she believed did not love her. She also experienced an apparently disastrous early marriage (at age 16) that ended in widowhood after a year; a happier second marriage also ended with the early death of the husband, and the second widowhood was fraught with unpleasant economic squabbles with her late husband's relatives. A third husband (much younger than herself) so mismanaged her estate that she finally decided to begin publishing novels. Writing *La gaviota*, a complex work of fiction, allowed her to be the outsider she was in so many ways—a woman author and intellectual in a patriarchal society, a half-German and quarter-Irish woman in a Spanish milieu— and to integrate the several cultural codes that she had learned in German, French, and Spanish intellectual circles.

Some of the strangeness of *La gaviota* derives from its having been written in French for a foreign audience; the footnotes and asides about matters obvious to the Spanish reader interrupt the narrative flow. There are also many other kinds of narrative deflections, such as comments on the construction of the novel (what would today be called metafictional elements). For example, in a footnote Fernán Caballero indicates that she had considered shortening the description of the convent because it was too wordy and not to the taste of the present generation, but she decided against it (126). These kinds of narrative intrusions are often at the center of discussions of romantic irony, and while they certainly contribute to the ironic effect of *La gaviota,* they are not its most important source. Rather, the irony derives from the constant clash of literary models. Böhl claimed to be faithfully describing real people, places, and customs, but literary language and recognizable generic types intervene. As Susan Kirkpatrick points out in her introduction to *Las Románticas: Women Writers and Subjectivity in Spain 1835–1850:* "Romantic irony plays with the gap between art and experience" (12), but Kirkpatrick does not apply the notion of romantic irony to *La gaviota.*[6] Fernán Caballero's often-stated rejection of the *romancesco* or imaginative romantic forms in favor of a literal transcription of local customs is belied in her reliance on romantic sentimentalism in a number of scenes and in her use of traditional romantic love plots and triangles (Stein and the Duke love Marisalada, but she loves Pepe, the bullfighter). The sentimentality, however, is, in its turn, countermanded by comic buffoonery.

The Romanticism of Byron, whom Böhl's mother translated, that of the Duque de Rivas, who prologued her novel *La familia de Alvareda* or that of José Zorrilla, whose *Don Juan Tenorio* was premiered about the time Böhl began working on *La gaviota,* was a masculine genre (generally favoring lyric and drama) in which the lone male psyche could vent its individuality and emotions (what Alan Richardson calls "colonizing the feminine"). Romantic irony, especially Fernán Caballero's, prefers dialogic and self-reflective (self-destructive) prose narrative and within that diffusing medium dilutes the self in favor of the community. Less than half of the narrative concentrates directly on the central female figure's story, and she is seldom the focalizer; communal scenes with the inhabitants of Villamar or the aristocratic circles of Seville dominate a sizable portion of the novel. Critics have noted the anti-romantic tenor of the dialogue about novel writing that comes about two-thirds of the way through *La gaviota* just before María meets Pepe Vera (Sevillian aristocrats opine that novels should avoid sentimentalism, seductions, and adultery), but in fact, romantic topoi are continually and subtly undermined throughout *La gaviota.* The protagonist herself is a complex parody of the romantic heroine. Full of contradictions and ambivalence, the singularly unlikable Marisalada is unique in the Caballero canon of female protagonists who generally personify feminine virtue. She is a wild, raw natural talent "beautiful daughter of nature" [bella hija de la naturaleza, 221], suggesting the chaos of which Schlegel wrote; she is tomboyish, abrupt, and completely devoid of feminine charm, but possesses an extraordinary singing voice. Momo, a simple country fellow, who despises her because she mocks his homely features, names her *la gaviota* (the sea gull) for her long legs and habit of scrambling across the rocks by the sea.

When we first see Marisalada, she lives in Villamar, a stultifying backwater village; she is very ill, perhaps dying. A mysterious foreigner appears as that unnameable romantic agent who will encourage the heroine's talent (one thinks, for example, of M. Paul in Charlotte Brontë's *Villette*), but a counter-romantic notion asserts itself at the same moment. Stein, the stranger, is a German doctor who has come to Spain to serve in the Carlist Wars; ill, he stumbles into Villamar on his way home, and the kindly villagers cure him. He, in turn, cures Marisalada, whose lovely voice seduces him into staying and marrying her (despite her cold, hard demeanor). Stein, who has musical knowledge, undertakes to train Marisalada's voice; the unromantic proposition is that German scientific expertise will tame wild, raw nature: "But what exceeded his expectations was how much he could get out of the extraordinary philharmonic faculties with which nature had endowed the fisherman's daughter. It was an incomparable voice, and it was not difficult for Stein, who was a good musician, to guide it appropriately, as one does the limbs of a grape vine, which are simultaneously flexible and vigorous, docile and strong."[7] Marisalda's wildness, however, is never fully contained by this unromantic "hero." The Duke of Almansa, who has land near the village, discovers Marisalada and sponsors her move to Seville and finally Madrid, where she becomes a famous opera star. There she falls in love with Pepe Vera, a bullfighter also associated with nature and wildness, who more closely fulfills the requirements of the dashing romantic male lead than either Stein or the Duke. When Stein discovers the adultery, he leaves for America, and when Pepe is gored to death shortly afterward, Marisalada suffers an illness in which she permanently loses her singing voice (aggravated by Pepe's insistence that she attend the bullfights, even though she is not well).

María's undramatic ending is also a response to romantic senti-mentality; she does not die when her adultery is discovered, nor does she commit suicide in the wake of her lover's death, her husband's departure, and abandonment by her admirer and benefactor, as romantic exaltation would dictate. She simply loses her operatic voice and returns to an ignominious life as a village barber's wife, playing out an eternal farce with Momo, a character borrowed from the Golden Age *gracioso* (fool) tradition (for example, he is sent to fetch Marisalada in Madrid when her father is dying, and upon seeing *la gaviota* on stage playing Desdemona, he believes her truly dead at the hands of the singer playing Othello). One of the closing scenes of the novel in which Momo appears with a toothache and swollen jaw underlines this farcical dimension:

> "What a horrendous vision!" exclaimed María, between guffaws. "They say the Sergeant of Utrera burst from ugliness. How is it that the same thing doesn't happen to you? You could scare fear itself. So your cheek is pregnant? Well, it will give birth to a melon, and you can put it in a sideshow. What a fright you are! Did you come to have your picture taken so they can put you in the *Ilustración*, which is always on the lookout for curiosities? "I came," said Momo, "to have your Ratón Pérez pull a bad tooth and not to have you annoy me with impudence, but you were a Sea Gull, you are a Sea Gull, and you will always be a Sea Gull!"[8]

Momo's refrain serves as a comic reversal of Shakespeare's wise fools who often prophesy impending tragedy, robbing Marisalada of the truly tragic end of a romantic heroine.

At punctuated intervals, metanarratives are insinuated to remind us of the traditional fate of those who transgress society's norms. Tía María recounts to her grandchildren the story of Medio Pollito, who overlooked his handicaps, disregarded his mother's advice, and went seeking adventure in the wide world. Medio Pollito was converted into a weathervane for his hubris. Early in his encounters with María, Stein hears her sing a ballad about a husband who killed his adulterous wife and her lover, and María plays Desdemona in Madrid, a motif that is repeated when María includes one of Desdemona's arias in the Duke's daughter's voice lessons. *La gaviota* is pregnant with romantic (*romancesco*) potential, but it is channeled into banality. As Schlegel would have it, the dialectic between chaos and order remains ever unresolved.

The first scene of the novel bears close scrutiny, for it carefully prepares the way for an ironic reading of the novel. The narrative situation in this prologue is a complex one by which the reader is distanced from the sentimental topic of the novel's plot. An extradiegetic narrator describes a ship on which most of the passengers are violently seasick; a more inauspicious beginning to a tale of adultery and punishment could hardly be imagined. Amidst this banal misery, the narrative eye is caught by a handsome young Spanish man, whose identity remains for the moment romantically mysterious, but who is unromantically described as being no social reformer: "That is to say, he did not hear the call to attack windmills, like Don Quijote,"[9] a favorite of the Romantics, especially the Germans. The Spaniard watches Stein render medical attention to an entire family, and two French travelers comment on the conversation these two men strike up in Latin, the only language they have in common. Stein tells his story to the Spanish gentleman (later revealed to be the Duke of Almansa). He could not find work as a doctor in Germany and so is going to Navarre to seek employment in the Carlist Wars. He interlards the narration of his story with sentimental, lachrymose embellishment—the pain of leaving his family and country, and their sorrow at his departure—all of which occasions the one Frenchman who understands Latin to explain to the other that Stein's narration has revealed him to be "a kind of weeping Werther" [una especie de Werther llorón 97], but his life and its conclusion contain nothing of Werther's passion or introspection.

The Frenchman ironically contradicts the narrator's assessment of the mysterious Spanish gentleman as no Quijote when he says "As for the Spaniard, I believe him a Don Quijote, protector of the weak, with a touch of Saint Martin, who shared his cape with the poor [the Spaniard has given Stein his cloak]."[10] The two Frenchmen decide to approach the Spaniard's servant to learn the mysterious gentleman's identity, and in the ensuing scene one hears loud echoes of the opening interview between the tavernkeeper Butarelli and Don Juan's servant Ciutti in José Zorrilla's *Don Juan Tenorio*. The theme of the conversation is the same (the identity of a mysterious nobleman), and the staccato rhythm of the question-answer format is identical. Fernán Caballero inverts the outcome of Zorrilla's dialogue, however, since the servant is completely forthcoming about who his master is, although the Frenchmen prefer not to believe him:[11]

"Has your master gone to bed?"
"Yes, sir," responded the servant, throwing his interlocutor a glance full of meaning.
"Is he rich?"
"I am not his administrator, only his valet."
"Is he travelling for business?"
"I don't believe he has any."
"Is he travelling for health?"
"He is in excellent health."
"Is he traveling incognito?"
"No sir: with his own name and surname."
"And his name is . . . ?"
"Don Carlos de la Cerda."
"Certainly an illustrious name!" exclaimed the painter.

> "Mine is Pedro de Guzmán," said the servant, "and I am at your service."[12]

One of the Frenchmen romanticizes the servant's very straightforward story, theorizing that he was lying to cover up the fact that the Spaniard is really a Carlist agent, while the other exclaims: "No certainly. . . . He is an Alonso Pérez de Guzmán, the Good, the hero of my dreams" [No, por cierto. . . . Es un Alonso Pérez de Guzmán, el Bueno; el héroe de mis *sueños*, 99].[13]

The self-consciously comic literaturizing (especially the exaggerated romanticizing) of the two male figures, one a potential Werther, the other either Don Quijote or Don Juan Tenorio, disappears from the next scenes of the novel. Stein's arrival at Villamar is couched in pure, unironized sentimentality. He has been cruelly dismissed from the government's army for having rendered medical assistance to a wounded Carlist soldier. As he makes his way to the coast, he is threatened by a bull while crossing a field. The small dog accompanying him and whom he had earlier wrested from the jaws of death now defends him from the bull but is mortally gored by the large beast (wild, raw nature is Stein's enemy throughout the novel).[14] Stein, weak and ill, finally arrives at a former convent inhabited by the generous Tía María and Fray Gabriel (the only monk remaining in the convent), who nurse him back to health, sacrificing their own scarce foodstuffs to succor him. The parodic frame, however, continues to exercise an impact when its tone is echoed in comic moments such as Fray Gabriel's simplistic mimicry of Tía María's folksy comments (a motif that runs through much of the novel), as well as in Momo's buffoonery. Every potentially sentimental scene is deflected by farce. For example, a squabble between Marisalada and Momo interrupts Stein's tender marriage proposal to María; another confounds the solemnity of their wedding celebration, and a third diffuses the sentimentality of their departure from Villamar for Seville.

When the setting shifts to the city, Rafael Arias becomes the agent of comic commentary; Rafael is in love, but he is the opposite of the Werther type of romantic hero: "Rita was the only woman her cousin Rafael Arias had seriously loved: not with a lachrymose and elegiacal passion, which did not correspond to his most anti-sentimental character, which among others dried up the native Levant, but with a lively, sincere and constant affection."[15] He engages in good-humored banter with Eloísa, who is completely smitten with French romantic novels (and who eventually enters into a disastrous marriage based on romantic principles with a suitor named Abelardo [!]). When Marisalada gives her first recital for the Duke's acquaintances, her attire is quite outlandish; her dress is too short and garish, and her hair is decorated with colorful ribbons and a white mantilla that makes her look even darker than she naturally is. Rafael humorously comments when she enters "If the bird's song is like its plumage, we'll have quite a jolly time."[16]

Caballero effectively overturned the male romantic models she had found in the Spanish, English, French, and German literature available to her through her international education.[17] The sentimental Werther, the repentant Don Juan, or the swashbuckling musketeers are domesticated and ironized within the multigeneric context of *La gaviota*. While both of the male strangers—Stein and the Duke—introduced in the prologue as potential romantic heroes represent disruptive forces that could shake traditional society in its foundations and do erupt into and violate the pastoral calm of traditional Villamar, neither fulfills the promise. Stein, in fact, does just the opposite as the scientific element that attempts to tame María's wildness. And the Duke facilitates the removal of that natural wildness to the city, but he is no more able to subdue it than is Stein. The opening dialogue with the servant that sets the Duke up as a potential Don Juan Tenorio is mocked when, like Zorrilla's character, he attempts to seduce Marisalada, his love object, with poetry. But, unlike Don Juan's successful letter to Doña Inés, Caballero's Don Juan is reduced to antipathetic banality when María's cold heart is completely impervious to the Duke's verses, although she is quite captivated by the jewelry he offers.

María, the female protagonist, is the satanic figure in *La gaviota*. She is allied with the destructive, unpredictable forces of the sea in a number of ways, beginning with her nicknames—Marisalada (literally, salty María) and "Sea Gull." Her father, whom she self-centeredly ignores, even when he is terminally ill, was shipwrecked by a treacherous sea, and thus he took up residence in Villamar. The sea is associated with the wider world beyond Villamar, which María avidly seeks: "in the immense extent of the ocean, as splendid as it is treacherous; sometimes docile and tranquil as a lamb; others agitated and violent like a fury, like those large and noisy existences that move in the world scene."[18] In his proposal of marriage to María, Stein points out that the sea's voice is full of enchantment and terror: "The waves are, María, those seductive and terrible sirens, in whose fantastic creation the Greek's florid imagination personified them; beautiful beings without heart, so seductive and terrible, that attracted a man with sweet voices in order to destroy him."[19] But María neither triumphs nor fails as a romantic Satan. Like Byron's *Don Juan*, the quintessence of romantic irony, she just sort of fizzles out. Nina Auerbach defines a "romantic structural irony," "a double imprisonment" (19) that fits Marisalada's situation; she escapes Villamar and the traditional female role that awaits her there, only to find a second internment in the same place. In another inversion of

Zorrilla's *Don Juan Tenorio*, she is an eternal outcast, but an ironically unheroic one. She reverts to Tirso de Molina's end for Don Juan (followed by Mozart), in which the satanic figure is condemned to hell, but her hell is to live the rest of her life without glory in a backwater village, married to a man who insists on playing the guitar and singing, even though he has no talent.[20]

Perhaps Fernán Caballero's status as an outsider, her inbetweeness, and her ambivalence come closest to Samuel Taylor Coleridge's orientation in romantic irony. According to Anne K. Mellor, Coleridge as a devout Christian, experienced a "guilt-ridden ambivalence" toward the romantic notion of a "dynamic, unconscious, amoral and abundantly creative force" (137). The ambiguous duality seems to operate in *La gaviota*; it reveals a strong urge to portray wild, raw nature as a fundamental source of life and art, alongside a contrary impulse to tame it and place it within a moral order. Parody, buffoonery, and farce further complicate and frustrate a reconciliation of these opposing impulses. Thus, Caballero created what I will call a "female romantic form" in which the collective prevails over the subjective, and in which irony, ambiguity, and ambivalence overshadow certainty. Her female romantic form appropriates male romantic tendencies, neutralizes them and subverts them to her own purposes. Chaotic nature in the guise of Marisalada does survive (although *manquée*), despite the several attempts by male-dominated civilization to destroy it. As a haunting echo and indomitable truth, Momo repeats at the end of the novel: "*Gaviota fuiste, Gaviota eres, y Gaviota serás*" (444).

NOTES

1. Fernán Caballero, *La gaviota*, edited by Julio Rodríguez-Luis (Barcellona: Labor, 1972). "conque Fernán se ha atrevido a pegar a U.? esto es una infamia y un atrevimiento del que no tenía noticia de Cecilia [*sic*] que desde ahora se intitulará a ese zoquete Fernán *no* caballero" (qtd. in Montesinos, p. 112). All translations of *La gaviota* are mine.

2. Numerous passages in Cecilia Böhl's correspondence attest to her deep ambivalence about her vocation as a writer. On the one hand, she proclaimed to detest the idea of women writers, while at the same time ironizing about male writers: "Comprendo perfectamente al barbero del Rey Midas; abundando en sus ideas me hice autor, autor con naguas [*sic*] que ha sido y es para mi el más antipático ser que puede darse. . . . En fin, si Hércules hilaba a los pies de Onfalia, era por amor, y el amor disculpa, no sólo las faltas, sino los ridículos que hace cometer; pero la péndola en mi mano no la disculpa nada, nada. Es mi sambenito voluntario, que yo ocultaba cuidadosamente, y que Mora, el solo que lo sabía, lo sacó a luz, no pudiendo resistir a los ruegos de la culta, disceta,

amable y simpática Condesa de Velle. Nunca se lo perdonaré, pues desprestigió a Fernán; porque no soy yo la sola a quién choca soberanamente la pluma en manos femeninas. Además no hay un pantalón que no se crea, en materia de escribir, superior a todas las enaguas, inclusas las de Mad. Staël." Alberto López Argüelles, *Epistolario de Fernán Caballero*, (Barcelona: Sucesores de Juan Gili, 1922), p. 30. [I perfectly understand King Midas's barber; saturated with his ideas, I became an author, an author in petticoats, which has been for me the most undesirable thing imaginable. . . . If Hercules knit at the feet of Omphale, it was for love, and love pardons, not only the errors, but the ridiculous acts, it makes one commit; but the pen in my hand cannot be pardoned by anything at all. It is my voluntary sign of penance, which I carefully hid, and which Mora, the only one who knew it, made known, unable to resist the pleas of the cultured, discreet, amiable and sympathetic Countess of Velle. I will never forgive him, because he lowered Fernán's prestige; because I am not the only one who is supremely disgusted by the pen in feminine hands. Besides there is not a pantwearer who does not believe that when it comes to writing, he is superior to all in petticoats, even Madame de Staël]. In another she asserts: "Falsas noticias me hicieron dar un paso, quizás, o sin quizás, inconveniente, para el severo juicio masculino que no suele hacer concesiones a los *imprudentes*, puede, pero, siempre nobles, sinceros y generosos brotes del corazón femenino." Argüelles, *Epistolario*, p. 90. [False information caused me to take a perhaps (or without perhaps) unfortunate step in the eyes of severe masculine judgment, which is not in the habit of making allowances for the *imprudent*, can, but always noble, sincere and generous buds of the feminine heart.] The ungrammaticality of this sentence could be an editorial error, or if correctly transcribed, could be an indication of the writer's wish to obfuscate her meaning.

3. *La gaviota*, Fernán Caballero's first published novel, was originally written in French and was translated for publication in installments by José Joaquín de Mora, who in the process effected a number of subtle changes, such as removing references to naked men. Fernán restored these omissions when she revised the novel for publication in book form in 1856. Unfortunately, the original manuscript is lost, and it is impossible to determine how many of the changes in the 1856 version were corrections of de Mora's tampering.

4. Caballero, *La gaviota*, p. 112. "Es que historicismo y folklorismo sean los dos polos entre los que se tiende el realismo de Fernán Caballero—y bajo todo ello late un corazón romántico."

5. Paul Olson in "Reacción y subversión en *La gaviota de Fernán* Caballero," indicates, for example, that the extreme reactionary position of characters like Tía María are presented as absurd exaggerations within the narrative context, and that the entire novel offers a subversive subtext, especially through a subtle and equivocal use of language that undermines an attempt to establish absolute conservative values in it.

6. Susan Kirkpatrick (p. 275) was the first critic to elaborate upon how Cecilia Böhl's ambivalent stance toward her vocation reveals itself in her literary creations, especially *Elia* and *La gaviota*. She points to the conflicting codes in the latter, in which a female artist can be genuinely successful, and yet is

eventually removed to the rural and domestic sphere. My reading departs from Kirkpatrick's in finding a more complex heteroglossia in the novel and less evidence that it "must be read as antifeminist and antiliberal."

7. Caballero, *La gaviota*, p. 205. "Pero lo que excedió sus esperanzas, fue el partido que sacó de las extraordinarias facultades filarmónicas, con que la naturaleza había dotado a la hija del pescador. Era su voz incomparable y no fue difícil a Stein, que era buen músico, dirigirla con acierto, como se hace con las ramas de la vid, que son a un tiempo flexibles y vigorosas, dóciles y fuertes."

8. Ibid., p. 444. "'¡Qué horrenda visión!' exclamó María, 'entre sus carcajadas. Dicen que el Sargento de Utrera reventó de feo. ¿Cómo es que no te sucede a ti otro tanto? Capaz eres de pegar un susto al miedo. ¿Con que tienes preñado el cachete? Pues parirá un melón, y podrás enseñarlo por dinero. ¡Qué espantoso estás! ¿Vienes a que te retraten para que te pongan en la *Ilustración*, que anda a caza de curiosidades?' 'Vengo, dijo Momo, a que tu Ratón Pérez me saque una muela dañada, y no a que me hartes de desvergüenza; pero Gaviota fuiste, Gaviota eres, y Gaviota serás.'"

9. Ibid., p. 91. "Es decir que no se sentía con vocación de atacar los molinos de viento, como don Quijote."

10. Ibid., p. 97. "En cuanto al español, le creo un don Quijote, protector de inválidos, con sus ribetes de San Martin, que partía su capa con los pobres."

11. Böhl played with references to *Don Juan Tenorio* in her correspondence as well. When discussing the government minister in charge of her husband's consular salary (the minister's surname was Tenorio), she referred to herself as the "Convidado de Piedra" (Stone Guest, Argüelles, *Epistolario*, p. 275).

12. Caballero, *La gaviota*, p. 98.

> "¿Se ha ido a la cama su amo de Ud.?"
> "Sí, señor, repsondió el criado, echando a su interlocutor una mirada llena de penetración y malicia."
> "¿Es muy rico?"
> "No soy su administrador, sino su ayuda de cámara."
> "¿Viaja por negocios?"
> "No creo que los tenga."
> "¿Viaja por su salud?"
> "La tiene muy buena."
> "¿Viaja de incógnito?"
> "No señor: con su nombre y apellido."
> "¿Y se llama . . . ?"
> "Don Carlos de la Cerda."
> "¡Ilustre nombre por cierto!" exclamó el pintor.
> "El mío es Pedro de Guzmán," dijo el criado, "y soy muy servidor de ustedes."

13. Rodriguez-Luis identifies the Duke and especially Stein as parodies of the male-romantic type, but he does not develop the idea. Biruté Ciplijauskaité notes a resemblance between Oswald of Madame de Staël's *Corinne* and the

Duke of Almansa (in terms of stature) and Stein (in all other aspects), but she does not consider the possibility of parody.

14. I am indebted to Javier Herrero, who has developed an elaborate network of metonymic relationships in the novel, for pointing out to me the coincidence of bulls and the sea in a number of passages. Herrero has indicated to me that he does not intend for the present to publish his interesting ideas, which tie together a large number of images and lead to a political reading of the novel. Pertinent to my study here, for example, is the fact that Stein is given refuge in the convent, whose walls are battered by the sea (in political terms, the convent has been appropriated by the government in its land redistribution policy). Stein, the unromantic and domesticated character, is thus associated with the emasculated institution where water is controlled and contained in a well, drawn by oxen (castrated bulls).

15. Caballero, *La gaviota*, p. 268. "Rita era la única mujer que su primo Rafael Arias había amado seriamente: no con una pasión lacrimosa y elegíaca, cosa que no estaba en su carácter, el más anti-sentimental que entre otros muchos resecó el Levante indígena, sino con un afecto vivo, sincero y constante."

16. Ibid., p. 336. "Si el gorjeo es como la pluma, es el fénix de estas selvas."

17. The serialized version of *La gaviota* contained a number of references to European romantic writers that Caballero edited out of the 1856 version. Julio Rodríguez-Luis includes these passages in the footnotes to his edition of the novel. For example, the early version contains a reference to followers of Byron and Lamartine: "¿Qué simpatía escitan [*sic*], qué noble sentimiento despiertan esos fraseólogos, lacrimosos y declamatorios, imitadores rastreros, copistas serviles de Byron y Lamartine?" (301, n. 22) [What sympathy do they excite, what noble sentiment do they awaken, these lachrymose and declamatory phraseologists, latent imitators, servile copiers of Byron and Lamartine?] Another mentions Alexander Dumas, Eugène Sue and George Sand in deprecatory terms (427, n. 20).

18. Caballero, *La gaviota*, p. 122. "en la immensa extensión del Océano, tan expléndido como traidor; unas veces manso y tranquilo como un cordero, otras agitado y violento como una furia, semejante a esas existencias ingentes y ruidosas, que se agitan en la escena del mundo."

19. Ibid., p. 222. "Las olas son, María, aquellas sirenas seductoras y terribles, en cuya creacion [*sic*] fantástica las personificó la florida imaginacion [sic] de los griegos: seres bellos y sin corazon [*sic*], tan seductores como terribles, que atraían al hombre con tan dulces voces para perderle."

20. Javier Herrero pointed out to me that Marisalada's ending is a hell, and Susan Kirkpatrick calls it a "comic hell" (267). I add the idea that, as a hell with ludic overtones, it is an inversion of the kind of hell to which Don Juan is consigned.

References

Argüelles, Alberto López. Ed. *Epistolario de Fernán Caballero: Una colección de cartas inéditas de la novelista.* Barcelona: Sucesores de Juan Gili, 1922.

Auerbach, Nina. *Romantic Imprisonment: Women and Other Glorified Outcasts.* New York: Columbia University Press, 1986.

Caballero, Fernán. *La gaviota.* Edited by Julio Rodríguez-Luis. Barcelona: Labor, 1972.

Carnero, Guillermo. *Los orígenes del romanticismo reaccionario español: El matrimonio Böhl de Faber.* Valencia: Universidad de Valencia, 1978.

Ciplijauskaité, Biruté. "*La gaviota* y la novela femenina de Francia." *LA CHISPA '83 Selected Proceedings.* Edited by Gilbert Paolini. New Orleans: Tulane University Press, 1983. pp. 61-69.

Herrero, Javier. *Fernán Caballero: Un nuevo planteamiento.* Madrid: Gredos, 1963.

Kirkpatrick, Susan. *Las románticas: Women Writers and Subjectivity in Spain 1835–1850.* Berkeley: University of California Press, 1989.

Montesinos, José F. *Fernán Caballero: Ensayo de justificación.* Berkeley: University of California Press, 1961.

Mellor, Anne K. *English Romantic Irony.* Cambridge, Mass.: Harvard University Press, 1980.

Olson, Paul. "Reacción y subversión en *La gaviota* de Fernán Caballero." In *Actas del 8 Congreso de la Asociación Internacional de Hispanistas.* Edited by A. David Kossoff, José Amor y Vázquez, Ruth H. Kossoff and Geoffrey Ribbans, 375–81. Madrid: Istmo, 1986.

Richardson, Alan. "Romanticism and the Colonization of the Feminine." In *Romanticism and Feminism.* Edited by Anne K. Mellor. Bloomington: Indiana University Press, 1988.

Rodríguez-Luis, Julio. "*La gaviota*: Fernán Caballero entre romanticismo y realismo." *Anales Galdosianos* 8 (1973): 123–36.

Schlegel, Friedrich. *Dialogue on Poetry and Literary Aphorisms.* Translated by Ernst Behler and Roman Stuc. University Park: Pennsylvania State University Press, 1968.

———. *Lucinde and the Fragments.* Translated by Peter Firchow. Minneapolis: University of Minnesota Press, 1971.

III

Institutional Interactions

Salonières and Schoolmasters

5

Lilian R. Furst

The Salons of Germaine de Staël and Rahel Varnhagen

In any consideration of cultural interaction in the Romantic Age, one major social institution immediately springs to mind: the *salon*. The *salon* was instrumental in bringing together men and women from different backgrounds, classes, and countries. The conversational exchange of views, which was the main occupation of the *salons*, was a salient medium for the discussion and transmission of innovative ideas. The growing internationalization of the *salon* at this period was of primary importance in furthering wider and freer cultural interaction than had hitherto prevailed. Given the limitations of space I have opted to focus on two outstanding *salons*: that of Germaine de Staël at Coppet, and that of Rahel Varnhagen in Berlin. These are the preeminent exemplars of the species at the time, and though neither is typical of the genre, an analysis of their functioning will give us an insight into the role of the *salon* in cultural interaction.

Both these *salons* flourished in the heyday of the Romantic Age: Rahel Varnhagen, or to be more accurate, Rahel Levin, as she was before her marriage to Karl August Varnhagen von Ense in 1814, presided over her *salon* from the mid-1790s to 1806, when the French occupation radically changed the atmosphere in Berlin, causing the cessation of the *salons*. As for Germaine de Staël, she was involved in a whole series of *salons* throughout her life, beginning with attendance at her mother's *salon* at age four! However, the one I want to examine is that held at Coppet in the years 1804–1810 because it was patently the most multicultural and the most literary of all her *salons*.

These two women could, at first glance, hardly seem more unlike. Germaine, as the only child of Louis XVI's powerful finance minister,

Jacques Necker, was born in 1766 into privilege and wealth. In her mother's *salon*, which reigned supreme in Paris from 1770 onward, she came to be on familiar terms with such eminent men as Denis Diderot, Jean d'Alembert, Georges-Louis Buffon, and Edward Gibbon, a former suitor of her mother's. During her teens, there was talk of marriage to William Pitt, the Younger, the British Prime Minister, but Germaine objected to the prospect of living in England. In January 1786, she married Eric Magnus, Baron Staël von Holstein, the Swedish ambassador to France, thereby securing for herself a diplomatic rank and position that were to be at least somewhat protective in the turbulent revolutionary years.

While Germaine was born into "the navel of the universe,"[1] Rahel Levin was destined from birth onwards to its periphery by her Jewishness. Her father, Markus Levin, was a prosperous jewelry merchant, who also arranged loans for actors and young noble spendthrifts, whom he would entertain in his home, which became a center of sociability for enlightened Jews and gentiles. But although her family was already quite far removed from traditional Judaism, Levin did not have the benefit of the select, indeed hyper-intellectual education that the French "female prodigy"[2] was given. Rahel's mother-tongue was Western Yiddish, of which even some of her later letters show traces.[3] Only in her early twenties, when she had met a number of intellectuals and nobles at the Bohemian spas, which she patronized in summers, did she engage tutors to make up for the deficiencies she then perceived in her knowledge of German, foreign languages, and mathematics. In the problems surrounding her marriage, Rahel offers another sharp contrast to Germaine. By refusing the Jewish businessmen proposed to her by her family, she both aggravated her tenuous relationship to her own community and risked isolation through rejection by the German upper classes. The precariousness of her social standing is confirmed by the two broken engagements she suffered, jilted in 1800 by Karl von Finkelstein after a protracted four-year courtship, and again in 1804 by Don Raphael d'Urquijo, secretary to the Spanish delegation in Berlin, to whom she was betrothed for two years. Eventually, in September 1814 she was baptized and married to Varnhagen von Ense, who was fourteen years her junior.

In other respects, too, these women were widely divergent. Germaine was of robust constitution, although she died at age fifty-one, whereas the always delicate Rahel survived to sixty-two. The latter never bore any children, and seems to have been remarkably chaste and cerebral in her friendships. By contrast, Germaine's love-life is notorious: of her three (possibly four) children, one at most may have been by her husband. Her roster of lovers included Charles-Maurice de Talleyrand, Mathieu de Montmorency, and Benjamin Constant. She was equally productive intellectually: her first novel, *Delphine*, appeared in 1802, and her second, *Corinne, ou l'Italie*, in 1807, was an immense success. She also published several treatises, of which two, *De la Littérature considérée dans ses rapports avec les institutions sociales* (1798) and *De l'Allemagne* (1810) achieved lasting fame. Rahel, on the other hand, left no formal writings, only a voluminous correspondence, edited shortly after her death by her husband as a memorial to her.[4]

I have begun with the differences between my two subjects largely because I want to elaborate on the similarities beneath the disparity. Neither of these women was blessed with physical beauty: the portraits of Germaine show her as inclined to corpulence, with short, plump arms and a soulful face; Rahel, on the other hand, was slight with a long nose and upper lip. Yet both wielded extraordinary power through force of personality, mind, and word, were famous during their lifetime, and have remained so ever since.[5] Their tremendous prestige is all the more curious insofar as both endured a painful marginalization. Rahel was doubly marginal by being Jewish and by defiantly discarding her heritage. Germaine, while born an insider, became an outsider through the enmity of Napoleon, who banished her from Paris and later from France altogether. Her incessant mobility and far-ranging travels are as much a product of this expulsion as of her innate restlessness. Each of these women in her own way was, therefore, under peculiar handicaps as a *salonière*, and each triumphed over adverse circumstances through sheer personal charisma.

Having introduced my two figures, let me now turn to their *salons*. Germaine de Staël and Rahel Levin operated in discrepant contexts. The *salon*, under female leadership, was a well-established tradition in France, flourishing particularly in the seventeenth century, as shown by Carolyn Lougee's study, *Le Paradis des femmes. Women, Salons, and Social Stratification in 17th Century France* (Princeton, N.J.: Princeton University Press, 1976). What is more, Germaine had the immediate example of her mother's *salon*, which she headed after the latter's death in 1794. Rahel, on the other hand, had only a single precedent in the *salon* run jointly by Henriette and Markus Hertz until his death in 1803; theirs was an exceptional, double *salon*, in which Henriette discussed poetry and novels with the young Romantics in one room while Markus lectured on reason, science, and the Enlightenment next door. However, the *salon* as a cultural practice was not a common form in Germany, and certainly not in the mode it assumed in Berlin in the final decade of the eighteenth and the opening years of the nineteenth century. Such *salons* as had existed—in Potsdam, Weimar, Jena, Leipzig, Heidelberg, and Darmstadt—were associated with princes' courts. The numerous *salons* hosted by middle-class Jewish women in Berlin in the 1790s and up to 1806 are an anomalous episode in German history, as has been documented by Deborah Hertz in her illuminating book, *Jewish High Society in Old Regime Berlin* (New Haven: Yale University Press, 1988). The sorry state of Berlin's intellectual institutions, devoid at that point of a university, a parliament, generous noble patronage, or even a vital publishing industry, created, paradoxically, a window of opportunity for a bevy of Jewish *salonières*, such as Amalie Beer, Sara Levy, Rebecca Solomon, and Philippine Cohen, besides Henriette Herz and Rahel Levin.

But even within their respective environments, Germaine de Staël and Rahel Levin departed from the norms more than they conformed to them. They went along with *salon* usage in upholding the custom of female sovereignty. Germaine admittedly made capital out of her husband's social position, but otherwise he played no significant role in her life; in November 1800 they were legally separated, and in May 1802 he died. Her wealth and her estate at Coppet were inherited from her father. As for Rahel, her *salon* reached its zenith long before her marriage. She began receiving in the mid-1790s while living as a rebellious spinster in an attic apartment of her family's grand house in the center of Berlin. Though not as affluent as the other hostesses of the period, she lived in easy circumstances, despite the limitations on her allowance from her brothers in the wake of family disputes. So both these women were financially as well as intellectually independent, each possessing a room of her own, to resort to Virginia Woolf's terms.

In both instances, too, their *salons* represented what might be called "neutral ground"—and this is their distinctive feature and their main departure from the norm. Instead of functioning as an extension of the social life of their time and place, the *salons* of Germaine de Staël and Rahel Levin were a kind of metonymic replacement. In Germaine de Staël's, this is to be taken literally for Coppet is just over the Franco-Swiss border in a spot safe from Napoleonic censorship. Rahel Levin's *salon* was metaphorically neutral territory as a Jewish home where nobility, intelligentsia, and artists could mingle as nowhere else. For this reason both these *salons* were conducive to extreme, quite unprecedented social heterogeneity, and became the seedbeds of cultural interaction. They were international and cosmopolitan, welcoming a wide spectrum of foreign visitors. As a result, they proved particularly consequential in implementing cultural interchange, notably between France and Germany.

In their overall figuration, these two *salons* run parallel: both were voluntary and unrestricted, yet relatively small and élite. Both had an artistic as well as an intellectual and social dimension: Germaine instigated theatrical performances, at which she often took the leading part, while Rahel arranged musical recitals in the course of the evening. Both *salons* depended on the extraordinary interlocutory powers of their hostesses, for whom conversation was nothing short of an art form. Of Staël J. Christopher Herold comments: "For Germaine, conversation was, next to love, the principal raison d'être." He adds: "Her emotional intensity and intellectual grasp, the improvisatory yet sure-footed rush of her eloquence, the electrifying enthusiasm she communicated for her ideals produced an effect on her audience that can be compared only to a rare musical experience."[6] No wonder that she took to the stage like the proverbial fish to water. Rahel, according to contemporary testimony, was far more low-key and restrained in manner. While Germaine domineered by her mere presence, Rahel would circulate quietly from one group to another, making introductions, animating discussions, and occasionally lingering to make signal remarks herself. Although her style was one of understatement, compared to Germaine's boisterousness, she was at least as adept at orchestrating her *salon*. Perhaps as a born outsider she never possessed the degree of self-assurance that is the insider's birthright, or perhaps it was more a matter of temperament. Be that as it may, the conversational brilliance of each of these women was absolutely decisive for the success of their *salons*.

In their practical organization and structure, the two *salons* were, however, utterly different. Both had internal complexities and tensions, but they, too, stemmed from predicaments peculiar to each one.

Germaine de Staël held court at Coppet, an estate on the lake shore about ten miles from Geneva in the Swiss canton that is now Vaud and then belonged to Berne. Her father had acquired the castle and barony in 1784, and during the chaos of the post-revolutionary years it became a safe haven from Napoleonic persecution. Coppet was, therefore, quite exceptional in the *salon* tradition insofar as it was in the country with no connection to either court or city. Because of its relatively remote location it was, perforce, mainly a residential *salon*. Its members fell into three major categories: first, local callers, who might come for merely a few hours as dinner guests or as spectators at the theatrical performances. The second group comprised transient visitors from all parts of Europe and even America; their stay might range from several days to several weeks. These included the Danish dramatist Adam Gottlob Oehlenschläger, the Danish poet Frederika Brun, who wrote in German, Prince August of Prussia, Friedrich Schlegel and his new wife, Dorothea, daughter of Moses Mendelssohn, a Russian nobleman, Prince Tuffiakin, François René Chateaubriand, François Guizot, Mathieu de Montmorency, Madame de Krüdener, Elisabeth Vigée-Lebrun, who painted Germaine's portrait as Corinne, the German philanthropist

Baron von Voght, the historian Johann von Müller, the Duchess of Courland, Prince Belmonte, Prince Sapieha, and an American art student, Mr. Middleton. This list of guests gives some idea of the motley array of birds of passage. The more or less permanent residents, who formed the core of the Coppet ménage were Germaine's cousin, Madame Necker de Saussure, her friend, the beautiful Julie Récamier, the novelist Benjamin Constant, August Wilhelm Schlegel, tutor to her children, Simonde de Sismondi, who was to write the monumental *History of the Italian Republics*, and a near neighbor, Charles-Victor de Bonstetten, who composed a travel book about Italy using the *Aeneid* as a kind of Baedeker. Between mid-morning breakfast and late afternoon dinner, the Coppet guests were left to their own devices, to write, to read aloud and discuss their own or others' works, or simply to engage in conversation, which often continued into the early morning hours since Germaine, an insomniac, liked to postpone the misery of bedtime.

However bizarre this set-up was, and despite the rivalries between lovers competing for the favors not only of Germaine de Staël but also of Madame Récamier, and notwithstanding the incessant undercurrent of political anxiety, there can be no doubt that Coppet was the central fulcrum for cultural interaction and for the transmission of German ideas to the French avant-garde at a time when the German romantic movement was in full flower while its French counterpart, held back by the Revolution and censorship as well as by a conservative attachment to the native neoclassical tradition, was still in a state of gestation. In that gestation, the Coppet *salon* played an absolutely crucial mediating, almost midwiferly role.

In comparison to Coppet, Rahel Levin's *salon* was in some respects far more conventional, in others, however, more of an infraction of social codes. It was more conventional than Coppet in its city center location, in its 5:00 P.M. meeting hour for tea and conversation, and in its openness to all comers without formal written invitation, simply by introduction through other habitués. Often introductions were effected by Gustav von Brinkmann, an amateur poet, who was secretary to the Swedish delegation in Berlin. Rahel had met him in the 1790s at Teplitz, and he was an invaluable intermediary between her and the gentile world at large. If the problems at Coppet were primarily of an amatory and political nature, in Rahel Levin's *salon* they centered on matters of etiquette and religion. It was unusual, to say the very least, for a young unmarried Jewish woman to be receiving the leading thinkers, artists, and nobles in her attic apartment. Among the regular guests were three sets of brothers: August Wilhelm and Friedrich Schlegel, Wilhelm and Alexander von Humboldt, and Ludwig and Christian Tieck, also Johann Gottlieb Fichte, Friedrich Schleiermacher, Johann von Müller, Friedrich von Gentz, Friedrich de la Motte Fouqué, Henrich von Kleist and Jean Paul Richter on occasion, members of the Prussian royal family such as Prince Louis Ferdinand and his sister, Princess Radziwil, aristocrats such as Count Alexander Tilly, a former page to Marie-Antoinette, the diplomat Peter von Gaultieri, Counts Dohna and Bernstorff, Wilhelm Burgsdorff, a Prussian state official, and the Prince de Ligne, a well-known wit, "master of the tone of the *ancien régime*,"[7] and finally such performing artists as the famous actors, Johann Friedrich Fleck and Friederika Unzelmann, and the great singer, Madame Marchetti. Noticeably underrepresented in Rahel's *salon* on the whole were women, except for a few close personal friends such as Pauline Wiesel. For a time Karoline von Humboldt, Wilhelm's wife, was on intimate terms with Rahel, but later she demonstratively distanced herself as a concomitant of her explicit antisemitism. Growing antisemitism after 1806 was one of the leading factors in the waning of Rahel's first and most brilliant *salon*. The two phenomena are closely connected, for antisemitism is an indication of a narrow, xenophobic mentality, inimical to the open-mindedness quintessential to the *salon* as an institution.

It is hard, indeed virtually impossible, to assess with any precision the impact of these *salons*. If only the tape recorder had been invented then so that we could have immediate access to some of those sparkling conversations! Lacking first-hand evidence, we have to depend on the testimony of witnesses and some not always reliable data. The fact that both these *salons* attracted such an illustrious assemblage of guests over so many years is the most telling proof of their magnetism and prominence. Gustav von Brinkmann, in an unpublished letter of May 5, 1801 to Julie Voss,[8] claimed that there was more wit on Rahel Levin's "Judensopha" (Jewish sofa) than in all the rest of Berlin. Backhanded though the compliment is, it nonetheless aptly summarizes the dominant position of Rahel's *salon* in the intellectual life of the time. Even Goethe enjoyed conversing with her in Karlsbad in 1795, and called on her in 1815 when she was in Frankfurt. As for Germaine's influence, perhaps the ambiguous title of Herold's biography *Mistress of an Age* does truly encapsulate her situation.

The two women met while Staël was in Berlin in 1804. The accounts are somewhat at variance: according to one source,[9] the indefatigable Brinkmann brought Staël to dinner at Dorothea von Courland's and arranged a long tête-à-tête between her and Rahel. According to an earlier source, the meeting took place at a soirée hosted by Brinkmann, who had invited the most distinguished and interesting people in Berlin to meet the French visitor. But once she was introduced to Rahel, Germaine ignored everyone else, retired into a corner with her, and engaged in a one and a half hour conversation with her alone. Germaine was deeply impressed by Rahel, and is reported to have said: "She is astonishing. I can only repeat what I have said a thousand times on this journey, that Germany is a mine of genius, whose riches and depth remain unknown as yet."[10] Rahel's reactions to her French interlocutor were more muted and mixed. Her correspondence contains almost fifty references to Staël: she praises her *Considérations sur les principaux événements de la révolution française* (1789), but is mostly critical of *De l'Allemagne*, and thinks that she has misread Rousseau.[11] Though discombobulated by Staël's whirlwind manner and want of repose, she nevertheless repeatedly expresses keen regret at her early death.

A "social phenomenon:" that is the phrase used by Thomas Carlyle to describe Rahel.[12] He defines that "phenomenon" in these terms: "That without beauty, without wealth, foreign celebrity, or any artificial nimbus whatsoever, she had grown in her silently progressive way to be the most distinguished woman in Berlin; admired, partly worshipped by all manner of high persons, from Prince Louis of Prussia downwards; making her mother's, and then her husband's house the centre of an altogether brilliant circle there." He designates her furthermore as "a woman of genius, true depth and worth" (33), who at the time of his writing in 1838 "seems to be still memorable and notable, or to have become more than ever so" (1). *Mutatis mutandis*, Carlyle's phrase is apposite to Germaine too. She, also, was a "social phenomenon," who gathered about her the leading minds of her day. The contributions made by these two women to cultural interactions in the Romantic Age are at once unique and parallel.

NOTES

1. J. Christopher Herold, *Mistress to an Age: A Life of Madame de Staël* (Indianapolis and New York: Bobbs Merrill, 1958), p. 28.

2. Renée Wintergarten, *Madame de Staël* (Leamington Spa: Berg, 1985), p. 19. Chapter 2 (18–25), "Education of a Female Prodigy," gives an account of her upbringing. She was introduced first to the Bible at age two, then to the masterpieces of seventeenth-century French literature along with more recent works of poetry and ideas. She was also taught Latin and English, which she spoke fluently by the time she was twelve. She read John Milton, Thomas Gray, Henry Fielding, and especially Samuel Richardson.

3. See Deborah Hertz, ed., *Briefe an eine Freundin. Rahel Varnhagen an Rebecca Friedländer.* (Köln: Kiepenhauer and Witsch, 1988).

4. *Rahel, Ein Buch des Andenkens für ihre Freunde,* 3 vols. (Berlin: Duncker und Humbolt, 1834; Reprint, Munich: Matthew and Seitz, 1983).

5. Proverbially, the three major forces in Europe at the turn of the century were said to be Napoleon, the Duke of Wellington, and Germaine de Staël!

Similarly, that phase in German cultural history has come to be known as "die Rahelzeit." The enormous amount of scholarly writing on Staël and, particularly more recently, on Rahel Varnhagen, too, testifies to their continuing interest for our age. Both are often seen as pioneers of women's emancipation.

6. Herold, *Mistress to an Age*, pp. 257, 72.

7. Ellen Key, *Rahel Varnhagen*, translated by Arthur G. Charter (New York and London: Putnam, 1913; Reprint, Westport, Conn.: Hyperion Press, 1976), p. 215.

8. Cited by Hertz, *Briefe an eine Freundin*, p. 257.

9. Ibid., p. 157.

10. Alfred Götze, *Ein Fremder Gast: Frau von Staël in Deutschland, 1803–4.* Jena: Verlag der Fromannscher Buchhandlung, 1928, p. 121; no source given. "Sie ist erstaunlich. Ich kann nur wiederholen, was ich schon tausendmal während meiner Reise gesagt habe, daß Deutschland eine Fundgrube an Genie ist, deren Reichtum und Tiefe man nirgends kennt."

11. *Rahel, Buch des Andenkens*, II: 540, and 218; III: 8 respectively.

12. Thomas Carlyle, "Varnhagen von Ense's Memoirs." *London and Westminster Review* 62 (1838): 24. I am grateful to Gregory Maertz for having so kindly sent me a copy of this review.

6

John L. Mahoney

The Rydal Mount Ladies' Boarding School
A Wordsworthian Episode in America

The following essay originated during my reading of Stephen Gill's biography of William Wordsworth, especially his account of the poet's last years at Rydal Mount. Now a celebrity, a Poet Laureate, although not an active one, honored with doctorates from Durham and Oxford, elected to the Royal Irish Academy, invited to the Queen's Ball in 1845, celebrated with a handsome new edition of his *Collected Works* "prefaced with an engraving of Wordsworth that makes him look like a poet from an antique world, and a picture of Rydal Mount,"[1] acclaimed by his contemporaries and visited by the famous and not-so-famous, he seemed almost like a gigantic father figure. And, of course, fan letters from all over the world greeted him.

What especially caught my attention in Gill's splendid account of the poet's final days of fame was a two-sentence account of a letter from "Mrs. Sarah P. Green of Charlestown, Massachusetts, which enclosed an advertisement for the Rydal Mount Ladies' Boarding School and her lecture entitled "Poetry of Nature." Dickens at his most creative could hardly have bettered either."[2] The description of the material was fascinating enough; the fact that it came from Charlestown, close to my birthplace, and its description of a school that neither I, my friends, nor the local historians knew much about, if anything, made the whole matter almost an obsession. While visiting the Wordsworth Library in Grasmere a short time later, I examined a packet of material including the letter, the advertisement, the lecture on "Poetry of Nature," and also a lecture entitled "Obsolete Idea."[3]

What follows is, however, much more than a recital of certain facts about the school. This essay is not only an account of dissension in a local Baptist community culminating in the resignation of its pastor, his

105

wife, and a large number of parishioners, but also the establishment of a new religious community nearby, and—most important—the establishment of a boarding school, along with a school for young children, taking its name from the home where Wordsworth lived from 1813 until his death in 1850.

First, there is the matter of the school itself. The advertisement— where it appeared is not mentioned—announces on December 18, 1845 the opening of the Rydal Mount Ladies' Boarding School in Charlestown (now a part of Boston), Massachusetts. A lithograph at the top of the page offers a romantic view of an elegant, two-story mansion with well-cut lawns and nicely spaced trees. Finely dressed young women stand in conversation or walk the pleasant greens. Outside what seems to be a brick and iron fence surrounding the mansion is a promenade-like street with elegantly dressed men and women and with young women on horseback. To the left and rear of the mansion is a considerably smaller building with what appear to be younger girls at play. The entire setting is inviting, the kind of picture then as now calculated to attract prospective students.

Below the lithograph are two sections, one a brief description of the "Rydal Mount Ladies' Boarding School," and the other a prospectus for "A School for Young Children," apparently the building attached to the mansion. The descriptions of each, without offering detailed information about the curriculum, are almost lyrical. We read that the school will be conducted by "Rev. Henry K. Green, whose attention is exclusively devoted to it, and Miss Mary H. Fales," and that it "has been opened at the residence of the former, in Charlestown, Mass." Few Boston mansions "are possessed of more attractiveness than the one which has been secured for this Institution." Only a few minutes walk from the central city, the "extensive grounds around it, abounding in fruit and shade trees, impart to it the united charms of elegance and seclusion."

The curriculum, while not listing particular subjects and requirements, assures potential students and their parents that the education received will have two special features, including "every branch, solid and ornamental, which pertains to an accomplished female education" (one suspects the hand of Sarah Green in the writing of the advertisement given her consistent and strong advocacy of the education of women). More interesting, especially when one considers the name of the school—Rydal Mount, the handsome residence of Wordsworth in the Lake District of England from 1813 to 1850—is the assurance that there will be particular concern with "the formation of manners, which are the results of habits rather than of precepts." This focus on habits has at least the ring of the Shaftesburian moral sense, of the Scottish critics' idea of taste, perhaps even of Wordsworth's confidence in the "Preface" to the 1800 *Lyrical Ballads* in a new poetry of feeling.

> For our continued influxes of feeling are modified and directed by our thoughts, which are indeed the representatives of all our past feelings; and as by contemplating the relation of these general representatives to each other, we discover what is really important to men, so by the repetition and continuance of this act feelings connected with important subjects will be nourished, till at length, if we be originally possessed of much organic sensibility, such habits of mind will be produced that by obeying blindly and mechanically the impulses of those habits we shall describe objects and utter sentiments of such a nature and in such connection with each other, that the understanding of the being to whom we address ourselves, if he be in a healthful state of association, must necessarily be in some degree enlightened, his taste exalted, and his affections ameliorated.[4]

The prospectus continues with strong assurance that "the *family* feature will be a prominent one in this establishment" and that "the boarding pupils will be members of Mr. G's family." Further, students who enroll can feel assured that "The Principals have had much experience in teaching either in colleges or select schools, and the best assistants will be obtained as circumstances may require."

Most surprising, even considering the prohibitively costly private secondary schools of the 1990s, are the fees ("Payment always in advance"). Board and tuition "in the English branches" for the year are $200 (more than $4,530 today)[5] with appropriate reductions for those who do not wish to board. "Languages, Music, and all the ornamental branches, at moderate prices."

Almost as interesting is the description of "A School for Young Children," "connected with this Seminary, to meet an exigency hitherto unsupplied by such Institutions." In rather ominous rhetoric, anticipating the reassurances of day-care facilities today, the advertisement recognizes how "Fashion and custom, the pressure of other duties, and the multifarious claims of Society have induced many parents to surrender their infant treasures, at the most susceptible period of childhood, to the irresponsible care and pernicious influence of mercenary domestics." Such care "increases the evil, till it assumes 'more heads than the beast in the vision.'"

Mrs. Sarah P. Green is the head of this school, and "The accommodations of the spacious house and grounds will secure to it all the attractions and benefits of rural seclusion, without collusion or contact with the RYDAL MOUNT SEMINARY." The emphasis in this school, as in the upper-division classes of the Seminary, again sounds quite romantic, with Mrs. Green committed to providing her charges "with the happiest and best influences of an intelligent and affectionate home," underlining her philosophy of making "their own affections and sense of happiness the agents of their moral and mental culture, by connecting their enjoyment and instruction" in order "to promote their highest interests, and prepare their minds to pursue with greater benefit the studies of their riper years." The tuition for this school—boarding and instruction—is again a formidable $200.

So much for advance publicity. What started with a certain enthusiasm at having made a modest Wordsworthian discovery turned to disappointment—albeit mild—at being able to learn so little about the educational dimension of the school, its origins, its curriculum, its history, and especially its Wordsworthian connections. That disappointment, however, gave rise to a new enthusiasm and a search that has generated a good amount of information—not nearly as much as one might like—about the Reverend Henry K. Green, Sarah P. Green, nineteenth-century Baptist history and controversy in Boston, and a theory of the case concerning the founding of Rydal Mount, Charlestown. And there are some rich possibilities for learning more. What follows is an account of the search and its current status. The ordering of the material might be described as following a principle of discovery rather than of strict logic.

First there are the players in the drama. We know nothing about Miss Mary H. Fales, Henry Green's associate at the school. We know very little about Sarah P. Green. She appears to have been the wife of Green although we have no formal record of the marriage and, as the drama is played out later, there is some reason to believe that there was a separation of some sort. We have her one letter—although a long and lavish one—to Wordsworth at "Rydal Mount, Westmoreland, England" dated February 16, 1846. The correspondence—one-way since, as far as we know, Wordsworth never replied—includes what seems to be an essay called "Poetry of Nature" and a lecture entitled "Obsolete Idea: Written for the soirée. Dec. 30th, 1845. By Mrs. S. P. Green." Apart from the information in the advertisement included among these materials, there is no specific mention of the school to Wordsworth. We are left to wonder about the particular circumstances of the founding of the school and its obvious commitment to Wordsworthian principles at least in its general plan of education.

The commitment to Wordsworthian principles is clear in Sarah Green's letter, and we begin with that letter. The impeccable handwriting—a pleasure for those who often struggle with the script of Wordsworth and his correspondents—is matched only by the ardor of the fan captivated by the poetry. The rhetoric is extravagantly effusive although, from the evidence we have, Green never traveled to the original Rydal Mount, never met the poet. She appears to be a woman of considerable education, a reader of poetry from Shakespeare to the Romantics, a writer of correctness and, in her better moments, of elegance.

Addressing Wordsworth as "reverend Sir," she proceeds. "I will not," she begins, "tarnish with the egotism of apologies, the tribute of homage, which owes its sentiments to the noblest impulses of a soul, enriched by your own genius with the gifts of immortal truth and beauty." The depth of her admiration is seen in her Hamlet-tinged high-flown "Apologies, 'weary, stale, flat, and unprintable' at any time, seem but idle phrase to a mind exalted by the purest enthusiasm of gratitude, ever kindled in a human spirit." What follows is a lengthy quotation (with one notable exception) from *Tintern Abbey*, beginning with "I have owed to thee [*sic*], / In hours of weariness, sensations sweet" and con-tinuing to the final tribute, "We see into the life of things" (ll: 26–48), with "thee" replacing "them" (the "beauteous forms" of nature) throughout. Fan letter indeed!

Just when the extravagance seems at its height, Green outdoes herself as she writes: "The offering of a reverential spirit will not, I trust, seem officious or intrusive to him, whose loftiest place of Fame 'will stoop to her' whose 'gentle admirations raise / Delight resembling love.'" And with still rising intensity, Green assures her reader that "A sense of delicacy will not permit me to add any personal details to the accompanying communications, which I trust, will not be wholly unin-teresting as the representative 'statue of a soul,' that owes the small portion of moral grace and symmetry it may possess to the reflected light of the 'vision splendid' which has illumined and expanded its intellectual existence." Green's closing, with its religious imagery, approaches idolatry. "The faint incense," she says, "of the tribute, and the memory of the giver, will soon fade from a path, so brilliant from its own Light and Beauty, but a distant votary will henceforth feel a new identity of interest and 'thou' shall still 'O, Poet! in thy favorite Isle / Quicken the Slothful and exalt the Vile.'"

The letter moves quickly to Green's essay, "Poetry of Nature." In reading it, one gets the sense of the disciple including a piece of his or her own work in a letter, hoping to receive some sort of approval or even response in a communication from the master. But, we remember, Wordsworth never responded. Green's argument is straightforward and properly Wordsworthian-romantic: "Of the infinite varieties of poetry, none is so rich in moral beauty, and so pure in its spiritual influence, as the unwritten music of *natural scenery*. The brightest visions of the Bard, and the glorious art of the Painter, have never summoned spirits so full of grace and power, as the living forms of sublimity and magnificence 'that we behold / From this green earth.'" Ironically she laces her argument with examples from poetry and painting stressing their power to capture the beauties of nature. She contends, for example, that nature is the source of art, arguing that "'the consecration, and the Poet's dream,' and the shadowy features of ideal grace, fade in the presence of Nature, whose elements of poetry are—mountains—oceans—forests—clouds—stars—suns, and rainbows, those 'shining ladders' of the soul, whence it beholds 'the light that never was, on sea or land.'" Religious imagery is still strong in Green's lyrical criticism as she speaks of the poet's "glorious ministry to dispense her [Nature's] purer influences, and reveal her higher analogies to her exiled children, whose toilsome paths lead far away from her vernal altars and sparkling fountains. . . . Dim, indeed, must be the eye that sees 'No splendor in the grass, no glory in the flower.'"

The man who remains unmoved by the magic of nature is not to be trusted. The ocean is the greatest manifestation of "physical greatness," and while Green does not elaborate on the sublime or on theorists like Edmund Burke and Immanuel Kant, the descriptions and examples—once again from poetry—clearly smack of the romantic sublime: "So wonderful in its fathomless depths, where 'nothing' in them . . . 'that doth fade, / But doth undergo a sea-change / Into something rich and strange.'" Wouldn't anyone, she argues, lay aside the poet's mantle to have a "sight of Proteus rising from the Sea; / Or hear old Triton blow his wreathed horn?" The question is posed using Wordsworth's own words from the sonnet proclaiming a weariness with the world and a desire to feel the intensity of myth in the imaginative capturing of the sea-gods Proteus and Triton.

Green goes a step further in her argument for a greater poetry touched by nature, contending that "to the moral mind, the Ocean had a sublimer element of power as the awful type of 'that immortal sea / Which brought us higher,' and while we contemplate the vastness of the mundane waters, our souls 'Can in a moment travel thither / And see the children sport upon the shore, / And hear the mighty waters rolling evermore.'" Sounding like a Wordsworthian conservationist and opponent of industrial development, she bemoans the turning of the ocean into "a highway of venal profit and wealth" and the forests, "the ancient temples of Nature into fire-wood for steam-ships and rail-roads."

Again the literariness of Green's argument emerges as she leaves "the grander aspects of natural scenery, to advert to the sweet and tender analogies of the 'Seasons' [James Thomson's poem] to the life and the social nature of man." For her, Winter, the final section of the poem, combines the softness of "fire-side enjoyments" with "elements of deeper power. Its sublimities of storm and desolation—its frosted landscapes, glittering in the rays of the morning sun—its palaces of ice and snow—looking as if 'Built of all precious substances—so pure / And exquisite' that they seem to the soul of man like a 'vision splendid' from 'that imperial palace whence he came.'" Green, needless to say, loses no opportunity to incorporate and adapt Wordsworth's poetry for her purposes.

From literary commentary Green moves to educational theory, certainly a subject of interest to many of the Rousseauistic Romantics, especially to Wordsworth. Combining a key strain of Rousseauism with an appropriate text from her favorite poet, she makes her case: "In training the youthful mind, it should be the aim of the parent and teacher to form an early taste for *natural scenery*, that its sweet and simple analogies, may lead their thoughts to the 'light that never was, on land or sea.' If the taste is early created, the scenery of earth, and the heraldry of the skies, may become the features of their own souls, moulding them to beauty and symmetry." She closes her argument with still another Greenian adaptation of Wordsworth, this time of the celebrated Dorothy passage in *Tintern Abbey*, but changing the singular "thee" for his sister to the plural "their" for Green's students. Hence, "when thy mind / Shall be a mansion for all lovely forms" is changed to include "their minds" and so forth until the end of the quotation when "Shall e'er prevail against thee, or disturb thy cheerful faith" becomes "against them" and "Their cheerful faith."

Green's glowing lecture ends on a more overtly religious note, this time with Alexander Pope the servant of her purposes. Granted the moral force of natural scenery, she argues, "The love of Nature, so pure in a religious sense, is debased into the grossness of materialism when it does not lead the soul 'from Nature up to Nature's God.'"

Included in Green's correspondence is a copy, already mentioned, of a lecture entitled "Obsolete Idea: Written for the soirée. Dec. 30th, 1845. By Mrs. S. P. Green." It is an interesting treatise for its time, brief and very much to its point concerning the importance of a certain kind of female education. The soirée is clearly the one referred to by someone signed simply "W." in the letters to the editor section of the *Boston Daily Evening Transcript* for December 31, 1845. More about the correspondent's remarks later.

The "Obsolete Idea" of the title is, as Green puts it, "One of those errors of a darker age," and "the belief that the training of a woman's intellectual nature unsphered her for the common purposes of life." If such elitism has developed, "it was a defect of education, for a well balanced mind derives its finer impulses and aspirations, from the domestic relations." Indeed such may be the case, she continues, for "even in this golden era of women's influence, she is often the victim of those narrow theorists who adapt their system to one aspect only of her nature, as it may happen to agree with their own peculiar tastes and prejudices." If woman is defined only in terms of her domestic tasks, "life to her, in its highest sense, must be 'a world without a sun,' where she will henceforth"—note what seems an especially inept allusion to Wordsworth's "A Slumber Did My Spirit Steal"—'Roll round in earth's diurnal course / With rocks, and stones, and trees'!"

Green, certainly a progressive on the subject, nevertheless seems to steer a somewhat middle course between a nineteenth-century feminist and a more traditional view of women's education, praising the professional ambitions of women without eschewing the domestic. She seems to be a good judge of the audience of the time as she speaks of the dangers of the extreme professional point of view. That "disproportionate share of cultivation" of the intellectual sacrifices "a woman's real dignity and happiness . . . to a false standard of taste and knowledge, which seals up all the sweetest fountains of tenderness and sympathy, and condemns her to a lot far more sad to see, than the barren and sordid toil of a mere house-keeper." With a touch of genuine humor— Green is an intriguing woman and the lack of hard information about her is a source of frustration—she continues to strike that balance of woman at work and at home: "Heavier, too, will be the sigh of the disenchanted lover as he contemplates the discomforts of his cheerless home, than even the mortified husband of a thrifty wife, who could "never get it out of his head, that once in the most moved part of a closet-sermon of his, on death and eternity, she looked thoughtfully downward, and at length said, 'Don't put on your left stocking tomorrow morning; I must first mend a hole in it'" (Green in a note at the bottom of her lecture page directs the reader to Jean Paul Richter's *Siebenkäs* as the source of the above). Green is optimistic about "a juster estimate of woman's real position in the scale of being" in spite of "hereditary prejudice" and "the conflicting systems of present theorists." When "soul, mind, and heart" are cultivated, she will then exhibit those Wordsworthian qualities which best distinguish the woman: "In whom all offices unite, / With all fine functions that afford delight."

So much for the Sarah P. Green correspondence with Wordsworth, although again there is no evidence that the poet ever responded. The difficult and fascinating problems involve a more detailed profile of the school, a better sense of the lives and backgrounds of its founders, and their connections with Wordsworth.

Upon returning from Grasmere, I began the process of dealing with such problems. To put it mildly, expectation was not matched by reality.

The then President of the Charlestown Historical Society, informed, courteous, and eager to help, had no knowledge of the workings of the school. Reference librarians at the Charlestown branch of the Boston Public Library provided a copy of *A Century of Town Life: A History of Charlestown, Massachusetts, 1775–1887* by James Hunnewell, which offered only the following information in a section on old houses in the city:

> At the end of the last century [18th], and in the earlier part of the present, mansion houses for single families were built on the slope of Breed's Hill [where the famous Battle of Bunker Hill was fought in the American Revolution and now the site of the impressive Bunker Hill Monument].

After a description of eight of the "notable" houses and of the Commandant's house at nearby Boston Navy Yard (still a large and busy facility), we receive our first bit of information:

> Nearly opposite to it [the Commandant's house] is the square wooden mansion (50 x 50 ft.) built by Nathan Tufts, placed far back from the street at the top of terraces covered by grass shaded by a few trees, and commanding a fine view towards the water. The grounds, although reduced in area, are still large. After the death of Mrs. Tufts (1843), who survived her husband eight years, the house was used for a boarding-school, and was called Rydal Mount.[6]

We also develop some chronological sense—while we know the date of the founding of the school, we are uncertain of how long it continued—as Hunnewell says: "Subsequently it was occupied for over a quarter of a century by the Rev. Thos. R. Lambert, rector of St. John's" (an Episcopalian church, still standing at Devens St., Charlestown). "Painted brown on the outside," he notes, "it is now [1888] in fine order."[7] *Fletcher's Charlestown Directory* (1848) lists "Rydal Mount Seminary, Chelsea St., opposite Navy Yard." Also at the Charlestown Library in *Indexes to Slides of Old Charlestown in Charlestown Branch Library, 43 Monument Square* is a "View East from the Monument [Bunker Hill] toward Rydal Mount and Navy Yard (Courtesy American Antiquarian Society)."[8]

A sense of place from the school advertisement, of exact location from city history, a photograph of the building—all of these, but still not a word about the nature of the school. The whole area along Chelsea Street now is an expressway. Furthermore, none of the many histories of private and public education offered any help in dealing with the school or its educational mission and practice.

What ultimately proved very helpful, although much more work with local history needs to be done, was the reference to the advertisement for Rydal Mount published in the *Boston Evening Transcript* for December 18, 1845. Reading in daily issues of the newspaper for 1845 and 1846 brought two important items to my attention.[9] The first is in many ways a strange editorial commentary of December 11, 1845. After opening with a word of strong support for education of the young, it proceeds to offer its recommendation "from having heard recently of a school opened in an adjoining town designed especially to bestow upon the pupils an elevated order of education, combining solidity with elegance, and fostering morality like a plant of beauty, to a bright expansion beneath the kindly influence of true, matronly teaching." In an amusing manner, the editorialist writes that "We are not at liberty to give the name of the school or of its government at present. Circulars and advertisements are in the course of preparation, however, which will be publicly distributed when the arrangements are perfected." More specifically, "A lady well connected, and educated herself on the most thorough system of domestic and intellectual education proposes shortly to open a boarding school for young children whose parents may choose to commit them to the maternal care and moral influences of such an Institution." All of this being said and then followed by what amounts to paraphrase of the advertisement already discussed, there can be little doubt that the School for Young Children at Rydal Mount, Charlestown and its leader Sarah P. Green are the objects of the remarks.

The *Boston Evening Transcript* is again helpful as it editorializes briefly on January 2, 1846 on a letter from a correspondent who had attended the soirée at Rydal Mount and alludes to the earlier cryptic remarks of December 11, 1845. The remarks are positive, assuring readers that: "From our knowledge of the Principals of this establishment and their admirable plans for the advancement of the young both in intellectual and moral education, we are confident that their school will be found to be the great *desideratum* for true domestic education—that which is emphatically both useful and elegant."

The letter to the editor, signed only "W" (Yes, we must resist at once the tendency to speculate wildly), although straightforward, seems almost to remind us of the age-old practice of the proprietor or friend writing to praise his or her own enterprise. "I had the pleasure," we read, "last evening of attending a literary soirée at the Mount Rydal School Charlestown." After some brief description of the attractive setting of the building, we are told, "The establishment is kept by the Rev. H. K. Greene [*sic*] and Miss Fales, and one of their principal—perhaps I may *say* the principal effort is, to render it a 'family school.'"

The first term of the school year had just ended and pupils seemed "at home and happy" and visitors "expressed great satisfaction with every arrangement." Christmas decorations were everywhere "interspersed with appropriate and classic inscriptions in letters of moss." Quotations from Milton, Pope, Edward Young, Kant, and, of course, Wordsworth are strategically placed, and "At the landing of the stairs, over the large window, opposite the door "Wordsworth / of Rydal Mount, Eng.'"

A "sumptuous and elegant" supper was served in the "upper hall of the school at which Mrs Greene [*sic*] delivered the following address to several of the pupils whose excellence was neatness and order, presenting to each a bunch of violets." It is, by any standard, an effusive speech of congratulations and counsel on manners and morals, and the letter writer quotes it in full (What modern editor would allow it?). Emphasizing the importance of women's education, she addresses her audience: "To adorn 'Rydal Mount' Seminary with a *cluster of stars* that will not be unworthy of the *sunlike* genius of its great namesake, and to show the defamers of our sex—'how divine a thing / A woman may be made' will crown you with honor and praise when this transient distinction has lost its charm and value."

Noting the presence of "parents and patrons" as signs of the "family school" that she regards as a distinctive feature of Rydal Mount, Charlestown, she sees all present involved in an "aim to unite the refinements of habit and good breeding with enjoyment and improvement." Still there is a sense of priorities as the academic and religious are set in perspective:

> But while we shall cultivate a love of the truly beautiful in art, taste and sentiment, and bestow a smiling benediction upon the higher aspirations of youthful ambition, we shall strive to inspire their minds with the noblest motives in the pursuit of knowledge and excellence, and to train their immortal spirits for heaven!

The correspondent closes this long account of the occasion with high praise, and recounts how "Miss Fales then delivered the red rose to several pupils for scholarship," and how one of the students responded with a poem of thanks on behalf of her classmates. Interesting for all students of the history of American education is the noting of speeches delivered after the dinner by Dr. E. Beecher, Rev. Dr. Vinton, Mr. Wells, and especially the Honorable Horace Mann. Mann was, of course, a member of the Massachusetts legislature, a secretary of the State Board of Education, and a major force in the development of public education in Massachusetts, although there is no mention of Rydal Mount in any of his writings.

So much for what can be learned about the school itself, about its Wordsworthian touches, its concern with both the professional and personal training of young women and children, its convictions concerning the education of the affections in a natural setting with students seen as part of the school family. Yet there are still so many unanswered, maybe unanswerable questions, which make this essay somewhat less than a definitive statement. What were the immediate circumstances surrounding the establishment of Rydal Mount? Why did local historians of the time and historians of American private elementary and secondary education fail to note it? What were the more specific features of its curriculum and instruction? How long an existence did it have? Who were the Reverend Henry K. Green and Sarah P. Green and Mary Fales? Why did Wordsworth, the squire of the original Rydal Mount in England, become their patron saint?

Most of these questions, in spite of the lack of information at this writing, need to be dealt with if we are to develop a more complete picture of this Wordsworthian episode in America. There may be a beginning—indeed a fair amount has been garnered in my travels, talks with residents of Charlestown, discussions with local clergy familiar with the religious situations of the time, and the scouring of archives with materials concerning local churches—in some preliminary findings or perhaps non-findings about the principal players in this episode.[10] Of Mary Fales virtually nothing is known except her role as assistant to Reverend Green in teaching the older students at Rydal Mount. Of Sarah P. Green we have her letter to Wordsworth locating her at the Chelsea Street school, Charlestown; her ideas on the educative power of nature; on the importance of women's education; on the need for a strong moral and religious dimension in superior instruction; and her devotion to, indeed at times almost embarrassing veneration of Wordsworth. Beyond that we have two interesting facts which we shall discuss in more detail later. The first is the listing "Green Henry K. Rev. h. Chelsea" in *Emmon's Charlestown Directory*.[11] The second, quite puzzling in the context of this story, is the record of a grave inscription in *A Documentary History of Chelsea, 1624–1824* which reads "In Memory of Sarah Green who died Aug. 17, 1852, aged 66."[12]

We have, however, in the course of this inquiry into the principals in the drama, learned a fair amount about Henry K. Green, which has been mildly helpful in dealing with the larger questions. Some records at the offices of the Baptist Convention of Massachusetts (Tremont Street, Boston) pinpointed Green as Baptist minister and pastor of the First Baptist Church in Charlestown from 1842–1844. More detailed records of the parish, now found in the Department of Special Collections of the Franklin Trask Library at Andover-Newton Theological

School in Newton, Massachusetts, shed further light on Reverend Green and his Charlestown pastoral service. And alumni listings of the various catalogues of the Andover Theological Seminary (the original name of the present institution), while incomplete, provided further and important biographical material.

First, in the *General Catalogue of the Theological Seminary, Andover, Massachusetts, 1808–1980*, Henry K. (middle name Knowles) Green, while listed as a member of the Class of 1830, is noted among "Non-Graduates" and as attending in 1827–1828. While there are gaps in his profile, it was a useful start in my inquiry. I learned that he came from "Waterford, New York" (no birth date is given although sometime between 1790 and 1800 would be a fair estimate), that he graduated from "Union" (Union College in Schenectady, New York) in 1822 and served as a "tutor at Columbian College [now George Washington University], D. C. 1826–1828." Ordained a Baptist minister in Salem, Massachusetts, September 12, 1828, he is listed as pastor at "First Baptist ch. Charlestown, Mass. 1842–1844; First Baptist ch. Trenton, N.J. 1850–1853; First Baptist ch. Brooklyn, N.Y.; Second Baptist ch. Danbury, Ct. 1858–1859." The record shows finally that he died in "Orange, N.J. Feb. 23, 1862."[13]

This information is, of course, incomplete and in many ways puzzling. The Andover-Newton archives have a file of correspondence concerning Green that adds to our knowledge of some of the gaps in his career listing in the Andover catalogue. First is a response to a letter of inquiry concerning Reverend Green and the Reverend Edmund Crawley from a J. W. Brown in Gaspreau, Nova Scotia to the Reverend C. C. Carpenter at Andover (dated simply January 28). In one paragraph, J. W. Brown states that "According to Saunders' History of Baptists of Maritime Provinces Rev. H. K. Greene was pastor of Granville St. Church, HX [Halifax] from October 1828 to March 1831. I cannot learn his middle name nor the place and date of his birth." Although no connection is made between Green and Crawley, it is interesting that Crawley also studied at Andover, was ordained roughly two years after Green in Providence, Rhode Island (1830), and succeeded Green as pastor of the Granville Street Church in 1830, resigning in 1839 to become professor at Acadia College (originally Queens College) in Wolfville, Nova Scotia. Crawley was a man of some distinction, honored with a D.D. from Brown University in 1844 and a D.C.L. from King's College in Windsor in 1847. Brown promises further information on Green, but there is no further correspondence in the file. What is interesting to note is that the Granville Street Church was originally an independent Episcopalian chapel with a strong educational thrust and many prominent people as parishioners. The church joined the Nova

Scotia Popular Baptist Association in 1828. It would seem that Green was present at the creation of a Baptist parish with more liberal, evangelical leanings than the sterner Calvinist Baptist might condone and that Crawley continued that tradition.[14]

Another response to a letter of inquiry about Green comes from G. N. Lasker of 18 Market Street, Trenton, New Jersey to Reverend A. H. Quint, D.D. of New Bedford, Massachusetts. It is an informative and intriguing letter although it stops just short of satisfying the curiosity it piques. After acknowledging Quint's inquiry, Lasker replies: "It is true that—Mr. Green was pastor of this First Baptist Church—for three years (from Jan 1st 1833). He was subsequently (1858–9) pastor of the Second Baptist Church Danbury Conn. Thence he went 'West' somewhere, & died. . . ." Quite a gap in his career listings, and quite a casual farewell!

Then, almost as an afterthought, "I might say however, (now it comes to me,) that he was pastor of the First Baptist Church, Brooklyn N.Y. between his pastorate here & in Danbury. Mr. Green had the reputation of being an able man. His sermons were admirably written, & he stood well as a thinker." We wonder, reading perhaps with a different sense of language today, what lies behind his next comment: "His domestic affairs were not always in a delightful state, & were sometimes embarrassing to him as a pastor."

Lasker's letter adds further details to the profile of Green, alludes to problems, although cryptically, and seems to establish (given the information that he was beginning a pastorate at Trenton in 1850) that he had left Rydal Mount and the School he and his wife had founded in 1845 after he left his pastorate at the First Baptist Church, Charlestown. Since Reverend Henry and Sarah P. Green lived in Chelsea in 1845, and since she was buried in Chelsea in 1852 while he was pastor of First Baptist Church in Trenton, New Jersey, is it too much to speculate that the domestic problems alluded to in Lasker's letter involved a separation of some kind, with Green leaving Charlestown, the school closing, and Sarah Green remaining behind?

The Franklin Trask Library Department of Special Collections at Andover-Newton Theological Seminary contains a minute-book with records of parish meetings of the First Baptist Church of Charlestown from 1828 to 1844, years during which Henry K. Green was pastor. While they offer little to illuminate the personal side of Green and his wife, they provide a fair amount of information about his coming to Charlestown, his pastorate there, and the fact of his leaving. What follows is an attempt to describe that pastorate which in its later years brings us close to the founding of Rydal Mount and his supervision of that Wordsworthian venture.

The Records of the First Baptist Church, Charlestown, Mass., 1824 note the resignation on September 19, 1841 of William Phillips as pastor after what is described as a happy five-year tenure. After the usual search processes of a parish committee, Henry K. Green of West Chester, Pennsylvania is called. This entry, then, places Green in Pennsylvania in 1841, part of the 1828–1842 period not covered in his profile in the Andover catalogue already cited. Green accepts the call in a glowing letter of December 23, 1841, closing with a prayer "that our union may promote the glory of the great Head of the Church, I subscribe myself 'Your servant for Jesus' sake,'" and signed "Henry K. Green." On January 7, 1842, Green was elected pastor by unanimous vote.

The next record we have in these minutes is a letter—nowadays we might call it "a progress report"—on his pastorate, again unanimously accepted by the parish. In this report is an account of how "The Female Seminary was visited by the spirit of the Lord, and several of the young ladies from other towns have been added to the church." This must be a reference to the Charlestown Female Seminary, founded by a much-loved pastor of the First Baptist, Charlestown from 1822–1836, and directed by Deacon Jones Fosdick. This seminary, one of the first for intellectual training of "Young Ladies," seems clearly an outgrowth of a vigorous Sunday School movement inaugurated by First Baptist and the Reverend William Collier in 1813.[15] Another school was founded after the Charlestown Female Seminary.

> In 1827 the school met in the building occupied by Miss Martha Whiting as an academy for young ladies, afterwards the "Charlestown Female Seminary." Dea. James Fosdick was superintendent of the male department, and Miss Whiting of the female. Miss Whiting and Miss Howe also gathered a school in connection with Mr. J. W. Davis and Mr. Joseph Watts in 1827 at Moulton's Point near the corner of Vine and Chelsea Streets, which became very prosperous for a term of years. Dea. Willard Knowles acted as superintendent. It was real missionary work which was entered upon there. It shows the vitality of the home church-life which could sustain a vigorous Sunday-school at such distance.[16]

Interestingly, as we will notice below, the school at Moulton Point was only discontinued when there was a division in First Baptist and the formation of a dissident congregation at the High Street Baptist Church in 1844, the year noted in the Andover catalogue as the year in which Henry K. Green finished his pastorate at First Baptist, Charlestown.

The minutes of First Baptist recount a controversy which certainly led to the parish division and the formation of a new congregation. That controversy revolved around one "Brother Swan," but may have been more broadly based in tensions between the more sternly Calvinistic and the more liberal Arminian elements in the parish. The parish minutes record that an invitation to Swan to join the parish was voted removed on November 18, 1842. Swan was apparently seen by some parish members as not possessing that purity of doctrine and practice expected of good members.

The minutes for December 17 record: "The Church received a communication from our Pastor [Green] asking to be Dismissed from the pastoral care of the Church." A vote for adjournment was passed so that the parish might consider the request, and the meeting was resumed on December 22, 1843, at which "after a protracted discussion in which the best Christian Spirit prevailed it was voted unanimously to request our Pastor to withdraw his request to be dismissed from the Pastoral care of the Church and to request the Society to concur." A day of fasting and prayer was declared for the first Monday of 1844 to reflect on the matter.

The case of Brother Swan remained an immediate sore spot, however, and on January 19 a motion to invite him brought "122 yeas & 72 nays." Although we find no information on the response to the vote, it is clear that Swan was not invited, for the minutes of March 29, 1844 speak of "existing differences between many members of this Church on different subjects, and as there is but little probability of coming together again and as many wish that a free Church be formed in this town."

The decisive point comes on April 22, 1844 as we read that "The two parts of the Church, having agreed to hold a united meeting for the purposes of making an amicable arrangement for forming a new Church. Rev. H. K. Green offered his resignation as Pastor—and his resignation was unanimously accepted." A long list of dismissed parishioners (those who resigned) follows, among whom is "Sarah P. Green" (obviously Green's wife at the time and soon to be a co-founder of the Rydal Mount School and a correspondent of Wordsworth); these members organize nearby as the Monument Square Baptist, later known as the High Street Baptist Church. In spite of the strife, the Monument Square Church requests First Baptist to send a delegate to a meeting to recognize a new church by that name. Henry K. Green became pastor of the new "High St. Church" and the "church building occupied by this group stood where Jordan Hall (Boys' and Girls' Club) is now located" (and still is today).[17]

Still all was not peaceful as the new church experienced difficulties. How long Green remained as pastor is unclear, but in 1850, with Green now pastor of the First Baptist Church in Trenton, New Jersey, seventy-one members of the High Street Church left and organized the Bethesada Baptist Church. The name was changed to Bunker Hill Baptist Church, and Reverend John Blain of the High Street Baptist was chosen pastor of Bunker Hill on February 28, 1850. The High Street Church disbanded in 1863, sold its property, and some of its members returned to the old First Baptist Church.[18] The First Baptist Church is now a modest residence at 4 Monument Square opposite the Bunker Hill Monument.

As for Reverend Green, we know that in 1845 he was pastor at High Street Baptist, that he remained a member of the Baptist Ministers Association;[19] that he and his wife founded the Rydal Mount Ladies Boarding School and School for Young Children, in part as a response to the demise of the Moulton's Point school, and in part as a more progressive, academically oriented, women-centered school committed to the training of the heart as well as the head in the Wordsworthian tradition. We know also that he headed the school until no later than 1850 when he took up a new pastorate in New Jersey. We know that Sarah P. Green probably remained in the area until 1852 when her burial is recorded in Chelsea where she had lived with her husband.

There is much more to learn about this Wordsworthian school in America, but whether the needed records can be found remains to be seen. As suggested above, this essay was inspired by the intriguing discovery of an unpublished letter and related materials in Grasmere, England. At this time it would seem that Rydal Mount in America had a life of five, certainly no more than seven years. In 1852, Reverend Green is elsewhere, his wife is dead, and there is no evidence of disciples carrying on "the glory and the freshness of a dream." But the power of Wordsworth's poetry for an American woman is a remarkable phenomenon in cross-cultural studies.

NOTES

* The author wishes to acknowledge the expert editorial assistance of Elaine Tarutis in the preparation of this essay.

† The author also wishes to acknowledge a grant from the American Philosophical Society which supported much of the research in this essay.

1. Stephen Gill, *William Wordsworth: A Life* (Oxford: Clarendon Press, 1989), p. 415.

2. Gill, *William Wordsworth*, pp. 412–13. This essay develops more fully the findings in my short article in *The Wordsworth Circle* 23 (Winter 1992): 43–48.

3. W. W. Ms. A. Green, S. P. 1,2,3. For permission to quote from these documents I am grateful to the Trustees of Dove Cottage. I am also grateful to

the always helpful Jeff Cowton, Registrar of the Wordsworth Library, Grasmere, who provided invaluable service during my visit and after my return.

4. William Wordsworth, *The Prose Works of William Wordsworth*, ed. W. J. B. Owen and Jane Worthington Smyser, vol. 1 (Oxford: Clarendon Press, 1974), p. 126.

5. I am grateful to my colleague Professor Joseph Quinn of the Department of Economics at Boston College for his answers to my questions concerning the value of 1845 dollars today.

6. James Hunnewell, *A Century of Town Life: A History of Charlestown, Massachusetts, 1775–1887* (Boston: Little, Brown, and Company, 1888), p. 87.

7. Hunnewell, *Century of Town Life*, p. 87.

8. I am grateful for the help provided by Maureen Marx and staff members of the Charlestown branch of the Boston Public Library.

9. My thanks to the reference staff of the Boston Athenaeum for directing me to the *Boston Evening Transcript* and for answering many questions about people and places in the educational system of nineteenth-century Boston.

10. Most helpful in providing information on Charlestown history and on Baptist ministers and activities of the time have been the following: John Alves; Rev. Stephen Ayres of St. John's Episcopal Church, Charlestown; Rev. Donald Dickinson of First Baptist Church, North Andover; Connie Hansen, Baptist historian par excellence; Maurice O'Shea, Vice President of Bunker Hill Community College, Charlestown; C. Allyn Russell; Kenneth Stone; and Rev. Jay Warden of the Diocesan Office of the American Baptist Church of Massachusetts.

This article could not have been written without the resources of the Department of Special Collections, Franklin Trask Library, Andover-Newton Theological Seminary and the expertise of Diana Yount in directing this author to key documents. Permission to quote from First Baptist Church, Charlestown records has been granted by the Trask Library.

11. Charles P. Emmons, *Emmon's Charlestown Directory* (Charlestown: Charles P. Emmons, 55 Main St., 1845), p. 31.

12. *A Documentary History of Chelsea, 1624–1824*. Collected and Arranged with Notes by Mellen Chamberlain. Vol. 2 (Boston: Printed for the Massachusetts Historical Society, 1980), p. 698.

13. *General Catalogue of the Theological Seminary, Andover, Massachusetts, 1808–1890* (Boston, Mass.: Thomas Todd, Printer, 14 Beacon St., 1909).

14. *Acadia Divinity College and the Baptist Historical Committee of the United Baptist Convention of the Atlantic Provinces* (St. John: 1988).

15. *First Baptist Church of Charlestown, 100th Anniversary. Dedication of the Church Edifice, November 13, 1861*. Pamphlet, January 12, 1961.

16. Pastor Geo. R. Horr, Jr., *Sermon on the Seventy-Fifth Anniversary of the First Baptist Sunday-School, Charlestown, Mass. April 15, 1888* (Boston: McDonald Gill and Company).

17. *First Baptist Church of Charlestown, 100th Anniversary*. Pamphlet, p. 7.

18. *145th Anniversary of the First Baptist Church* (Charlestown, Massachusetts: 1946). Pamphlet.

19. *Bunker Hill Baptist Church, Declaration of Faith and Covenant.*

IV

Interactive Legacies

Rousseau and Staël in England

7

Annette Wheeler Cafarelli

Rousseau and British Romanticism

Women and the Legacy of Male Radicalism

> *Men have had every advantage of us in telling their own story. Education has been theirs in so much higher a degree; the pen has been in their hands.*
>
> —Jane Austen,
> Persuasion

> *J'ai peutêtre fait périr dans l'opprobre et dans la misére une fille aimable, honnête, estimable, et qui surement valoit beaucoup mieux que moi. . . . Beaucoup d'autres meilleures choses étoient à ma portée; ce ruban seul me tenta, je le volai, et comme je ne le cachois guéres on me le trouva bientôt. On voulut savoir où je l'avois pris. . . . je dis . . . que c'est Marion qui me l'a donné. . . . et moi avec une impudence infernale je confirme ma déclaration, et lui soutiens en face qu'elle m'a donné le ruban. . . . Elle continua de se défendre avec autant de simplicité que de fermeté, mais sans se permettre jamais contre moi la moindre invective. Cette modération comparée à mon ton décidé lui fit tort.*
>
> —Jean-Jacques Rousseau,
> Confessions

Modern scholars have often inspected the place of Jean-Jacques Rousseau in the writings of the familiar British male Romantics.[1] As is

often the case in charting national literatures, comparatists from abroad—
in this case looking across the channel from France in the service of
proving Rousseau's international reputation—have most systematically
chronicled the presence of foreign literatures in Britain.[2] But worldwide
studies of Rousseau, by concentrating almost entirely on the male
literary tradition, have by and large neglected to analyze his ambiguous
radical legacy for women writers.[3] Although his ubiquity among the
familiar poets and the lesser known British male Romantics offers an
impressive view of the breadth of Rousseau's impact on libertarian
thought and the vogue of sensibility, in practical terms such studies are
more helpful in measuring the prestige of Rousseau than in giving a fair
picture of the British Romantic Age: an era in which women writers
were filling the literary marketplace in unprecedented numbers and
declaring their entitlement to respond to the male writers who dominated the intellectual purview and symbolized the high literary tradition.

This paper will concentrate on the female reaction to Rousseau in
Britain in the Romantic Age. Like the familiar male romantic writers,
radical British women of the late eighteenth and early nineteenth
centuries were also listening to international currents; but their
approval of Rousseau was never without an amalgam of misgivings. The
women who voiced the most antipathy to Rousseau were not Burkeites
trying to crush progressivism (the profile generally associated with male
opponents to Rousseau), but, rather, the most radical feminist
commentators who were demanding equality for women within a
dissident program of revolutionary change. Paradoxically, the conservative women who most opposed radical politics were in reality the
most likely to conform to Rousseau's prescriptions for women, despite
their claims of repugnance for Rousseau.

Women writers cast their public commentaries on Rousseau chiefly
in two genres already well established as avenues for female participation in the arts, the novel, and pedagogic writings—realms already
securely associated with professional women. Thus, the two key texts for
women were Rousseau's novel *Julie, ou la Nouvelle Héloïse* (1761) and his
educational treatise *Émile, ou l'éducation* (1762).[4] The plot of Julie suc-
cumbing to a liaison with her tutor Saint-Preux, and afterwards settling
into an exemplary marriage amid sub-alpine scenery with the older
Wolmar in perfect amity with her former lover, to whom she professes
her enduring passion before expiring, gave rise to a wide variety of
novelistic sentimental duos and triads set amid inspirational scenery.
With book five of *Émile*, Sophie was seen as the sequel to Julie, and the
explicit theories of education in *Émile* were viewed as systematizing the
implicit ones of *Héloïse*; as Rousseau himself observed, the key concepts
of *Émile* were prefigured in *Héloïse*.[5]

Despite its encouragement of observational theories of education, *Émile* presumed a heavily gendered division of the sexes that denied women the benefits of his program of natural education. His advocacy of a separate and unequal homebred education for female children turned back the clock on the previous half-century's efforts at educational reform to enhance female education.[6] Based on his primary assumption of the innate difference of men and women, Rousseau's *Émile* insisted upon the sophism of separate educations.[7] The business of women is marriage, childbearing, obedient subjugation, and above all, pleasing men.[8] Once the mother has fulfilled her duty to procreate and lactate, she turns the education of sons over to the father or governor.[9] Rousseau's strict division between male and female training is well known: the boy enjoys liberty, the undivided attention of an entirely dedicated tutor whose own life is subordinated to his charge (regardless of numerical practicalities); the girl leads a sequestered life, toying with dolls until she can become doll-like herself in a preoccupation with clothing and self-adornment.[10] Not for her the outcries against political injustice, since she has been trained to docility and constraint: it is the law of nature for her to be subordinate to her husband, she is made to obey men and to yield even to their injustices.[11] Any other action is a deplorable attempt to "usurp" male rights.[12] In the phrase often quoted among British women in the Romantic Age, with no small degree of ire, Rousseau states the Englishwoman should be trained to please her future husband as if cultivating her talents for a harem.[13] It is a curious feature of Rousseau's British legacy that this image gave rise to one of those anomalous moments when left- and right-wing women found themselves in agreement: neither side was willing to pledge itself to Rousseau. To examine the legacy of Rousseau among British women writers is in fact not to celebrate Rousseau as a radical, but rather to see how Rousseau, in spite of himself, gave rise to feminist radicalism.

Rousseau embeds proscriptions against women's intellectual activities in virtually all his writings: in *Émile* forbidding women adequate education to engage his texts; in *Héloïse* barring young women from novel reading; and in the *Rêveries* reprimanding women for inquiring into the truth of his *Confessions*.[14] The influence of Rousseau on the subject of women prevailed to such an extent that protests based on his own libertarian theories in the second discourse *Sur . . . l'inégalité* (1755), and *Du Contrat Social* (1762) had little force against documents such as *Héloïse, Émile,* and *La Lettre à d'Alembert* (1758),[15] which advocated an unbridgeable intellectual distinction of the sexes and identified domesticity as the sole glorious pursuit of women. The famous story of Marion, Rousseau, and the stolen ribbon (which among women quickly became the most talked about episode of the first volume of the

Confessions) emblematized the powerlessness of women to oppose him. The statement of male narrative, however duplicitous or misleading, has an implicit and unassailable credibility precluding any opposition, however legitimate; like Marion trying to clear herself of Rousseau's imputations, the attempt at defense, counterargument, and self-advocacy by women Romantics contradicting Rousseau was a Sisyphean effort against the authority of male testimony.[16]

Rousseau's *Héloïse* swept England in the 1760s, and its immense vogue generated plot and scenic elements throughout the late eighteenth-century British novel. Its popularity is evident in the masses of novels featuring Julies, Julias, Julianas, and Juliettes (the novel reading Henry Tilney in Austen's *Northanger Abbey* asserts: "Do not imagine that you can cope with me in a knowledge of Julias and Louisas")[17]; and the abundance of Rousseauvian landscapes, whether Alpine fantasies or domesticated as English Lake or Irish countryside, as in the works of Ann Radcliffe, Charlotte Smith, and Sydney Owenson Morgan. More daring were the various triads that were modeled on the threesome of Saint-Preux, Julie, and Wolmar; more didactic were those depicting educational schemes modeled on Émile and Sophie.

On one level, Rousseau was merely returning to England the motif of seduction and its consequences that he had borrowed from the previous continental vogue of Samuel Richardson's *Clarissa*. In terms of reception history, *Héloïse* was first accepted as an antidote to *Clarissa*, showing how women who transgress can be rehabilitated; it was only later that it came to be condemned as a prescription for female transgression with impunity. The year of its translation, the *Critical Review* reported that Rousseau's novel showed how reputation could be regained by moral behavior: Rousseau "hath taught us the means of retrieving the esteem of mankind, after a capital slip in conduct." Richardson and Rousseau were equal partners in a commendable enterprise: "The one renders his heroine proof against all the assaults of temptation, thereby proposing a perfect pattern for the imitation of her sex; the other describes her subject to human frailty, lest, by elevating virtue too high, we should be discouraged from attempting to climb the steep ascent." For early readers, Rousseau provided a salutary motto of virtue redeemed.[18]

There does not seem to have been a time when fiction was not regarded as potentially hazardous to young minds; certainly it was a view that increased as novels began to multiply in the late eighteenth century. By the time Clara Reeve published an early history of the genre, *The Progress of Romance* (1785), she deemed it necessary to more carefully monitor the reading of *Héloïse*: "It is dangerous to criticise a work that has been so much, and so justly admired.—It is a book that speaks to the heart . . . when reflexion comes afterwards, and reason takes up the reins, we discover that it is dangerous and improper for those for whose use it is chiefly intended, for young persons." Reeve still justifies the book, however, by restoring it to a particular socio-historical milieu:

> Rousseau saw that the women on the Continent . . . as soon as they were married . . . encouraged gallants; of the two evils he thought a single person's indulging a criminal passion, of less pernicious consequence to society, than a married woman who commits adultery:—upon this principle he wrote this book.—He puts the character of a woman who encourages lovers after marriage, in opposition to one who having committed the greatest fault before marriage, repents, and recovers her principles.

Given that "it is a dangerous book to put into the hands of youth," because "it awakens and nourishes those passions," Reeve suggests that the best plan would have been to have promulgated an abridged and altered form: "to make the two Lovers, stop short of the *act*, that made it criminal in either party to marry another," regretting that in its mischievous present form, "those who write only for depraved and corrupted minds, dare appeal to *Rousseau* as a precedent."[19]

In the wake of the French Revolution, the proper mediation of potentially hazardous material was not sufficient. The evangelical Hannah More named *Héloïse* the most dangerous of the entire corpus of corrupt novels; her 1797 *Strictures on the Modern System of Female Education* declared,

> Novels . . . are daily becoming vehicles of wider mischief. . . . Rousseau was the first popular dispenser of this complicated drug. . . . He does not paint an innocent woman ruined, repenting, and restored; but with a far more mischievous refinement, he annihilates the value of chastity. . . . He exhibits a virtuous woman, the victim not of temptation, but of reason—not of vice, but of sentiment—not of passion, but of conviction; and strikes at the very root of honour, by elevating a crime into a principle.

Hannah More was one of many counterrevolutionary voices that complained women learned from Rousseau to reason themselves into deplorable sexual mores. In the hands of the "seducing" Rousseau, "there never was a net of such exquisite art, and inextricable workmanship, spread to entangle innocence, and ensnare inexperience . . . unhappily, the victim does not even struggle in the toils, because part of the delusion consists in his imagining that he is set at liberty."[20] In 1804, the *Anti-Jacobin Review* used the familiar argument that Rousseau himself warned young women away from romance reading in the preface to *Héloïse*, and declared that those who become accustomed to fiction become "unfit to perform the duties of their station"; Eaton Stannard Barrett's *The Heroine* (1813) warned against the seductive genre of novels with the syllogism, "What St. Preux is to Heloise, the book is to the reader."[21]

Frances Brooke's epistolary novel, *The History of Lady Julia Mandeville* (1763), was quick to join the Julie vogue. The tender Lady Julia is barely allowed a letter to sully the purity of the beau ideal (the *Critical Review* called the novel "as sentimental as Rousseau, and as interesting as Richardson")[22] and when her devoted Harry impulsively meets his end in a duel over her, Julia expires from sensibility.

In another rather harmlessly denatured triad, Sydney Owenson Morgan's *The Wild Irish Girl* (1806), depicts father and son as the English Wolmar and Saint-Preux who compete unbeknownst to one another for the Glorvina of the title. At novel's end, Lord M. senior safely resigns this Julie to his son, in whose hands the complete epistolary narrative lodges. Glorvina, called a "child of Nature," has been raised in pure uncontaminated isolation (though she has been taught Latin, among other things, to the anxiety of her suitor). Posing as a drawing tutor, her young admirer brings a copy of *Héloïse*, "a book which Glorvina had *not*, yet *should* read, that she may know herself, and the latent sensibility of her soul." Presumably he speaks for Morgan in saying,

> Let our English novels carry away the prize of morality from the romantic fictions of every other country; but you will find they rarely seize on the imagination through the medium of the heart; and, as for their heroines, I confess, that though they are the most perfect of beings, they are also the most stupid.

But as with the familiar British novel heroine, silence is golden—despite her *Héloïse* initiation, Glorvina has little to say for herself, so we can only judge of her intelligence and sensibility as we are told. The eponymous hero of her first novel *St. Clair*, dies in a duel with his beloved's fiancé, against whom he had earlier defended *Héloïse*; Olivia in turn dies of sensibility, voicing remorse for her equally pure engagement to the Colonel ("he was not a St. Preux") and infatuation for St. Clair ("the first impulse of my passions").[23]

As Morgan suggests, the Julies of Anglophonic fiction tended to be morally purer than Rousseau's. What she fails to mention is that when heroines failed to be morally exemplary, the scandal was cast back upon their female authors for knowing more than they should. Yet, throughout the 1790s, radical women writers risked experimenting with the Julie triad to study the plight of the compromised woman amid the realities of social endurance. In Helen Maria Williams's *Julia* (1790),[24] for example, Frederick Seymour finds himself attracted to Julia rather than to her cousin whom he marries; in a reversal, Williams puts this Saint-Preux to death at the end, a "young man, who fell the victim of that fatal passion, which he at first unhappily indulged, and which he was at length unable to subdue." It is not without a warning, however, that "women have even greater reason than men to fortify their hearts against those strong affections, which, when not regulated by discretion, plunge in aggravated misery that sex." Her heroine, rather than compromise the purity of her passion, never marries—though such was a typical vow for heroines in the British novels of the period (for example, Charlotte Smith's *Ethelinde*); few plots, however, actually required them to fulfill it.

Mary Hays's more controversial *Memoirs of Emma Courtney* (1796)[25] included a preface in which Hays also cautioned that the book was intended "as a *warning*, rather than as an example." Emma, excessively attached to books and circulating libraries, confesses her ambivalent experience of *Héloïse*: "with what enthusiasm, did I peruse this dangerous, enchanting, work!" The book presages her infatuation with Augustus Harley "the St Preux, the Emilius of my sleeping and waking reveries," with whom she offers to live, herself "Rousseau's Julia." Secretly married to another, Harley reveals his enduring passion for Emma before expiring, but not before Emma is forced to abandon her infatuation—without any actual illicit activity—in the face of a different marriage, in which she herself is wronged. Twice the book boldly upholds her friend Mary Wollstonecraft, though the character Emma is careful to say that her own conduct "*is not what I would recommend to general imitation.*"

As has often been noted, Wollstonecraft's posthumously published novel, *The Wrongs of Woman; or Maria* (1798) radicalizes her earlier sentimental tale, *Mary* (1788).[26] The preface to the earlier work declares its "heroine" is not a Clarissa or a Sophie, although the title page bears a motto from *Héloïse*; but she, like the later Maria of *The Wrongs of Woman*, still indulges in the reading of sentimental novels, the excesses of which Wollstonecraft warns of in her *Vindication of the Rights of Woman* (1792).[27] The preface of *The Wrongs of Woman*, states its intention of "exhibiting the misery and oppression, peculiar to women that arise out of the partial laws and customs of society." This unfinished novel, now familiar to feminist readers, shows Maria placed by her husband in a madhouse and figuratively imprisoned, "bastilled," by the institution of marriage: "Was not the world a vast prison, and women born slaves?" But she succumbs, like many women, to the pitfall of relying for distraction and escape on the misleading fictions of Rousseau, "the Prometheus of modern sentiment" (musing "how difficult it was for women to avoid growing romantic, who have no active duties or pursuits"). A fellow prisoner lends her Rousseau's *Héloïse*: "it seemed to open a new world to her—the only one worth inhabiting" and she imagines him a Saint-Preux or "an ideal lover far superior . . . the demi-god of her fancy." They escape, elope, and, as indicated in the notes sketching her intended plan, the novel was to have documented the arduous compassionless path of the divorce courts and civil actions for damages, only to find her at the end deserted by her paramour: "her lover unfaithful." This Henry Darnford is a far cry from the Saint-Preux she imagined, and the chronicles of betrayal recounted by Maria and the maidservant Jemima hardly inhabit the sentimental world of *Héloïse*; as Jemima says of the realities of her downfall and the delusions of fiction, "I have since read in novels of the blandishments of seduction, but I had not even the pleasure of being enticed into vice."

All three of these radical women writers suffered from a public scorn that novelists of purely sentimental convention would never know. The story has often been told of the consequences of Wollstonecraft's relationship with Gilbert Imlay and the ostracism she suffered upon marrying William Godwin—which far from legitimating her, only revealed the unsanctioned status of the child she bore before Imlay deserted her for another. Williams's long residence in France and illicit liaison with a married man drew down the scorn of conservatives; Hays was denounced for the autobiographical dimension of her own misplaced, though innocent infatuation. Wollstonecraft was obliged to defend Hays to Godwin, of all people, with the reminder of her own past: "You termed Miss Hay's [*sic*] conduct insanity when only her own happiness was involved. . . . my old wounds bleed afresh. . . . One word more—I never blamed the woman for whom I was abandoned. I offered to see, nay, even to live with her, and I should have tried to improve her." That Godwin revealed her proposed Rousseauvian triad in his 1798 *Memoirs* of Wollstonecraft shows the extent of his blindness about the impact of his and Rousseau's theories on women; this, along with denominating her "a female Werter," and publishing her letters to Imlay as an authentic declaration of Rousseauvian passion, acted much to the detriment of her reputation.[28]

Elizabeth Hamilton's *Memoirs of Modern Philosophers* (1800) was one such contentious response, linking Godwinian utopian idealism and Rousseauvian sentimentalism in her ridicule of improvident declarations of passion and politics.[29] Mary Hays is parodied as Bridgetina Botherim, for her philosophical aspirations as well as her rapturous forwardness in wildly calling out for "the St. Preuse of my affections"; she gives *Héloïse* to the susceptible Julia, who promptly elopes with a worthless impostor. The comedy ends with Julie perishing penitent, though Bridgetina remains throughout a headstrong figure of ridicule. She indefatigably argues there should be no distinction of the sexes, in response to the authoritative charge that Wollstonecraft intended to "unsex women"; she decries against marriage ("Why was I doomed to come into the world in such an age? Why was I born when an absurd, an unnatural institution ties up the hearts of men") while praising Rousseau and "the sublime virtues of his Eloisa." A rather less visionary character replies, "was she not a wanton baggage who was got with child by her tutor?" Yet a strangely mixed picture emerges from this peculiar reactionary novel; for when another sober character blames Rousseau's "system of female education" ("A creature instructed in no duty but the art of pleasing, and taught that the whole end of her creation was to attract the attention of the men, could not be expected to tread very firmly in the paths of virtue"), and another asks "what Rousseau would have done with all the ordinary girls, for it is plain his system is adapted only for *beauties*; and should any of these poor beauties fail in getting husbands, GOD help them, poor things! they would make very miserable old maids," their refutations are not so removed from modern objections to Rousseau's Sophie.

Above all, the Rousseauvian document that had the most impact for women in Britain was *Émile*. Harold Silver argues that the Rousseaumania between the 1760s and 1790s played a important role in European libertarian thought as the principle of natural education was taken up by followers in Britain.[30] It is clear that the majority of male commentators—and many female commentators—accepted Rousseau's distinction between the sexes. Indeed, the English reading public purchasing the translated *Émile* found that book five on Sophie was important enough to warrant a place in the title, *Emilius and Sophia*. Yet for women, any explicit program of following Rousseau's segregated education was to their disadvantage, and although British women sought to lay claim to radical reform by refuting Rousseau, they found the Rousseauvian argument about the natural station of women used to suppress their dissent.

Stéphanie Félicité de Genlis was responsible for putting into currency a vast number of fictionalized Rousseauvian educational systems, drawing considerable publicity from her real life role as governess to the children of the Duc de Chartres (to become the Duc d'Orleans), including one of mysterious birth said to be her own. Her most famous work was *Adèle et Théodore, ou Lettres sur l'éducation* (1782), which orchestrated object lessons to teach children such things as shunning irrational fears ("we shall accustom them as Rousseau advises"), although it is throughout made clear that girls should be raised on the expectation of preparing for a dependent life. Thus, little blushing Adèle, equipped with her Rousseau-prescribed doll, is praised for her "modesty and simplicity," and raised with minimal reading so that "she will have but few ideas but they will be rational ones." It is hardly surprising that another educator, the onetime governess Charlotte Brontë, should assign to Mr. Rochester's fastidiously dressed French-educated illegitimate daughter, whom Jane Eyre has the task of improving, the name of Adèle.[31]

In Britain, the archetypal British Rousseauvian response was Thomas Day's *The History of Sandford and Merton* (1783–1789),[32] in which the coddled Tommy Merton, indulged with the prosperity of the family sugar fortune, is contrasted to the hardy Harry Sandford, raised by the clergyman Mr. Barlow in a natural upbringing of practical experiential lessons. A few pages suffice to praise Miss Simmons who has none of the dreaded "accomplishments" but instead "rational and useful knowledge." Thereafter many books written for children featured male and female Barlows entrusted with guiding their young charges through a choreographed empirical education, including Wollstonecraft's *Original Stories* (1788), Laetitia Barbauld and John Aikin's *Evenings at Home* (1792–1796), Charlotte Smith's series of *Rural Walks* (1795), and Maria Edgeworth's *The Parent's Assistant* (1796).

But the clergymen and educators such as John Gregory, James Fordyce, John Bennet, John Burton, and Thomas Gisborne (names now familiar largely due to modern reprints prepared for scholars studying the impact on the novel of the much bruited "conduct literature") are only a few of the many male writers of books of female guidance who advocated the highly gendered Rousseauvian education in which middle-class and aristocratic women were encouraged to direct their training to please men.[33] Implicitly, of course, such programs were designed to optimize their matrimonial chances and thus minimize the threat of having to live alone, or worse, having to generate an income through the scanty labor options available for single women to prevent any further decline down the social scale.

Day's dichotomy of corrupt luxurious education and Rousseauvian natural education in *Sandford and Merton* popularized educational plans as a common motif in fiction. These city mouse/country mouse pairings had initially found their way into the intellectual marketplace with Henry Brooke's *The Fool of Quality* (1766–1770), which features a sturdily brought up child of nature, raised away from his aristocratic background, who confers the wisdom of his native intelligence on all who surround him. Elizabeth Inchbald, who began a translation of Rousseau's *Confessions* in 1790, wrote one such sequel in *Nature and Art* (1796).[34] The young Harry, raised bookless, speaks the pure ingenuous truth ("He would call *compliments, lies—reserve* he would call *pride—stateliness, affectation*—and for the words *war* and *battle,* he constantly substituted the word *massacre*"). His cousin, the urbanely corrupt young William, in graphic contrast, seduces and refuses to marry the villager Agnes Primrose, who is driven to prostitution and crime, and is finally condemned to execution by her seducer (whose punishment is the humiliation of divorce from a wife who remarries a libertine). But Lois Whitney points out what is true of many such Rousseauvian schemata: primitivism in *Nature and Art* is "a confusion of several points of view"; the Rousseauvian exemplar is educated by his father on a remote island, but the surrounding savages' wrongful behavior suggests their social isolation does not equally guarantee their moral perfection.[35]

Lying behind all of these experiments is the idea of the guardian trying to synthesize a primitive state by holding a ward in artificial isolation. Inchbald's 1788 play *The Child of Nature*, loosely adapted from Stéphanie Félicité de Genlis's *Zélie, ou l'ingénue* (1781),[36] features a Marquis Almanza who keeps confined in his castle an orphan Amanthis whom he "has brought up from her infancy . . . and has never suffered any living creature to behold." The Marquis prohibits all books except those he himself has written. Unlike the euphemisms which shrouded Day's experiment, Almanza's uncle demands, "Who is that young woman you keep in a part of this house? Is she your mistress, or your daughter, or one whom you mean to marry, and by so doing bring disgrace upon your family?" The play takes place at the very moment she is introduced to the world ("Today, I restore Amanthis to that liberty she has never remembered, of course, not once regretted"), and certainly leads us to wonder what exactly is a state of nature, if being held in complete seclusion duplicates it. The same day witnesses the return of her exiled father in disguise, and we also may wonder at the merits of praising Amanthis for her blind obedience to the total stranger who announces himself her closest relation. Almanza and Amanthis marry under the closing benediction: "To love with sincerity and judgment, is only reserved for superior minds; few beings, such as Almanza and his Child of Nature." Inchbald interjects the term "child of nature," and her abridgement converted the five act sentimental drama of a man fallen in love with his ward into a popular fable-like afterpiece.[37]

The term "child of nature" afterwards became common to describe the sequestered upbringing of many ingénues. Morgan's wild Irish girl has been mentioned. In Charlotte Smith's novel *The Young Philosopher* (1798), the "simple yet well-informed child of nature" Medora marries the forthright young philosopher Delmont, whose mother "had formed a new way of educating children"—the two, uninfluenced by fashion or wealth, after many old world trials leave for the uncorrupted new world of North America. In the preface, Smith declares her admiration for Wollstonecraft's *Wrongs of Woman*; of even more interest is the novel by Wollstonecraft's friend Eliza Fenwick (who along with Mary Hays, tended Wollstonecraft's final days). Fenwick's *Secresy: Or, the Ruin on the Rock* (1795) features a sequestered education gone awry. The "child of nature" Sibella Valmont is raised by her uncle in seclusion; he protects her fortune, but she falls susceptible to the blandishments of Clement Montgomery, her uncle's illegitimate son; he deserts her and she is left the naïve victim of her "erroneous education." Fenwick utterly disavows the simple sequestered upbringing so mistakenly idealized in the wake of Rousseau. However, in Jane West's *A Tale of the Times* (1799), the "genuine child of Nature" Lucy Evans tries to advise her friend the Countess Geraldine who regardless becomes "the third Eloisa" when a seducing proponent of the new "philosophy" undermines her virtue. They appear at a masquerade attired as Perdita and Florizel, characters from Shakespeare's *The Winter's Tale*, still a potent allusion to the notorious liaison two decades earlier of Mary Robinson and the Prince Regent.[38]

The subplot of Maria Edgeworth's *Belinda* (1801) in which the unsteady but improving hero Clarence Hervey educates an orphan ward Virginia as a "child of nature," was based on the unsuccessful educational experiment of her father's friend Thomas Day in raising two orphans as Sophies. Navigating between the sophisticated charms of Lady Delacour and the pliant Virginia (named after Bernardin de Saint Pierre's *Paul et Virginie*), Harvey comes to realize that "in comparison with Belinda, Virginia appeared to him but an insipid, though innocent child." He marries the less indolent but equally insipid Belinda, concluding "Nothing could be more absurd than my scheme of educating a woman in solitude to make her fit for society." Yet, as with the Inchbald play, the fictional world takes up the question of Virginia's injured reputation that commentators on Day were so eager to gloss over regarding Day's orphans: "When a man marries, he sets up new equipages, and casts off old mistresses"; "Nobody will visit her, to be sure"; "Her reputation is injured—fatally injured." As is well known, educational schemes lie at the center of Maria Edgeworth's own fiction as well as the many educational manuals and children's stories she wrote with her father Richard Lovell Edgeworth. R. L. Edgeworth's preface to the first series of *Tales of Fashionable Life* (1809) testified, "It has been my daughter's aim to promote, by all her writings, the progress of education from the cradle to the grave," and she prefaced her novel *Belinda* calling it "a Moral Tale—the author not wishing to acknowledge a Novel." In 1783, her father set her the task of translating *Adèle et Théodore* (abandoned when it was preempted by another edition). The first two chapters of Edgeworth's first published work, *Letters for Literary Ladies* (1795) are usually described as depicting the debate between Thomas Day and R. L. Edgeworth over what should constitute the educational program of his eldest daughter. Although modern readers are eager to confer the victory in the debate on the less conservative voice (R. L. Edgeworth's), the dialogue is at best ambiguous, since neither offers a radical advocacy of women's education. Both disavow being "a champion for the rights of woman." Certainly the caution that Rousseau's plan "would overturn the world, would make every woman a Cleopatra, and every man an Antony," imputes to Sophie capabilities far beyond what Rousseau envisioned. To confute any suspicion of irony, the next section, the "Letters of Julia and Caroline," confirms the conventionalities, with the even-keeled Caroline cautioning against the excessive sensibility of the flighty Julia, who dies penitent after her implicitly adulterous transgressions.[39]

Rousseau's *Émile* called attention to the professionalization of education and to an occupation women were traditionally associated with through their link with children. By the end of the eighteenth century, writing about teaching was also a common field for the professional and occasional woman writer. It is important to make finer distinctions than are usually made in discussing what have often been reductively grouped as conduct or courtesy books. By the late eighteenth century it is important to distinguish two separate kinds of material, the educational manual or treatise addressed to educators (guardian, governess, tutor) whether parental or professional, and the conduct book addressed to pupils (often depicted as young relations). If its antecedents lie in the lofty tradition of Baldassare Castiglione, and the more questionable contribution of the fourth Earl of Chesterfield, the conduct book for women of the Romantic Age signaled a relatively humble enterprise, concerned with etiquette rather than educational reform, confirming women's modesty in not aiming for a more ambitious audience. The conduct book was a coaching manual for the socialization of the young (and those with hopes for upward mobility), but it essentially instilled the status quo. The educational treatise, however, was in the position of theorizing the role of pedagogy as well as giving practical instructions, and thus by the turn of the century it had emerged as a chief genre for women writers. Many continued to use the epistolary format often associated with the humbler conduct literature, but the writing of educational treatises entailed the professionalization of pedagogy. It dignified an avenue for middle-class women who lacked financial provision that was close enough to traditional domestic tasks as not to compromise their reputations, one of the handful of occupations available to women who were neither laborers nor aristocrats. Rousseau had opened the door to ideological innovations among radical women that he did not anticipate and certainly would not have welcomed. For radical women the educational treatises became a vehicle for polemical subterfuge, an acceptable genre through which women could enter the forum of public debate. Yet, these works illuminated an interesting cultural dividing line, because they elicited a backlash of conservative answers that sought to reclaim women for their traditional station in life.

Catharine Macaulay's *Letters on Education* (1790)[40] was responsible for opening up the serious discussion of Rousseau's educational theories to women, taking up for women Plato's task of forming "the children of the state." The "sagacious Rousseau" is credited in a limited regard—the pleasure of education, the importance of not swaddling infants, of letting children play—but with the caveat that she would "advise every tutor to read his Emilius with care; yet let him not be so charmed with the eloquence and plausibility of the author, as to adopt altogether the rules laid down in this work on the subject of instruction" (000–00). Macaulay's treatise authorized women to oppose the central Rousseau-vian doctrine, "the absurd notion, that the education of females should be of the opposite kind to that of males."

Many of the ideas associated now with Wollstonecraft were developed from seeds in Macaulay, a strong advocate of coeducation: "let your children be brought up together; let their sports and studies be the same"; "confine not the education of your daughters to what is regarded as the ornamental parts of it, nor deny the graces to your sons." Girls are to learn Latin,[41] reduce their "accomplishments" and novel reading, and above all she specifies, "lest you should mistake my plan, that though I have been obliged (in order to avoid confusion) to speak commonly in the masculine character, that the same rules of education in all respects are to be observed to the female as well as to the male children."[42] Similarly, Wollstonecraft followed Macaulay's declaration, "the character of our species is formed from the influence of education," in refusing to attribute to nature an inferiority which is the product of a second class education. Macaulay rejects the notion of "the supposed intrinsic character of women," asserting that "nature is charged with all those imperfections which we alone owe to the blunders of art." In the epistolary chapter entitled "No Characteristic Difference in Sex" she says the there is too much "false speculation on the natural qualities of the female mind," and she does not hesitate to identify the source of the sophistry: "Among the most strenuous asserters of a sexual difference in character, Rousseau is the most conspicuous. . . . [H]e sets out with a supposition, that nature intended the subjection of the one sex to the other; that consequently there must be an inferiority of intellect in the subjected party."

Macaulay, like Wollstonecraft was to do, repeatedly alluded to the passage famous in Rousseauvian pedagogy at the turn of the century, that a woman should cultivate talents "in order to please her future husband . . . as a young Circassian cultivates hers to fit her for the harem," the words, she says, of a "licentious pedant." It is their "sensuality" and "tyranny over women" that leads men to extol "a false idea of female excellence," and to ordain an education that tends "to corrupt and debilitate both the powers of mind and body," and thus fulfill the weakest stereotypes. Providence did not intend women for "the condition of slavery," she writes, but "it is a long time before the crowd give up opinions they have been taught to look upon with respect." There are some commentators who have suggested Wollstonecraft was overvaluing Macaulay when she said she wrote with Macaulay's approbation in mind,[43] but what readers often fail to realize is the revolutionary place of Macaulay in defying both conservative and radical male commentators in order to devise an independent feminist educational rhetoric—and the lengthy siege necessary "before the crowd give up opinions."

Like many women of the period, including Maria Edgeworth, Hannah More, Sarah Trimmer, and Laetitia Barbauld, Mary Wollstonecraft was throughout her life involved in the production of educational materials—children's tales (*Original Stories*, 1788), an anthology of improving extracts (*The Female Reader*, 1789), two educational treatises, (*Thoughts on the Education of Daughters*, 1787, and *A Vindication of the Rights of Woman*, 1792). Of these women she was by far the most radical feminist and the radicalization of her works was historically linked to the rising tide of Rousseau. We need to look at how she advanced Macaulay's critique to understand the complexities of Rousseau's presence in Britain.

Her first publication, *Thoughts on the Education of Daughters* (1787)[44] adumbrated in brief the principles she was to develop in her later *Vindication of the Rights of Woman* (1792). Like many other educational works of the period, the book contained the usual opposition to superficial "accomplishments," but it was strengthened by its realistic concern for preparing women for the possibility of earning a living, not merely awaiting a marriage. Yet, she was careful to stipulate "no employment of the mind is a sufficient excuse for neglecting domestic duties." Wollstonecraft's *A Vindication of the Rights of Men* (1790), the first published reply to Edmund Burke's *Reflections on the Revolution in France*, reflects the historical moment in bringing forward Rousseauvian rhetoric in its call for the "liberty of reason" and the "rights which men inherit at birth." But in terms of gender issues this work offers no critique of Rousseau, and its selective use of texts such as *Lettre à d'Alembert*, for example (she denounces those who aestheticize politics by shedding tears over novels), avoids feminist controversy.

There are only a few references to Rousseau in Wollstonecraft's surviving letters—her first reading of *Émile* in 1787, lending Godwin *Héloïse*, comparing herself to the "*Solitary Walker*."[45] Wollstonecraft actually esteemed aspects of his system of boys' education in *Émile*, the doctrine of natural rights, the social contract, and the essay on inequality, but as she asks of *Héloïse*, "Whoever drew a more exalted female character than Rousseau? though in the lump he constantly endeavoured to degrade the sex." When she started reading *Émile* in 1787, she said, "I . . . love his paradoxes"; by the time of the *Vindication* she was denouncing Rousseau for his "unintelligible paradoxes."[46]

Between the *Thoughts* and the *Vindication* was the watershed of the revolution, and all its Rousseauvian associations. The *Vindication*, however supportive of the revolutionary age, is framed as a systematic refutation of Book five of Rousseau's *Émile*. Although she endorses his principle of achieving virtue through reason ("this was Rousseau's opinion respecting men: I extend it to women")[47]—she demands the extension of Rousseau's libertarian rhetoric to women: "I wish to . . . make women rational creatures, and free citizens"; women shall not "be excluded, without having a voice, from a participation of the natural rights of mankind." In terms of pedagogy, however, it is necessary to "proceed on a plan diametrically opposite to that which Rousseau has recommended": it is Sophie and "the principles on which her education was built, that I mean to attack."

Wollstonecraft's negative critique of Rousseau is profoundly indebted to the intervention of Macaulay's *Letters on Education*: "Rousseau, and most of the male writers who have followed his steps, have warmly inculcated that the whole tendency of female education ought to be directed to one point:—to render them pleasing."[48] Much of what she says echoes Macaulay's imagery with emphasis: "tyrants and sensualists" try to keep women in the "bondage of ignorance," subjected to restraint and an "enervating" education that trains them to be weak, passive, and accommodating themselves to their husband's tastes. The wife is a "house slave" and "play-thing," with "submissive charms," "gentleness, docility, and a spaniel-like affection." According to Wollstonecraft, the corrupt values of a segregated female education created in Sophie the same falsely idealized model of docile, submissive, superficiality as John Milton extolled in Eve; but it ignored the demographic reality that left many women single or widowed. Without training and without employment, an unmarried sister (the situation of so many of Jane Austen's characters) is an unwelcome dependent, "viewed with averted looks as an intruder" within the family, and with suspicion when she tries to find work outside it.

In developing an educational and social program to give women more opportunities, Wollstonecraft discards Rousseau's idea that girls innately want to "sit still" to play with dolls, and his "his ridiculous stories, which tend to prove that girls are *naturally* attentive to their persons." William Godwin's *Memoirs* of Wollstonecraft testified "Dolls and the other amusements usually appropriated to female children she held in contempt"; Mary Hays afterwards reported Macaulay's childhood indifference to dolls.[49] Like Macaulay, Wollstonecraft was an advocate of coeducation, and an opponent of the concept of a domestic station assigned by nature: "the sexual distinction which men have so warmly insisted upon, is arbitrary." The political double standard by which Rousseauvian rebellion was extolled as libertarian in general terms, but as a usurpation of the male domain when attempted by women, was a particular target of Wollstonecraft. "Women cannot be confined to merely domestic pursuits," she wrote: the actual tyrants and usurpers of rights are men, whose "scepter, real, or usurped, extends not to me." Wollstonecraft refuted the common counterfeminist charge that the claim for women's rights sought to establish a female empire: "I do not wish them to have power over men; but over themselves."

Wollstonecraft's most famous opponent was Hannah More, and the polarity between the two has often been observed.[50] More's early *Essays on Various Subjects: Principally Designed for Young Ladies*,[51] prescribes conventional female behavior but without assuming any opposing discourse. There is no question that "girls should be taught to give up their opinions," should not be "contentious," should "acquire a submissive temper and a forbearing spirit" because "a girl who has docility, will seldom be found to want understanding enough for all the purposes of a social, a happy, and a useful life." It is a testament of the intervention of Rousseau's association with the French Revolution, that the revised educational precepts of the *Strictures on the Modern System of Female Education* (1797), which supplanted the *Essays* in publishing terms, takes up a position squarely within post-Rousseauvian opposition. Yet, even as she denounces him, her own program for girls of "early habitual restraint" inculcating the "submissive" is altogether consonant with Rousseau's dictates. In More's revised treatise, the same principles prevail with emphasis—docility, obedience, and books reading only so far as it promotes domestic life—preparing not for "brilliant adventures" but for a life largely "dull, obscure and uninteresting."

In cautioning that society must raise neither "Amazons nor Circassians," More placed her two targets together. Despite Wollstonecraft's program of opposition, she was paired as the counterpart of Rousseau in rebellion, and despite the many silent allusions to Wollstonecraft's *Vindication*, More claimed not to have read her: she wrote Horace Walpole August 18, 1792, "I have been much pestered to read the *Rights of Woman*, but am invincibly resolved not to do it. . . . I have as much liberty as I can make a good use of." He wrote "my dear Saint Hannah," August 21, assuring her that he, too, refused to read the "philosophizing serpents." Although Wollstonecraft goes unnamed, the title of *Strictures* echoes the *Vindication*'s subtitle *With Strictures on Political and Moral Subjects*, and Wollstonecraft rises up as "*The Female Werter*," who proclaims with "more presumption than prudence, *the rights of woman.*" Wollstonecraft set up Eve as Milton's equivalent of Sophie, and equally contemptible; More extolled Eve, and while her politics condemned Rousseau, her educational precepts inculcated a pliant Sophie. More's denunciation of the "revolutionary spirit" of clamoring for "*rights*" directly countermands Wollstonecraft's closing demand for a "REVOLUTION in female manners." But More illuminates the political moment of the late 1790s in reporting, "open rebellion had ceased, yet the female claim had not been renounced . . . the imposing term of rights has been produced to sanctify the claim of our female pretenders" with their "presumptuous vanity dishonourable to their sex."

When Wollstonecraft opened her *Vindication* vowing to address the "rights and duties" of women, she was pointing to a dichotomy that spoke volumes in the era where radical writers invoked rights, and conservatives dwelt on duties. Not unexpectedly, Hannah More emphasized women's duties to counteract the radical claims: "*They* little understand the true interests of woman who would lift her from the important duties of her allotted station. . . . Nor do they understand her true happiness, who seek to annihilate distinctions. . . . Each sex has its proper excellencies . . . original marks of difference." By restoring the innate division of the sexes (silently overlooking its conspicuous association with Rousseau), More seeks to cancel the language of liberty and rights with the language of duty and distinction. Women are enjoined to seek no "empire." They must yield to "the Salique law of intellect" (an expression making clear her alliance with the French monarchy rather than the revolution); for a woman to attempt to rival male abilities is merely "subversive of her delicacy as a woman."

Anxious to oppose the moral liberties of *Héloïse*, More concurs with the training manual of Sophie.[52] Female knowledge is "for home consumption" only. She assures men they will benefit when women are taught to eschew the claim of rights ("with the improvement of the other sex . . . they themselves will be sure to be gainers by it") and "to put an end to those petty and absurd contentions for equality which female smatterers so anxiously maintain." Like Macaulay and Wollstonecraft, she rejects the idea of women being raised for the harem, but her principles endorse the fundamental view that women and men have "naturally" and innately different traits—women are "little accustomed to close reasoning," "their judgement *naturally* incorrect," their "irregular fancy," easily endangered by novels, requiring "ballast." The political climate had changed a decade later; More evidently deemed it morally safe enough by 1808 not only to write a novel, *Coelebs in Search of a Wife*, sending the hero off like Émile to search for a perfect wife, but to compare his admiration for Milton's Eve as the model for his spouse, to Sophie's infatuation with the fictional Telemachus. All was secure enough to endorse certain of Rousseau's pedagogic programs such as giving children simple toys (although the *Christian Observer* gave the usual disclaimer, "novels are mischievous, but we cannot allow this work to be called a novel").[53] With the era of revolution safely suppressed, Rousseau was no longer a threat; by the 1830 reprint of collected works, the "Female Werter" who demands "the rights of woman," needed to be annotated with the name Mary Wollstonecraft.

In the eagerness to restore women to the history of the Romantic Age, many critics have been unwilling to confront the reality that among women political radicalism in Britain did not always mean feminist radicalism. Laetitia Aikin Barbauld was at the center of pro-revolutionary Dissenting circles, but her libertarian principles did not extend to the advancing the education of women. In the *Vindication*, Wollstonecraft condemned Barbauld's poem "To A Lady" for telling women "your best, your sweetest empire is—to please." Barbauld later answered Wollstonecraft in another poem "The Rights of Woman," in which she urged women to "abandon each ambitious thought," and (like More and other conservatives), represented women who seek "rights" as striving to make "Man thy subject" and to rule with the claim, "thy rights are empire." It is in the context of figures such as Barbauld that we may understand Wollstonecraft's need to declare in the *Vindication*, that she was no longer an advocate of "the wonders" of private education. Barbauld, turning down Elizabeth Montagu's offer to sponsor her to run a women's college, deemed homebred education adequate and answered, "young ladies, who ought only to have such a general tincture of knowledge as to make them agreeable companions to a man of sense . . . should gain these accomplishments . . . from conversation with a father, a brother or friend." Despite her own liberal—and Latin—education, she, like More, saw herself as unique: "Too great a fondness for books is little favourable to the happiness of a woman. . . . My situation has been peculiar and would be no rule for others." In her essay "On Female Studies," she further proclaimed, "Men have various departments in active life; women have but one . . . to be a wife, a mother, a mistress of a family."[54]

Clara Reeve's *Plans of Education: With Remarks on the Systems of Other Writers* came out the same year as Wollstonecraft's, and although she acknowledges the presence of Macaulay and the reputation of *Émile*, she was a moderate in pedagogy: "Though there is much to be disapproved in Rousseau's system, there is also much to be approved, and some things to be admired." Although the treatise centers on the usual opposition to mere "accomplishments," the epistolary plot of the treatise presumes that at least some women will be relegated to finding work as companion or educator. As had Macaulay, she declared "the health of a state" contingent on "the education of youth." The practical Reeve was one educator, however, who did not overlook the obvious drawback of educational systems that required parents wholly devoted to the relentless task of orchestrating pedagogy. Noting that *Adèle et Théodore* had been criticized for "being calculated only for people of high rank and fortune," she concludes "I cannot suppose it was ever designed to be strictly and literally followed"; and with an eye to the parental saturation point of the notorious British experiments in Rousseauvian natural education, she argues "in defiance of Rousseau and all his disciples—that some restraint is absolutely necessary in the education of the youth of both sexes."[55]

R. L. Edgeworth also alluded to the all-encompassing school-mastering required by the Rousseauvian scheme. He wrote in the preface to *Harry and Lucy*,

> Perhaps parents may pity the father and mother, in "Harry and Lucy," as much as they pity the children; and may consider them as the most hard worked, and hard working people, that ever existed, or were ever fabled to exist. They may say, that these children never had a moment's respite, and that the poor father and mother had never any thing to do, or did any thing, but attend to their children, answer their questions, and provide for their instruction or amusement.[56]

Edgeworth, however, who had four wives and twenty-two children to practice on, had at his side his eldest daughter, who assisted him in all his educational projects. In the current process of historical revaluation, Maria Edgeworth has been the subject of considerable intellectual revisionism in the last few decades. But throughout the great novelistic output, which has been recently rediscovered for the classroom, she upholds an essentially conservative position, and indeed, the high copyright payments and the wide distribution of her novels of manners cannot be detached from their affirmation of the status quo. In works such as *Belinda* (1801), *The Modern Griselda* (1805), and *Leonora* (1806), the wife is made entirely responsible for the success of the marriage and the happiness of the husband, as well as for driving him to and drawing him from the path of dissipation.

The belief that women are responsible for making the marriage is testified in the first educational treatise she wrote with her father, *Practical Education* (1798),[57] which asserted "a mother ought to be answerable to her daughter's husband" to ensure that her daughter's "imagination must not be raised" above "domestic life." Unlike More, the Edgeworths were not afraid to utter the name Rousseau—"we shall not, like many who have spoken of Rousseau, steal from him after having abused him . . . whenever Rousseau is in the right, his eloquence is irresistible." Children are given the Rousseauvian sequestered education (forbidding contact with servants and interfering guests), which curtails all input but that of the dedicated educator. Edgeworth's youthful susceptibility to Rousseau is tempered, although not especially to the advantage of girls. Dolls "boast of such an able champion in Rousseau" though they must not be allowed to foster vanity and love of finery. *Robinson Crusoe* (one of the only books Rousseau allows Émile), incurs a dangerous "taste for adventure," making it a book actually better suited to girls alone since "to girls this species of reading cannot be as dangerous as it is to boys; girls must very soon perceive the impossibility of their rambling about the world in quest of adventures." Romance reading can be equally misleading for girls, and it is necessary to replace the "*stimulus* of dissipation or of romance" with "proper objects," to make them contented to "enjoy the happiness which others describe."

The Edgeworths used Rousseau against the radical program by reasserting the necessity of segregated education. What is curious about the position of the Edgeworths is how they proclaimed as advances ideas which determinedly backpedaled from the radical forefront.[58] Although the generic masculine "*he*, has been used for grammatical convenience" (and "not at all because we agree with the prejudiced, and uncourteous grammarian, who alerts 'that the masculine is the more worthy gender'"), an alert pronoun is as far as the Edgeworth program goes. A sharply gendered education is advocated with utter complacency ("From the study of the learned languages women by custom, fortunately for them, are exempted"), and unlike the empiric education of boys, girls "*must* trust to the experience of others" rather than experimenting themselves. They must behave with "timidity," "reluctance to act," and "caution," since "they cannot rectify the material mistakes in their conduct." Rousseau had said in *Émile*, one stain ruins a woman's reputation; in contrast, Wollstonecraft's *Vindication* asserted men should be compelled to support the women whose reputations they ruin, and Macaulay declared with the irony of experience, "let her only take care that she is not caught in a love intrigue, and she may, lie, she may deceive, she may defame . . . yet preserve . . . her reputation."

Like More and Barbauld, the Edgeworths answer Wollstonecraft, but are unwilling to articulate her or Macaulay's presence directly, as if passing over their names silences them for posterity. *Practical Education* firmly opposes those "writers who advise that no difference should be made in the educating of the two sexes." Holding to the pretense of defending the best interests of women, they discountenance the doctrine of rights in favor of duties: "We cannot help thinking that their happiness is of more consequence than their speculative rights, and we wish to educate women so that they may be happy in the situations in which they are most likely to be placed." Like other conservatives, girls should be "inured to restraint" and learn to bear "reproofs," their "discontents" obviated by indulging them in so few hopes they will have few disappointments. Read in isolation, the Edgeworths have been praised for discrediting "accomplishments" ("tickets of admission to fashionable company" which "are supposed to increase a young lady's chance of a prize in the matrimonial lottery"), but opposing accomplishments in educational treatises was as uncontroversial and as universal as opposing lying (Wollstonecraft as well as More decried the acquisition of accomplishments as trifling). Although the Edgeworths describe the market as "overstocked," the young women of *Practical Education* are nevertheless given an education, as in other conservative treatises, directed at marriage and designed to make them pliable to the "tastes of the individuals with whom they are to pass their lives," a training that will prepare them for "*domestic happiness.*" This, the Edgeworths proclaim, to be a "new vocabulary"—instead of "'success in the world'" or "'fortunate establishments,'" the new model of "*domestic happiness*" will govern women's lives.

Indeed, the "new vocabulary" was no more than that: an old program with a new name. The revival of Sophie masqueraded as a new domesticity, omitting her creator in Britain, lest his name suggest unwelcome liberties. Reactionary measures armed with a new restrictive code provided a similar ideology of redomestication in France and America. Mary Shelley, for example, who had learned her first lesson of Rousseau from the enthusiasm of Lord Byron and Percy Bysshe Shelley,[59] is a conspicuous example of the confusion brought about by the mixed intellectual signals surrounding Rousseau. Preoccupied with glorifying her husband's values after his sudden drowning, Mary Shelley's essay in

The Liberal, "Mme d'Houdetot" (1823), sentimentalized the French-woman's inspirational role for Rousseau's Julie; she had different feelings when Shelley had earlier suggested a triad with his friend Thomas Jefferson Hogg.[60] One of the pieces she wrote for *The Cabinet of Biography* (1838–1839) was a brief life of Rousseau which praised his "sincere love of virtue" and declared his *Émile* to be "a book that deserves higher praise," completely neglecting her mother Mary Wollstonecraft's critique of Rousseau. This sentimental essay is largely a veiled reverie in which Mary Shelley indulges a selective identification with the Rousseau legend: "his birth cost the life of his mother" (as had hers); she commiserates with Julie and "the fault of an unmarried girl"—once her own case as she waited to marry Shelley.[61] Mary Shelley succumbed early on to the renewed vocabulary of domesticity, to the surprise of others still toiling in the radical struggle. Frances Wright, founder of the Nashoba community in Tennessee, initiated a corre-spondence with her in the 1820s, knowing of her radical family connec-tions. Mary Shelley wrote back, "I am so much of a woman, that I am far more interested in you" than in Nashoba; and she counseled Wright's friend, the utopian socialist Robert Dale Owen, "Do not imagine that she is capable always of taking care of herself. . . . She is too sensitive & femi-nine not largely to . . . desire to find a manly spirit where on [to] lean."[62]

If the history of British radical education for women was answered with a rhetoric of redomestication, one of Rousseau's famous paradoxes surfaced to confound even the most conservative educator. Only a fragment of the novelistic sequel to *Émile* that Rousseau began was actually written, but this fragment entitled *Émile et Sophie, ou les Solitaires* implicitly refutes the educational program so carefully prescribed for Sophie, since her sequestered upbringing makes her vulnerable to tedium and seduction. When it was first published in 1782 as part of the twelve-volume collected works, the *New Review* wrote of *Émile,* "the reader of that novel [*sic*] certainly did not expect to hear of Sophia's falling a victim, in the same manner as Clarissa, to the machinations of a Lovelace"; the reviewer cited how well Rousseau's *Émile* bore "his dishonor" as an illustration of "the advantages of his system in preparing a man for bearing up against all the accidents of fortune."[63] But at least one woman writer commented on it as evidence of the disadvantages of Rousseau's system for women. Claire Clairmont, who became stepsister to Wollstonecraft's two daughters when Godwin remarried, wrote: "Sophie is the most finished of Coquettes—Emile is astonished at her infidelity—'he is sure that as Sophie has proved weak there can be no truth in woman.' It is indeed partial to judge the whole sex by the conduct of one whose very education tended to fit her more for a

Seraglio than the friend & equal of Man." Indeed it was Claire Clairmont, not Mary Shelley, who defied all social conventions—bearing a child with Byron, remaining unmarried, working lifelong as governess, companion, and teacher—and who resisted the new vocabulary of domesticity, upheld the revolutionary rhetoric of women's rights, and reappropriated Rousseau's harem for a new women's state: "Our conversation at table was very amusing—We agreed to form a state upon the Turkish model, only that the tables should be turned and the men shut up in harems and kept by the women."[64]

The redomestication of women that was taking hold by the early decades of the nineteenth century and was so firmly reasserted as to reductively emblematize the Victorian era was neither a new ideology nor can we regard it as an unprecedented sentimental upsweep. As in France, the backlash to the increasing radicalism reasserted domesticity as a form of social control in response to the late century feminist alignment. The cult of redomestication arose not in response to the end of useful labor for women (a view that idealizes eighteenth-century cottage labor and alleges that a new ideology of household use was needed to supply the empty days of women no longer valued in home production of income), but because radical women were calling attention to the surplus woman problem and the need for more employment opportunities for women, realizations that were becoming increasingly more visible with factory work. Women could not forego gainful employment simply because industrialization removed forms of cottage and agrarian labor—but the rediscovered doctrine of the domestic station of women could be used to silence the clamor of middle-class feminists, and the theories of Rousseau could surface anew cloaked under the new goal of "domestic happiness."

NOTES

1. Irving Babbitt, *Rousseau and Romanticism* (1919; reprint, New York: Meridian 1962); Margery Sabin, *English Romanticism and the French Tradition* (Cambridge, Mass.: Harvard University Press, 1976); Edward Duffy, *Rousseau in England: The Context for Shelley's Critique of the Enlightenment* (Berkeley: University of California Press, 1979).

2. See Henri Roddier, *J.J. Rousseau en Angleterre au XVIIIe siècle* (Paris: Études de littérature étrangère et comparée, 1950); Jacques Voisine, *J.J. Rousseau en Angleterre a l'époque romantique* (Paris: Didier, 1956).

3. Since this essay was written, two recent books of note have helped illuminate Rousseau's impact on British writing: on women novelists, Nicola Watson, *Revolution and the Form of the British Novel, 1790–1825* (New York: Oxford

University Press, 1994), and on the male poets, Thomas McFarland, *Romanticism and the Heritage of Rousseau* (New York: Oxford University Press, 1995).

4. Rousseau's works were usually translated into English with great rapidity, within a year or less; see Roddier, *J. J. Rousseau en Angleterre*, pp. 397–403, and Voisine, *J. J. Rousseau en Angleterre*, pp. 449–51. French citations are taken from the four volume *Oeuvres complètes* (Paris: Gallimard, 1969). The initial translations of the key texts appeared as follows: *Julie ou la nouvelle Héloïse* (1760), translated in 1761 as *Eloisa, or a series of Original Letters*; *Émile, ou de l'éducation* (1762), translated in 1762 as *Emilius and Sophia: or a New System of Education* (1762); *Les Confessions*, Part one (first six books, along with *Les Rêveries du promeneur solitaire*, 1782), translated in 1783 as T*he Confessions of J. J. Rousseau with the Reveries of the Solitary Walker*; Part two (second six books, 1788), translated in 1790 as *The Confessions . . . Part the second.*

5. Rousseau, *Confessions*, Book 9, "tout ce qu'il y a de hardi dans l'*Émile* étoit auparavant dans la Julie," I:407.

6. On Rousseau and women's educational history in Europe, see Josephine Kamm, *Hope Deferred: Girls' Education in English History* (London: Methuen, 1965); Phyllis Stock, *Better Than Rubies: A History of Women's Education* (New York: Putnam's, 1978), p. 106; Mary Jo Maynes, *Schooling in Western Europe: A Social History* (Albany: State University of New York Press, 1985), pp. 34–40.

7. Rousseau, *Émile*, Book five, IV: 700: "l'homme et la femme ne sont ni ne doivent être constitués de même . . . ils ne doivent pas avoir la même éducation."

8. ———, *Émile*, Book five, IV:693, "la femme est faite spécialement pour plaire à l'homme. . . . la femme est faite pour plaire et pour être subjuguée"; IV: 698, "Les femmes, dites-vous, ne font pas toujours des enfans? Non, mais leur destination propre est d'en faire"; IV: 736, "Toutes les réflexions des femmes . . . doivent tendre à l'étude des hommes."

9. The mother instills incorrect values, such as her opposition to teaching Émile a trade, *Émile*, Book three, IV: 470.

10. Rousseau, *Émile*, Book five, IV:706–7, "la poupée est l'amusement spécial de ce séxe. . . . elle attend le moment d'être sa poupée elle-même."

11. ———, *Émile*, Book five, IV:709–10, "il faut les exercer d'abord à la contrainte. . . . Il résult de cette contrainte habituelle une docilité dont les femmes ont besoin toute leur vie, puisqu'elles ne cessent jamais d'être assujeties ou à une homme ou aux jugemens des hommes. . . . faite pour obéir . . . elle doit apprendre de bonne heure à souffrir même l'injustice"; IV:750, 865.

12. ———, *Émile*, Book five, IV:700; IV:731; IV:767.

13. ———, *Émile*, Book five, IV:716 "Je voudrois qu'une jeune Angloise cultivât avec autant de soin les talens agéables pour plaire au mari qu'elle aura, qu'une jeune Albanoise les cultive pour le Harem d'Ispahan." The William Kenrick translation, *Emilius and Sophie*, popularized this phrase as follows: "I would have a young Englishwoman cultivate her agreeable talents, in order to please her future husband, with as much care and assiduity as a young Circassian cultivates her's, to fit her for the Haram of an Eastern bashaw."

14. Rousseau, *Émile*, Book five IV: 798, says it is not worth teaching girls to read at a young age ("il y en a bien peu qui ne fassent plus d'abus que d'usage

de cette fatale science"); the first preface to *Héloïse*, II:6, says proper young women should not read novels ("jamais fille chaste n'a lu de romans"); in the *Rêveries*, Walk four, I:1034, a pregnant newlywed insinuatingly asks Rousseau if he has children in order to see him lie, given the impropriety of his uttering the truth in front of her ("on la provoquoit même pour jouir du plaisir de m'avoir fait mentir").

15. Rousseau, *Le Second discours: Sur l'origine et les fondements de l'inégalité parmi les hommes* (1755), translated in 1762; *Du Contrat social* (1762), translated in 1764 as *A Treatise on the Social Compact; La Lettre à d'Alembert* (1758), translated in 1759 as *A Letter from M. Rousseau of Geneva to M. d'Alembert of Paris, concerning the Effects of Theatrical Entertainments on the Manners of Mankind.*

16. Rousseau, *Confessions* Book two, I:84–85, *Reveries*, Walk four, I:1024, 1032. An interview Maria Edgeworth held with Élisabeth Sophie d'Houdetot testified to Rousseau's misleading persuasiveness: "She said that he did not steal the ribbon as he declared in his confessions—that whilst he was writing so finely upon Education he left his own children in a foundling hospital and that he defended this with so much eloquence that even those who blamed him in their hearts could not find tongues to answer him," letter from Edgeworth to Mary Sneyd (10 January 1803), *Maria Edgeworth in France and Switzerland: Selections from the Edgeworth Family Letters,* edited by Christina Colvin (Oxford: Clarendon Press, 1979), pp. 74–76.

17. Jane Austen, *Northanger Abbey* (London: Murray, 1818). James H. Warner argues that Rousseau's sentimentality, most fully embellished in *Héloïse*, was at the core of his appeal in Britain, not his political theories, "Rousseau's Reputation in England," *Modern Language Notes* 55 (1940): 272, 280; "Eighteenth-Century English Reactions to the *Nouvelle Héloïse,*" *PMLA* 52 (1937): 803–19. Male novelists also used the Rousseauvian echo, for example, Henry Brooke, *Juliet Grenville, or the History of the Human Heart* (London: Robinson, 1774), Henry Mackenzie, *Julia de Roubigné* (London: W. Strahan, 1777), Donatien de Sade, *Juliette* ([n.p.] Holland, 1797).

18. *Critical Review* 12 (1762):204–5.

19. Clara Reeve, *The Progress of Romance,* vol. II (Colchester: Keymer, 1785; reprint, New York: Facsimile Text Society, 1930), pp. 13–18.

20. Hannah More, *Strictures on the Modern System of Female Education* (London: Cadell and Davies, 1797).

21. *Anti-Jacobin Review and Magazine* 19 (1804):425–26; Eaton Stannard Barrett, *The Heroine* (London: Colburn, 1813; revised 1814, 1815).

22. Frances Brooke, *The History of Lady Julia Mandeville* (London: Dodsley, 1763); *Critical Review* 16 (1763):45, and her 1760 translation of Marie Jeanne Riccoboni's *Lettres de milady Juliette Catesby* ([n.p.] Amsterdam, 1759).

23. Sydney Owenson Morgan, *The Wild Irish Girl* (London: Phillips, 1806); in *St. Clair* (said to have been published in Dublin in 1802, reissued London: Harding and Highley, 1803), Colonel L— complains that women "prefer being the elegant, the impassioned, the highly gifted, but criminal Eloisa, to the formal, uninteresting, but virtuous Clarissa."

24. Helen Maria Williams, *Julia* (London: Cadell, 1790).

25. Mary Hays, *Memoirs of Emma Courtney* (London: Robinson, 1796).

26. Mary Wollstonecraft, *Mary* (London: Johnson, 1788); *The Wrongs of Woman*, edited by William Godwin (London: Johnson and Robinson, 1798). See, for example, Tilottama Rajan, "Wollstonecraft and Godwin: Reading the Secrets of the Political Novel," *Studies in Romanticism* 27 (1988):228–29.

27. Wollstonecraft, *Vindication*, V:194, 256–57.

28. Wollstonecraft, 4 July 1797 letter to Godwin, *Collected Letters of Mary Wollstonecraft*, edited by Ralph M. Wardle (Ithaca: Cornell University Press, 1979), p. 404; William Godwin, *Memoirs of the Author of a Vindication of the Rights of Woman* (London: Johnson and Robinson, 1798); Gary Kelly, "Godwin, Wollstonecraft, and Rousseau," *Women and Literature* 3 (1975):21–26, argues it was Wollstonecraft who inspired Godwin's commitment to Rousseau. Babbitt, *Rousseau and Romanticism*, p. 78, writes, "Werther, one should recollect, is only a German Saint-Preux"; on the parallel impact of Goethe when *The Sorrows of Young Werther* (1774) became available in English (1779), see Syndy McMillen Conger, "The Sorrows of Young Charlotte: Werther's English Sisters 1785–1805," *Goethe Yearbook* 3 (1986):21–56.

29. Elizabeth Hamilton, *Memoirs of Modern Philosophers* (London; Robinson, 1800); for other novelistic parodies, see B. Sprague Allen, "The Reaction Against William Godwin," *Modern Philology* 16 (1918):57–75.

30. Harold Silver, *English Education and the Radicals 1780–1850* (London: Routledge and Kegan Paul, 1975), p. 18; W. A. C. Stewart and W. P. McCann, *The Educational Innovators: 1750–1880*, vol. 1 (London: Macmillan, 1967), pp. 25–33.

31. Stéphanie Félicité de Genlis, *Adèle et Théodore, ou Lettres sur l'éducation* (Paris: Lambert and Baudouin, 1782), translated as *Adelaide and Theodore; or, Letters on Education* (London: Cadell, 1783); Samia I. Spencer, "Women and Education," pp. 91–92 in *French Women and the Age of Enlightenment*, edited by Samia I. Spencer (Bloomington: Indiana University Press, 1984), pp. 91–92, observes that when the French Academy in 1783 was awarding its first *Prix d'utilité*, it was given not to *Adèle et Théodore* but to *Les Conversations d'Émilie* (1774) by Louise d'Epinay (who provided for Rousseau the country retreat known as l'Hermitage, where he lived in 1756–1757 while first formulating *Héloïse*).

32. Thomas Day, *The History of Sandford and Merton*, 3 vols (London: Stockdale, 1783, 1786, 1789).

33. See, for example, James Fordyce, *Sermons Addressed To Young Women* (London: Printed for A. Millar and T. Cadell, 1766); John Gregory, *A Father's Legacy to His Daughters* (London: W. Strahan, 1774); John Burton, *Lectures on Female Education and Manners* (London: J. Johnson, 1793); John Bennett, *Strictures on Female Education* (Norwich: E. Bushnell, 1787); Thomas Gisborne, *Enquiry into the Duties of the Female Sex* (London: T. Cadell and W. Davies, 1797); for a general discussion of their relation to Rousseau, see Dorothy Gardiner, *English Girlhood At School* (Oxford: Oxford University Press, 1929), pp. 442–53.

34. Elizabeth Inchbald, *Nature and Art* (London: Robinson, 1796).

35. Lois Whitney, *Primitivism and the Idea of Progress* (1934; reprint, New York: Octagon, 1973), pp. 129–31.

36. Elizabeth Inchbald, *The Child of Nature* (London: Robinson, 1788), adapted from de Genlis's *Zélie ou l'ingénue* in *Théâtre de société* (Paris: Lambert and

Baudouin, 1781); quotations from the acting copy printed in *The London Stage*, vol. II (London: Sherwood, Jones, 1825).

37. On its popularity among women's plays, see Judith Phillips Stanton, "'This New-Found Path Attempting': Women Dramatists in England 1660–1800," in *Curtain Calls*, edited by Mary Anne Schofield and Cecilia Macheski (Athens: Ohio University Press, 1991), p. 333.

38. Charlotte Smith, *The Young Philosopher* (London: Cadell and Davies, 1798); Eliza Fenwick, *Secresy: Or, the Ruin on the Rock* (London: for the author, 1795); Jane West, *A Tale of the Times* (London: Longman and Rees, 1799).

39. Maria Edgeworth, *Tales of Fashionable Life* (London: Johnson, 1809); *Letters for Literary Ladies* (London: Johnson, 1795); *Belinda* (London: Johnson, 1801; revised 1810). On the *Belinda* variants, her father's role in making revisions, and the biographical sources for *Literary Ladies*, see Marilyn Butler, *Maria Edgeworth: A Literary Biography* (Oxford: Clarendon Press, 1972), pp. 173, 282–86, 494–95.

40. Catharine Macaulay, *Letters on Education: with Observations on Religious and Metaphysical Subjects* (London: Dilly, 1790).

41. Mary Wollstonecraft did not know Latin and it does not appear in her educational advice. Among dissenting educators and academies in the late eighteenth century there was a pronounced trend away from the Latin education associated with the elite schools and toward the new alternative scientific education pioneered by the commercial and manufacturing middle classes; see John Lawson and Harold Silver, *A Social History of Education in England* (London: Methuen, 1973), pp. 206, 218–19.

42. Mary Wollstonecraft's *Vindication*, 5:175, followed Macaulay's rejection of the generic masculine in its praise of her: "I will not call hers a masculine understanding, because I admit not of such an arrogant assumption of reason," although in her earlier review, *Analytical Review* 8 (1790):241, of the book she had called Macaulay "this masculine and fervid writer"; see Bridget Hill, *The Republican Virago: The Life and Times of Catharine Macaulay, Historian* (Oxford: Clarendon Press, 1992), p. 143.

43. See for example, Katherine M. Rogers, *Feminism in Eighteenth-Century England* (Urbana: University of Illinois Press, 1982), p. 204.

44. Mary Wollstonecraft, *Thoughts on the Education of Daughters* (London: Johnson, 1787).

45. Mary Wollstonecraft (letter to Everina Wollstonecraft) 24 March 1787, and (letter to William Godwin) 1 July and 17 August 1796, Wollstonecraft *Letters*, (Ithaca, N.Y.: Cornell University Press, 1979), pp. 145, 331, 337. It has often been mentioned that Wollstonecraft failed to comment on the radical women's societies during her residence in France (December 1792 to April 1795). Her infatuation with Imlay and her pregnancy impeded her contacts with women of the revolutionary societies. Her child, however, was a barometer of the French state: in 1794 her nurse told her "Frenchwoman like, that I ought to make children for the Republic," and a few months later Wollstonecraft said of her daughter, "to honour J. J. Rousseau, I intend to give her a sash, the first she has

ever had round her—and why not? for I have always been half in love with him."
(letter to Ruth Barlow) 20 May 1794, (letter to Gilbert Imlay) 22 September
1794, Wollstonecraft, *Letters*, pp. 255, 263.

46. Mary Wollstonecraft, (letter to her sister Everina) 24 March 1787,
Wollstonecraft, *Letters*, p. 145; *An Historical and Moral View of the French Revolution*
(London: J. Johnson, 1794), *Works* VI: 62; *Analytical Review* notices of Rousseau,
VII: 49, 228.

47. Macaulay's *Letters on Education* had stated, "there is but one rule of
conduct for all rational beings."

48. Wollstonecraft's *Vindication* declares, excepting Macaulay "all the writers
who have written on the subject of female education . . . have contributed to
render women more artificial, weak . . . useless."

49. Mary Hays, *Female Biography; or, Memoirs of Illustrious and Celebrated Women
of all Ages and Countries*, vol. 5 (London: Phillips, 1803), pp. 287–307.

50. Contemporary observers made the same pairing; Richard Powhele's *The
Unsex'd Females* (London: Cadell and Davies, 1798) positioned Hannah More
and Mary Wollstonecraft "diametrically opposite."

51. Hannah More, *Essays on Various Subjects: Principally designed for young
ladies* (London: Wilkie, 1777) was later omitted from her collected works in
favor of the *Strictures on the Modern System of Female Education*, 2 vols. (London: T.
Cadell and W. Davies, 1799), although it enjoyed various uncopyrighted reprints
later in the nineteenth century, once the matter of refuting Rousseau ceased to
be a pressing issue.

52. The conservative Elizabeth Hamilton, *Letters on Education* (Bath: 1801),
Letter I, concurred with More on a separate education for women ("Nature . . . .
has sufficiently qualified us for the sphere in which she evidently intended we
should move"), but even she rejected Rousseau's use of dolls as encouraging
girls to dwell on appearance and personal vanity.

53. Hannah More, *Coelebs in Search of A Wife* (London: Cadell and Davies,
1808); *Christian Observer* 8 (1809):109; Rousseau also cited the exemplary
conjugality of Milton's Adam and Eve, *Émile*, Book five, IV: 762–63, 790.

54. Mary Wollstonecraft, *Vindication* 5: 123; Laetitia Barbauld, "To a Lady,
with some painted flowers," *Poems* (London: Johnson, 1773), and "The Rights of
Woman," *Works*, edited by Lucy Aikin, vol. I (London: Longman, 1825), pp. xvi;
"On Female Studies," *A Legacy for Ladies*, edited by Lucy Aikin (London:
Longman, 1826).

55. Clara Reeve, *Plans of Education* (London: Hookham and Carpenter,
1792), pp. 29, 45, 51.

56. R. L. Edgeworth, *Harry and Lucy* (London: Johnson, 1801, first edition
of *Early Lessons*).

57. R. L. Edgeworth, *Practical Education* (London: Johnson, 1798); she had
earlier written *Letters for Literary Ladies* (London: J. Johnson, 1795); and *The
Parent's Assistant: or Stories for Children* (London: J. Johnson, 1796).

58. Contemporary observers were cynical about the Edgeworths' self-
esteem. *The Quarterly Review* 23 (1820:541–42) questioned questioned the

achievements proclaimed in Edgeworth's *Memoirs*; Coleridge had heard "that the Edgeworth's [*sic*] were most miserable when children; and yet the father in his book is ever vapourizing about their happiness," (letter to his wife) 19 September 1798, Butler, *Maria Edgeworth*, p. 51.

59. Byron's *Childe Harold* chronicled their lake Geneva trip, as did Shelley's 12 July 1816 letter to Thomas Love Peacock on the "sacred name of Rousseau" and 18 July 1816 to Thomas Jefferson Hogg I:493–94 "Rousseau is indeed in my mind the greatest man the world has produced since Milton," *Letters of Percy Bysshe Shelley*, edited by Frederick L. Jones, vol. 1 (Oxford: Clarendon Press, 1964), pp. 480–88, 493–94.

60. *The Liberal* 2 (1823): 67–83. Some kind of triadic arrangement seems to have been suggested involving Shelley, his first wife Harriet, and Thomas Jefferson Hogg, although Shelley recanted in a 16 November 1811 letter to Hogg, *Letters of Percy Bysshe Shelley*, I: 184: "I am not jealous, I perfectly understand the beauty of Rousseau's sentiment; yet Harriet is *not* an Heloissa, even were I a St. Preux. . . . She is prejudiced; tho' I hope she will not always be so. . . . If *she* was convinced of its innocence, would I be so sottish a slave to opinion as to endeavour to monopolize what if participated would give my friend pleasure without diminishing my own?" We know from Harriet Shelley's 20 November 1814 letter to Catherine Nugent, that she was outraged at the subsequent suggestion that she, Mary, and Shelley all live together "I as his sister, She as his wife? He had the folly to believe this possible," *Harriet Shelley's letters to Catherine Nugent* (London: privately printed, 1889) pp. 57–59. Mary Shelley seems to have been equally recalcitrant about the suggestion that Hogg be included in some kind of triad with Shelley and herself, 1 January 1815 letter to Hogg, *Letters of Mary Wollstonecraft Shelley*, edited by Betty T. Bennett, vol. 1 (Baltimore, Md.: Johns Hopkins University Press, 1980), p. 6.

61. Dimysius Lardner, ed., *The Cabinet of Biography: Eminent Literary and Scientific Men of France*, (London: Longman 1838–1839), pp. 111–174. Mary Shelley claims the English objection to Julie was not her transgression but her marrying a different man.

62. Mary Shelley, 12 September 1827 letter to Frances Wright, 9 November 1827 letter to Robert Dale Owen; in a 11 June 1835 letter to Maria Gisborne, she wrote, "You speak of women's intellect . . . there is in me a vacillation, a weakness. . . My Mother had more energy of character—still she had not sufficient fire of imagination," and argued that there were fundamental gender divisions: the female "sex . . . makes us quite different creatures—better though weaker but wanting in the higher grades of intellect," Mary Shelley, *Letters*, II: 4, 17, 123, 246.

63. *New Review* 2 (1782):12–24.

64. Rousseau, *Émile et Sophie, ou les Solitaires* (1782), translated in 1783 as *Emilius and Sophia or a New System of Education to which is now first added: The sequel; or, the Solitaries*. On Rousseau's plans for the unfinished *Émile and Sophie*, see Joel Schwartz, *The Sexual Politics of Jean-Jacques Rousseau* (Chicago: University of Chicago Press, 1984), pp. 96–97, 170; and Charles Wirz, "Note sur *Émile et Sophie,*

ou les solitaires," *Annales de la Société J. J. Rousseau* 36 (1963–1965):291–303. Claire Clairmont, 9 September 1814 and 29 December 1826, *Journals of Claire Clairmont,* edited by Marion Kingston Stocking (Cambridge, Mass.: Harvard University Press, 1968), pp. 39–40, 405.

8

Kari Lokke

Sibylline Leaves
Mary Shelley's *Valperga*
and the Legacy of *Corinne*

In her author's Introduction to *The Last Man*, Mary Shelley claims to have discovered this novel inscribed on the leaves of the Cumæan Sibyl and to have given English dress to the "obscure and chaotic" Latin verses of the ancient prophetess.[1] Meena Alexander in *Women in Romanticism* associates this underworld Sibylline cave issuing prophecies of doom with the unfinished tale "Cave of Fancy" of Shelley's mother, Mary Wollstonecraft, who died from complications giving birth to her daughter.[2] Certainly the Bay of Naples, leading to the dark cavern of the sibyl, is for Shelley a preeminently female realm: "the blue and pellucid element was such as Galatea might have skimmed in her car of mother of pearl; or Cleopatra, more fitly than the Nile, have chosen as the path of her magic ship" (1). And clearly the Sibyl is a figure of the literary mother or mothers whose wisdom, written on "thin, scant pages" has been hidden or misunderstood in ages past.[3] As the narrator observes, "this was certainly the Sibyl's Cave; [though] not indeed exactly as Virgil describes it," (3) for the Sibylline leaves seem to represent a collective effort spanning centuries and nations:

> What appeared to us . . . astonishing was that these writings were expressed in various languages: some unknown to my companion, ancient Chaldee, and Egyptian hieroglyphics, old as the Pyramids. Stranger still, some were in modern dialects, English and Italian. (3)

It is the daughter's task to give "form and substance to the frail and attenuated Leaves of the Sibyl" even at the risk of "distortion and diminution of [their] interest and excellence," for these leaves are now "unintelligible in their pristine condition" (4).

Perhaps as the daughter of a literary mother, Shelley was particularly sensitive to the idea of the legacy of a tradition of women writers. There is, in fact, another woman besides Wollstonecraft whose writing also strongly influenced Mary Shelley and that is Germaine de Staël, perhaps the most renowned woman writer of her age. From the incorporation of the portrayal of German scientific and illuminist communities in *De l'Allemagne* into *Frankenstein* to the essay on Staël which concludes Shelley's contributions to *Lives of Eminent Literary and Scientific Men of France*, Germaine de Staël claimed a significant presence in Mary Shelley's intellectual life. This powerful presence is furthermore convincingly articulated by Doris Kadish who, in *Politicizing Gender*, reads Shelley's *The Last Man* as an allegory of the French Revolution which promotes heroic, visionary images of the woman writer suggested by similar allegorical strategies in *Corinne*.[4]

Similarly in Shelley's second novel, *Valperga: Or, the Life and Adventures of Castruccio, Prince of Lucca*, completed in 1821, the shaping influence of Staël's *Corinne* is strongly present and the similarities between the two novels are striking.[5] Italy is the setting for both novels, a backdrop which allows both authors to celebrate the Italian potential for political independence and indirectly to condemn Napoleonic tyranny. Each author provides a powerful critique of the romantic hero; through the character of Oswald, Staël reveals the weakness and the submission to an oppressive paternal authority at the heart of romantic melancholy. Shelley, through the character of Castruccio, exposes the destructive brutality of Byronic self-worship. Perhaps most interestingly, the plot of each novel revolves around a love triangle in which two women who are in love with the same man come, in the end, to forge a strong bond of sympathy and understanding with each other. Furthermore, as Emily Sunstein asserts in her biography *Mary Shelley: Romance and Reality*, Corinne, the inspired Italian improvisatrice, is clearly a literary model for Beatrice, the tragic sibylline prophetess of *Valperga*.[6] Finally, *Valperga*'s stoical heroine Euthanasia can be read as Shelley's response to the emotional self-destruction of Staël's Corinne.

While emphasizing Staël's strong influence on Shelley, I intend this essay not as an influence study but rather as a study in philosopical and aesthetic affinity and conflict between members of two generations and two nationalities of women Romanticists. Analysis of Staël's and Shelley's conceptions of selfhood and transcendence as revealed in these two novels will bring into focus the uniqueness of each of these women Romanticists as well as suggesting commonalities between them. The obvious similarities between *Corinne* and *Valperga* provide a rich field of comparisons—a locus of specifically feminine and feminist cultural interaction—facilitating critical delineation of each author's distinctive contributions to a women's Romanticism that overlaps with but is also distinct from the European Romanticism that till recently has been seen as preeminently and almost exclusively male.

Examining *Valperga* as a response to and an appropriation of Staël's representation of female genius and its affinities with explicitly feminine conceptions of the visionary and the transcendent brings into focus Staël's role as an originary figure in the history of Western women's self-definition of poetic identity. Staël's cultural impact on other women writers extends well beyond the boundaries of the French national literary tradition to the English writers Jane Taylor, Felicia Hemans, Letitia Landon, George Eliot, and Elizabeth Barrett Browning, and to the Americans Harriet Beecher Stowe, Margaret Fuller, and Willa Cather.[7] It is as if the overpowering and troubling combination of inspiration, strength, and self-destructiveness in Staël's *Corinne* cannot be ignored; the novel, its author, and its heroine demand a response, requiring interaction and reaction from future women writers seeking literary models and mothers.

Much recent and exciting work on women in Romanticism has emphasized these writers' preoccupations with mundane daily life and the domestic, their refusal of the visionary and the transcendent and their identification of the immanence of their bodies with nature.[8] This essay complements such work by illuminating a powerful and international strain of romantic writing by women that seeks to redefine rather than reject or deny the transcendent in terms of collective creative and visionary capacities beyond the individual ego. Thus, Staël and Shelley might be considered as central contributors to the feminine tradition that Margaret Homans delineates in the conclusion of *Women Writers and Poetic Identity*, which "holds that the transcendence the Romantics sought was impossible under the conditions of romantic egotism and is only possible through collectivity."[9]

Staël and Shelley do indeed envisage selfhood, female selfhood in particular, as multiple and collective, both energized and threatened by the conflicts and tensions this multiplicity generates. The central female characters in each novel are represented as facets of a single, whole self. At first it might seem that the dark half-Italian Corinne and the blond English Lucile merely reinforce and correspond, in their complementarity, to the stereotypes of the seductress and virgin. Lucile is pure, virginal, retiring, an embodiment of strict morality and domestic virtues. She is represented symbolically by Corregio's Madonna in the museum scene near the conclusion of the book. When we first see Corinne, on the other hand, she is dressed as Domenicinos's sibyl, and glorying in a public celebration of her poetic genius; she is being crowned with Roman laurels as Tasso and Petrarch before her. Sexually experienced even before she falls in love with Oswald, Corinne has left her deceased English father's home and abandoned his name rather than be confined in the narrow domestic world ruled by Lady Edgermond, her stepmother and Lucile's mother. Lucile seems the archetypal wife and Corinne, as descendant of Italy's Renaissance courtesans, the mistress, for Staël makes it clear that Corinne does *not* wish to marry Oswald.[10]

Yet, the fact that Corinne and Lucile are half-sisters suggests that they are in a sense parts of one self in need of integration. And in the novel's conclusion, Staël self-consciously and explicitly undermines the artificial opposition between virgin and seductress, wife and mistress, mother and artist as she brings Lucile and Corinne together in mutual sympathy.[11] Though jealous of the love Oswald feels for Corinne, Lucile astutely recognizes that her own interests lie with her sister:

> Now Lucile was . . . dissatisfied with Oswald for his cruelty to a woman who loved him so much; and it seemed to her that for the sake of her own happiness, she should fear a man who had thus sacrificed another woman's happiness. The gratitude and interest she had always felt for her sister intensified the pity Corinne inspired. Far from being flattered by the sacrifice Oswald had made for her, Lucile was tortured by the idea that he had only chosen her because her position in society was better than Corinne's. (384)

In the final scenes of the novel, Corinne reciprocates Lucile's sympathy and "generously strove to make Lucile happier with Oswald:" "You will have to be you and me at the same time" (413), Corinne says to her sister, knowing that she herself is near death. Imagine, for example, what the experience of reading *The Red and the Black* would be, if Madame de Rênal and Mathilde de La Mole were to establish an intimate and loving friendship in the concluding scenes of the novel!

Perhaps most significant in its implications for Staël's conceptualization of female selfhood and genius is the fact that Juliette, Lucile's daughter by Oswald, resembles Corinne, through uncanny prenatal influence: ". . . the little girl looked like Corinne: Lucile's imagination had been absorbed with memories of her sister during pregnancy, and Juliette . . . had Corinne's hair and eyes" (386). When Oswald sends Juliette to Corinne for music and Italian lessons, the notion of a legacy of female genius becomes explicit as young Juliette exclaims: "She promised to teach me everything she knows. She says she wants me to be like Corinne. What is Corinne, father? The lady didn't want to tell me" (410–11). Corinne, the essence of female genius, though unspeakable, indefinable and vulnerable, nevertheless lives on in Juliette. For her music lessons, she held "a lyre-shaped harp made for her size, in the same way that Corinne held it, and her little arms and pretty expression imitated Corinne perfectly" (411).

If Germaine de Staël defuses the destructive opposition between mother and mistress, private wife and public genius with the hope embodied in Juliette, symbolically the daughter of both Lucile and Corinne, Mary Shelley presents three female characters who embody three different stages of woman's life and three different responses to male domination. The key to the symbolic significance of these women is their striking names—Beatrice, Mandragola, and Euthanasia, Countess of Valperga—clearly chosen, in conjunction with their tragic fates, as explicit challenges to patriarchal literary, religious, and political traditions. The title of the novel sets *Valperga*, the domain of the heroine, in opposition to its subtitle *The Life and Adventures of Castruccio, Prince of Lucca* just as it sets visionary possibilities against historical realities. Indeed, Tilottama Rajan suggests that in its "deferred utopianism," *Valperga* "may very well be the first feminist historical novel."[12]

With the three female characters of *Valperga*, Mary Shelley sets women, whether in youth, maturity, or old age, in radical opposition to male power and privilege and to the values which represent and sustain them. Beatrice is the martyred child or virgin, Euthanasia the mature woman of wisdom, and Mandragola the embittered crone or witch. Mandragola responds to oppression with vengeful fury, Beatrice, with the extremes of submission and revolt, and Euthanasia, with a delicate balance of philosophical resignation and carefully reasoned resistance. All three women are connected through their relation to the title character, Castruccio, Prince of Lucca, a fourteenth-century historical figure later celebrated in Machiavelli's biography of him.[13] Euthanasia is betrothed to him from childhood, though because he is a Ghibeline and she a Guelph, she eventually refuses him when he becomes the tyrannical leader of the opposing faction. Beatrice enters an obsessive love relationship with Castruccio that ends with his abandonment of her. And Mandragola studies him from afar as a fascinating embodiment of the power denied her by patriarchal society. In effect, the essence of female characterization in *Valperga* is to provide a picture of the sociopolitical origin and psychological significance of these three female archetypes.

The youngest of these three women, the prophetess Beatrice, might be said to be modeled after what Shelley perceived as Corinne's propensity for both divine ecstasy and self-destructive despair. Beatrice's description of her first encounter with Castruccio is a clear echo of Corinne's first meeting with Oswald during her triumphant coronation in Rome: "It appeared to me a dispensation of Providence, that I should have met him at the full height of my glory, when I was burning with triumph and joy."[14] She is furthermore named for the tragic historical figure made famous in the English speaking world by Percy Bysshe Shelley, Beatrice Cenci, who was put to death for having her father Count Cenci murdered after being raped by him. In fact, as James Rieger points out in *The Mutiny Within*, Mary Shelley's research for *Valperga* was an important source for her husband's tragedy which was indeed her favorite of his works.[15] When Beatrice first appears in *Valperga*, her beauty, dark and essentially Italian like that of Corinne, strikes Castruccio as "exquisite and almost divine":

> Her deep black eyes, half concealed by their heavy lids, her curved lips, and face formed in a perfect oval, the rising color that glowed in her cheeks which, though her complexion was pure and delicate, were tinged by the suns of Italy, formed a picture such as Guido has since imagined, when he painted a Virgin or an Ariadne, or which he copied from the life when he painted the unfortunate Beatrice Cenci. (II: 17–18)

If Percy Shelley's Beatrice Cenci rises up against the triple tyranny of paternal, papal, and divine authority, Mary Shelley's Beatrice implicitly asserts the possibility of a female-centered religion in the face of institutionalized Catholicism. Beatrice is, in fact, the daughter of Wilhelmina of Bohemia, a visionary who believed herself to be "the Holy Ghost incarnate upon earth for the female sex" so that her tenets would supersede those of Jesus Christ and her female companion Magfreda would "succeed to all the power and privileges of the Roman pontiff" (II: 26–27). After Wilhelmina dies and Magfreda is burnt at the stake by the Inquisition, the orphaned Beatrice is raised by a benevolent Catholic bishop who inculcates her with his orthodox beliefs only to have her fulfill the promise of her destiny as prophetess and heretic.

Unlike the sibylline Corinne, who is presented as genuinely gifted with supernatural enthusiasm, Beatrice is merely deluded into believing that her personal fantasies and desires are divinely inspired.[16] "She, most unfortunate, mistakes for the inspirations of Heaven the wild reveries of youth and love" (II: 69). Convinced that she and Castruccio are destined to be together for eternity, she becomes his lover only to descend into utter despondency when he abandons her to return to his political ambitions and to Euthanasia. Beatrice represents the dark side of the premonitory powers of the unconscious, for her one genuinely prophetic dream predicts her imprisonment in a Gothic chamber of horrors from which she will emerge mad, a convert to the Paterin heresy that claims the spirit of evil rules on earth.[17] In Beatrice, Shelley seems to have pictured the fate of a woman, who through her mysterious and parthenogenic origin, is irrevocably outside societal and patriarchal order.

Beatrice seeks to serve God and ends up cursing him, perhaps because, ignorant of her maternal heritage, she conceives of God as male. The second significant female character in *Valperga* Mandragola, on the other hand, is totally devoted to the demonic. This witch takes her name from the magical and phallic mandrake root and recalls the Machiavelli play of the same name.[18] Her "fiendish love of mischief" is, in fact, Shelley asserts, a love of power she does not possess: "It was believed that the witch loved evil as her daily bread, and that she had sold her soul to the devil to do ill alone; *she* knew how powerless she was; but she desired to fill in every part the character attributed to her" (III: 117). Through Mandragola as well as through Beatrice, Shelley represents the destructive potential of woman's justifiable but mis-directed anger. This is explicit in Shelley's depiction of Mandragola:

> She had been young once; and her nature, never mild, had been turned to ferocity by wrongs which had been received so long ago, that the authors of them were all dead, and she, the victim, alone survived. Calumny had blasted her name; her dearest affections had been blighted; her children torn from her; and she remained to execrate and to avenge. (III: 116)[19]

Significantly, Mandragola is incapable of love for other women and is ultimately responsible for Beatrice's death from shock when she lures her to a meeting with Castruccio, who is accompanied by his political ally the Monk Tripalda who turns out to have been one of Beatrice's sadistic torturers. Thus, the evil Tripalda becomes a kind of double for Castruccio and Castruccio's seduction of Beatrice a symbolic rape.

Though Mandragola destroys Beatrice with her nihilistic anger and will to power, Euthanasia comes close to saving her through love and wisdom. Euthanasia, Countess of Valperga, the fair heroine, tells her tale in a chapter entitled "Euthanasia's Narrative," a bright version of Staël's chapter "Corinne's Story" in which Corinne tells the tale of her self-exile from England in order, after her English father's death, to escape the repressive influence of her stepmother and the judgment of Oswald's father that her genius, "passionate character" and "impetuous imagina-tion" (329) make her a kind of enchantress unfit to be the wife of his son. Euthanasia, on the other hand, is the beloved favorite daughter of a benevolent philosopher father, an idealized Godwin figure. Through her readings of the ancient Romans and of Dante she is "irresistibly forced to connect wisdom and liberty together" (I: 196), to value reasoned judgment over passion, and to commit herself to the Guelph republican cause, for, as Shelley writes, she loved "the very shadow of freedom with unbounded enthusiasm (I: 187). This enthusiasm, in fact, shows her to be a sister soul of Corinne despite their differences. For, like Corinne in Rome, Euthanasia is beloved in Florence for her "beauty, her accomplishments, and the gift of flowing yet mild eloquence" (I: 167). Like Corinne, she seems divinely inspired: "the sweet words of this celestial girl . . . seemed as a link to bind . . . earthly thoughts to heaven" (I: 168); "her conversation appeared one strain of poetry" (188). Furthermore, it is the Countess of Valperga, not Beatrice, who is repeatedly associated in the novel with Dante's muse of the same name, as if to emphasize the intellectual and political awareness essential to the cultural role Dante attributes to his Beatrice.

Euthanasia first meets Beatrice when the fallen prophetess visits her castle on a pilgrimage to Rome and the Countess offers her consolation, but the prideful Beatrice continues on her pilgrimage during which she is abducted and held captive by the Gothic torturers who eventually cost her both sanity and life. Freed from her torturers, she is imprisoned by the Inquisition to silence her heretical cursing of God as the spirit of evil and cruelty, as "a father that . . . torments his children" (III: 45). Hearing Beatrice's tragic history and her execration of God as a spirit of malice, Euthanasia responds with "deep interest" in her: "She felt that they were bound together, by their love for one who loved only himself" (III: 53). Here Shelley takes an important step beyond Staël by suggesting that Euthanasia's love for Beatrice supplants her pain over the loss of Castruccio: "The feelings of her heart were so completely absorbed in pity and love for Beatrice, that the painful ideas of many years' growth seemed rooted out by a new and mightier power" (III: 61). Ultimately, as Tilottama Rajan asserts, "Euthanasia's bond with . . . Beatrice is the affective core of Mary Shelley's novel," (64) "the most compelling part of the novel" (63).

Significantly, the Countess's namesake is Saint Valperga (Walperga), an eighth-century English abbess of the Germanic convent at Heidenheim and protectress against witchcraft.[20] That her saint's day is May Eve or *Walpurgisnacht*, date of the pagan festival of sacred springtime marriage, suggests that she represents Christianity's attempt to incorporate these pagan rituals into itself while claiming to transcend them. For Mary Shelley, the Countess of Valperga represents woman's claim to the consolations of a realm and a sisterhood beyond the immanence of nature and the negative pleasures of vengeance. Just as the relics of Saint Valperga's bones were buried in a celebrated pilgrimage site, a cave near Eichstätt that was said to exude a miraculous healing oil, so Euthanasia seeks to enlighten Beatrice with an Allegory of the Cave that is the philosophical heart of the novel, a representation of Shelley's ideal vision of the secrets of the sibyl's cave. It is as if Shelley is suggesting that it is indeed a pilgrimage to Valperga rather than to Rome that Beatrice needs.

Euthanasia pictures Consciousness with sensation and the emotions of Love and Hate, Joy and Sorrow, as a sentinel at the entrance to the cave of the human mind. In the vestibule, "still illumined by the light of day, sit Memory with banded eyes, grave Judgement bearing her scales and Reason in a lawyer's gown" along with Hope and Fear, Religion and Charity. "Within, excluded from the light of day, Conscience sits, who can see indeed, as an owl, in the dark. His temples are circled by a diadem of thorns, and in his hand he bears a whip; yet his garb is kingly and his countenance, though severe, majestical" (III: 100). There is another inner realm, beyond this male domain of Ethics and Morality, of God the Father and the Son. This inner cave, both surpassingly beautiful and terrifyingly hideous, is the realm of madness and heresy, but also of Poetry, Imagination, and Heroism.

> [Here] the highest virtues dwell, and . . .find a lore far better than all the lessons of the world; and here dwells the sweet reward of all our toil, Content of Mind, who crowned with roses and bearing a flower-wreathed sceptre, rules, instead of Conscience, those admitted to her happy dominion. (III: 102)

Spiritual transcendence, for Mary Shelley, then, is pictured as beyond personal emotion, a deep self-knowledge and peace of mind, as a goddess who is reminiscent of the visions of meditative Eastern mysticism. Poetry and imagination, not morality or conscience, dwell in this realm, the horrors of which are dispelled when it is "lighted by an inborn light" (III: 101). The particular beauty of *Valperga* is that in Euthanasia Shelley has created a woman who has achieved this state of philosophical wisdom at the novel's conclusion. As William D. Brewer suggests, *Valperga* is a portrait of "the triumph of Euthanasia's mind," an affirmation of the value of her utopianism in the face of "historical chaos:"

> And, if the present looks hopeless, one can still look forward, as Euthanasia does, to a positive future: "what would not this world become, if every man might learn from its institutions the true principles of life, and become as the few which have as yet shone as stars amidst the night of ages?" (I: 197)[21]

Furthermore, Euthanasia's state of mind is clearly not equivalent to resignation or quiescence, for Euthanasia's final significant act is to join

a conspiracy against Castruccio, in an effort to overthrow his tyranny
and at the same time to protect him from would-be assassins. After the
conspiracy is betrayed by Tripalda and Castruccio sentences her to exile,
Euthanasia drowns in a storm on the sea voyage to Sicily. En route to her
death, she is granted a final vision of sublime harmony, with the sky a
loving mother smiling on its child:

> The eternal spirit of the universe seemed to descend upon her, and she
> drank in breathlessly the sensation, which the silent night, the starry
> heavens, and the sleeping earth bestowed upon her. All seemed so
> peaceful, that no unwelcome sensation in her own heart could disturb
> the scene of which she felt herself a part. . . . "What a brave canopy has
> this earth, and how graciously does the supreme empyrean smile upon
> its nursling!" (III: 255–56)[22]

Despite the loss of all her loved ones, the slaughter of her supporters,
and the razing of her magnificent castle, Euthanasia retains the virtues
that are her dominant characteristics till the end of her life: enthusiasm,
or inspired love of divinity and nature; unfailing, supreme courage in
the face of grave dangers; and self-respect or, as Shelley writes, "self-
approbation," "the sweetest and most secure happiness" (III: 183)
possible on earth.

Euthanasia, then, is Mary Shelley's answer to Corinne whose fate in
Staël's novel is ultimately that of Beatrice and Mandragola. In her anger,
Corinne refuses to see Oswald before she dies and, despite assertions
that she has forgiven him, curses him in witchlike fashion to the pain
and unhappiness of his guilty conscience. And finally, like Beatrice,
Corinne chooses a self-willed death in response to a betrayal of love.
Thus, Shelley concludes rather harshly in her judgment of *Corinne* in
Lives of Eminent Literary and Scientific Men of France.

> Mme de Staël was naturally led to portray death as the result of sorrow;
> . . . She might also wish to impress on men an idea of the misery which
> their falsehood produces. . . . For the dignity of womanhood, it were
> better to teach how one, as highly gifted as Corinne, could find
> resignation or fortitude enough to endure a too common lot, and rise
> the wiser and better from the trial. (332)

I have no doubt that Staël did, in fact, very much wish to "impress
upon men an idea of the misery their falsehood produces." Beyond that,
however, I suspect that she would indeed have been very sympathetic to
Shelley's response to her book. For Staël gives us in Corinne a character
who, like Euthanasia, achieves an impersonal state of grace, but is

unable to sustain it, in part because of emotional excess but more importantly because she feels herself and her genius condemned by what Staël so presciently terms "the whole of paternal authority" (357). Of her state of mind during improvisation, Corinne says:

> At such times it seems to me that I am experiencing a supernatural enthusiasm, and I sense full well that what is speaking within me has a value beyond myself. . . . I am a poet when I admire, when I scorn, when I hate—not out of personal feelings, not for my own cause, but for the dignity of the human race and the glory of the world. (45)

This capacity for the transcendence of personal emotion is destroyed by the melancholy and grief which has afflicted Corinne in precisely the manner delineated by Sigmund Freud's "Mourning and Melancholia."[23] The roots of Corinne's melancholy are identification with the lost object of her affections, Oswald, and with his judgments and his repressed anger directed inward—precisely the mechanisms described in Freud's essay. Just as Oswald's melancholy results from his identification with his father, so Corinne comes to identify with Oswald's judgment of her and to decide that it is Lucile rather than she who is worthy of Oswald. Unlike male poets, who are rendered eloquent by their melancholy, Corinne has lost the gift of improvisation at the novel's conclusion:

> Unable to divert her thoughts from her own plight, she portrayed her suffering. But no longer were there any general ideas or the universal feelings that correspond to all men's hearts; it was the cry of grief, ultimately monotonous as the cry of birds in the night, too fervent in expression, too vehement, too lacking in subtlety: unhappiness it was, but it was not talent. (368)[24]

Corinne derives its psychological power from an unrelenting depiction of its heroine's self-destructive internalization of the patriarchal values and modes of thinking and feeling represented by Oswald and the deceased father who haunts his conscience: obsession with duty, propriety, and violence to feelings and desires. Staël reveals that even her female genius Corinne is unable to sustain her own celebration of pleasure and the moment, unable to resist the hegemony of melancholy, repression, and guilt that has afflicted Oswald since the death of his father. When she leaves the land of her mother, Italy, to seek Oswald in Scotland, she ends up not with her beloved but rather at her *own* father's grave and it is here that she decides to sacrifice herself in order to make possible the conventional marriage between the virginal, submissive Lucile and the man Corinne passionately loves.

Thus, in the end, the remarkable poet and prophetess is reduced to vengeance and rage, wishing on Oswald the kind of unhappiness that he has caused her:

> Is it possible that you still look for what is called happiness? . . . Do you know that I would have served you like a slave? Do you know that had you loved me faithfully, I would have bowed down before you as before a messenger from heaven? Well, what have you done with so much love? What have you done with an affection unique in this world? With an unhappiness just as unique? Therefore do not lay claim to happiness, do not offend me by thinking you may win it still. (409)

It is Corinne's end, so troubling to feminist readers today, that Mary Shelley rewrites in *Valperga* by enabling her own heroine to transcend her need for Castruccio and find peace of mind within herself and bliss within nature at the conclusion of her novel.[25] Shelley's ambivalent response to *Corinne*, in fact, establishes a pattern of future feminist cultural interaction with Staël's powerful novel.[26] Thus, though Margaret Fuller, dubbed a "Yankee Corinna" herself, writes vividly and beautifully of Staël as a "benefactress" to American women, as the beams of her intellect rendered "the obscurest school-house in New England warmer and lighter to the little rugged girls . . . gathered together on its wooden bench," she ultimately concludes that Staël "could not forget the Woman in the thought; while she was instructing you as a mind, she wished to be admired as a Woman; sentimental tears often dimmed the eagle glance."[27] In her *Memoirs* Fuller even takes Corinne as a symbol of feminine spiritual weakness and philosophical incapacity:

> No Sibyls have existed like those of Michel Angelo; those of Raphael are the true brides of a God, but not themselves divine. It is easy for women to be heroic in action, but when it comes to interrogating God, the universe, the soul, and, above all, trying to live above their own hearts, they dart down to their nests like so many larks, and if they cannot find them, fret like the French Corinne.[28]

Corinne creates an anxiety of influence that is the inverse of the Bloomian sort in which it is the perceived weakness of Staël's fictional artist—taken as a picture of Staël herself and of women artists in general—that haunts future women writers.

In the light of this intercultural women's tradition of response to Staël's *Corinne*, Mary Shelley's accomplishment in creating a female character who does indeed "live above her own heart" as a paragon of emotional detachment, philosophical power, and meditative vision is truly impressive. Finally, Shelley's Euthanasia dies having redefined the mission of her namesake, Saint Valperga, but also having leant renewed significance to her first name meaning good or painless death. Given this tragedy and that of her other female characters, Mary Shelley seems to be suggesting that this death with moral and spiritual integrity is the most a woman can hope for in a world run by men like Tripalda and Castruccio who value power and domination above all else. Thus, the death of Euthanasia, like that of Staël's Corinne, is, in a sense, the only statement of political protest left to her.[29] Furthermore, in its passionate cry of anger and outrage, *Corinne* is also paradoxically a tribute, like *Valperga*, to the wisdom and necessity of philosophical and meditative detachment, *the* central theme of Staël's non-fiction works from the beginning to the end of her life.[30] Ultimately, through her legacy to Juliette and to future women writers, Staël's heroine remains true to her refusal of a patronym and to her name chosen from the Greek poetess and mentor of Pindar. Thus, beyond Corinne's ostensible individual defeat, Staël envisages collective, historical transcendence of destructive emotion and traditional patterns of female dependence and limitation. Similarly, the women of *Valperga*, whose extravagant names rewrite mythic and literary traditions, suggest the necessity of examining and redefining the values and qualities which determine canonization, both literary and spiritual.

NOTES

1. Mary Shelley, *The Last Man*, edited by Hugh J. Luke (Lincoln: University of Nebraska Press, 1965), p. 4. A nightmarish tribute to the powers of the priestess of Apollo, this novel is an apocalyptic vision of the destruction of the human race by plague in the twenty-first century. All parenthetical references to *The Last Man* are to this edition.

2. Meena Alexander, in *Women in Romanticism*, writes: "The cave itself, in a kind of imaginative extremity, is both the womb of Mother Nature and the tomb of all mothers" (London: Macmillan, 1989), p. 185.

3. See Sandra M. Gilbert and Susan Gubar, "The Parables of the Cave," in *The Madwoman in the Attic: The Woman Writer and the Nineteenth-Century Literary Imagination* (New Haven: Yale University Press, 1979), pp. 93–104.

4. Doris Y. Kadish, *Politicizing Gender: Narrative Strategies in the Aftermath of the French Revolution* (New Brunswick, N.J.: Rutgers University Press, 1991), pp. 15–36.

5. Mary Shelley read *Corinne* at least twice—in 1815 while nursing her firstborn daughter, who died before she was a month old, reinforcing the association of death and motherhood that was to haunt Mary Shelley her whole life, and later with Percy Shelley in Naples during the months following the loss of

her second child in September 1818. *Valperga* is, in my opinion, a fascinating and neglected novel. Emily Sunstein in *Mary Shelley: Romance and Reality* (Boston: Little, Brown and Co., 1989) agrees: "*Valperga*, an undeservedly little-known work of rich Romanticism, serious philosophy, and fine scholarship, is her epic of this period when she found meaning in what she had been through since Clara and William died" (188). Similarly, Frederick L. Jones, editor of *The Letters of Mary Shelley*, vol. I (Norman: University of Oklahoma Press, 1944) writes, "[Mary Shelley's] creation of *Frankenstein* at the age of eighteen is a marvel known to many; but few if any are aware that *Valperga*, her second novel, excels the first almost as much as *Alastor* surpasses *Queen Mab*" (xxx).

6. The historical model for Beatrice, as Emily Sunstein suggests, was the millenarian Joanna Southcott "who claimed to be the New Savior sent to raise women and redeem humanity; she attracted thousands of followers during Mary Godwin's girlhood until her death in 1814, following a hysterical pregnancy that was supposed to deliver Shiloh, the second Christ" (53).

7. For a full discussion of the actual historical legacy of *Corinne* in women's writing of the nineteenth and twentieth centuries, see Madelyn Gutwirth, *Madame de Staël, Novelist: The Emergence of the Artist as Woman* (Urbana: University of Illinois Press, 1978), pp. 260–309. For Staël's influence on Felicia Hemans' aesthetics and politics, see Nanora Sweet, "History, Imperialism, and the Aesthetics of the Beautiful: Hemans and the Post-Napoleonic Moment," in *At the Limits of Romanticism: Essays in Cultural, Feminist, and Materialist Criticism*, edited by Mary A. Favret and Nicola J. Watson (Bloomington: Indiana University Press, 1994), pp. 170–84.

8. Anne K. Mellor, *Romanticism and Gender* (New York: Routledge, 1993). Mellor writes, for example, that "the women writers of the Romantic period for the most part foreswore the concern of their male peers with the capacities of the creative imagination, with the limitations of language, with the possibility of transcendence or "unity of being," with the development of an autonomous self, with political (as opposed to social) revolution, with the role of the creative writer as political leader or religious savior" (2). See also, Stuart Curran "Romantic Poetry: The I Altered," *Romanticism and Feminism*, edited by Anne K. Mellor (Bloomington: Indiana University Press, 1988), pp. 185–207.

9. Margaret Homans, *Women Writers and Poetic Identity* (Princeton, N.J.: Princeton University Press, 1980), p. 233.

10. Corinne's reasoning is as follows, "For her part, she had not wanted the marriage tie to Oswald, and had she been certain he would never leave her, she would have been happy with that alone; but she knew him well enough to know that he conceived of happiness only within domestic life, and that he could never renounce the ideas of marriage without loving her less;" Germaine de Staël, *Corinne, or Italy*, translated by Avriel H. Goldberger (New Brunswick, N.J.: Rutgers University Press, 1987), pp. 277–78. All parenthetical references to *Corinne* are to this edition.

11. For an insightful discussion of the complexity of conflicts and interrelations between Corinne and Lucile, see Gutwirth, *Madame de Staël, Novelist: The Emergence of the Artist as Woman*, pp. 202–57.

12. Tilottama Rajan, "Mary Shelley's *Mathilda*: Melancholy and the Political Economy of Romanticism," *Studies in the Novel* 26, no. 2 (1994): 62.

13. In another connection to Staël, Shelley discovered Castruccio in the *Histoire des républiques italiennes du moyen âge* of Staël's close friend Simonde de Sismondi. For a study of the historical and political significance of *Valperga*, see Joseph Lew, "God's Sister: History and Ideology in *Valperga*," in *The Other Mary Shelley: Beyond Frankenstein*, edited by Audrey A. Fisch, Anne K. Mellor, and Esther Schor (New York: Oxford University Press, 1993), pp. 159–81.

14. Mary Shelley, *Valperga: or, The Life and Adventures of Castruccio, Prince of Lucca*, vol. 3 (London: G. and W. B. Whittaker, 1823), p. 69. All parenthetical references to *Valperga* are to this edition.

15. James Rieger, *The Mutiny Within: The Heresies of Percy Bysshe Shelley* (New York: George Braziller, 1967), pp. 121–28.

16. For a discussion of Beatrice as a rewriting of the Cassandra figure, an emblem of the female artist, see Barbara Jane O' Sullivan, "Beatrice in *Valperga*: A New Cassandra," in *The Other Mary Shelley: Beyond Frankenstein*, edited by Audrey A. Fisch, Anne K. Mellor, and Esther Schor (New York: Oxford University Press, 1993), pp. 140–58.

17. Percy Shelley compared Mary to a Paterin in her response to the deaths of her children. See Sunstein, *Mary Shelley: Romance and Reality*, pp. 162–63, and James Rieger, *The Mutiny Within*, pp. 112–28, for a discussion of the significance of Paterin heresy for both Percy and Mary Shelley's art. Beatrice is frequently read as Mary Shelley's critique of Percy Shelley's "unchecked imagination." See Jane Blumberg who, in *Mary Shelley's Early Novels* (Iowa City: University of Iowa Press, 1993), reads Beatrice as an embodiment of "the potential end result of the unrestrained and impractical Romantic imagination" (100). Rieger provides a more nuanced and subtle reading of Beatrice as a character who ultimately loses faith in the imagination so that it is denied, loses its healing power, and inevitably returns as terror. Euthanasia's parable, with its glorification of poetry and the imagination as productive of the highest virtues and the greatest terrors, supports Rieger's reading.

18. In Machiavelli's play, a young and virtuous wife is literally compelled by her stupid husband, greedy mother, and hypocritical priest to enter into an adulterous relationship with a young lover. The play ends with a cynical "happily ever after" when the young woman accepts the fact that her secret and deceitful sexual pleasure is dictated by a corrupt society. Mary Shelley's Mandragola is, however, too angry to be able to use others to her advantage.

19. Shelley, *Valperga*, III: 116. Like Beatrice and Euthanasia, Mandragola clearly embodies a side of Mary Shelley and an aspect of her experience, for Mary Shelley herself had experienced all the traumas and injustices listed here.

20. Donald Attwater, *The Penguin Dictionary of Saints* (Baltimore: Penguin, 1965), p. 339.

21. William D. Brewer, "Mary Shelley's *Valperga*: The Triumph of Euthanasia's Mind," *European Romantic Review* 5, no. 2 (1995): 144.

22. This vision of nature is challenged by the subsequent portrayals of nature as a cruel stepmother, suggesting Shelley's conflicted response to maternal nature

imagery. Mandragola's dwelling place, for example, is also depicted in fig-urations of a maternal nature.

23. In "Mourning and Melancholia," *Collected Papers*, translated by Joan Riviere, vol. 4, (New York: Basic Books, 1959), Freud writes of "an identification of the ego with the abandoned object. Thus, the shadow of the object fell upon the ego, so that the latter could henceforth be criticized by a special mental faculty like an object, like the forsaken object. In this way, the loss of the object became transformed into a loss in the ego, and the conflict between the ego and the loved person transformed into a cleavage between the criticizing faculty of the ego and the ego as altered by the identification" (159).

24. See Juliana Schiesari who argues in *The Gendering of Melancholia* (Ithaca, N.Y.: Cornell University Press, 1992) that male melancholia is made "to repre-sent a sensitive or exquisite illness characterized by representation itself, whereas the "lower" [female] form (depression) remains characterized by an incapacity to translate symptoms into a language beyond its own self-referentiality as depression" (16). Schiesari's assertion that women's "melancholia, or depres-sion, can be shown to be a perpetual mourning for the barred status imposed upon them" (17) by patriarchal society perfectly describes Corinne at the end of the novel.

25. For an excellent analysis of the problematical conclusion of *Corinne*, see Ellen Peel, "Corinne's Shift to Patriarchal Mediation: Rebirth or Regression?," *Germaine de Staël: Crossing the Borders*, edited by Madelyn Gutwirth, Avriel Goldberger, and Karyna Szmurlo (New Brunswick, N.J.: Rutgers University Press, 1991), pp. 101–12.

26. An interesting pattern emerges in the differences between the responses to *Corinne* of later women poets and those of women writers of fiction. Poets—Hemans, Landon, and Browning—seem more willing to accept Staël's conflation of the poetess and the abandoned woman, whereas prose writers—Shelley, Eliot, and Fuller—are more sharply critical of Staël's definition of the female artist. This difference, linked to genre, is worthy, I think, of further exploration. Bettine von Arnim provides a refreshingly irreverent portrait of her meeting with Staël in *Goethe's Correspondence with a Child* (Boston, Mass.: Ticknor and Fields, 1859), pp. 40–41. And in *Günderode* (Boston: T.O.H.P. Burnham, 1859), she describes *Delphine* as "most absurd" (230) and finds the novel wearisome despite the fact that it is "written by the best authoress in Europe" (235).

27. Margaret Fuller, *Woman in the Nineteenth Century* (New York: Norton, 1971), p. 94.

28. Margaret Fuller, *The Woman and the Myth: Margaret Fuller's Life and Writings*, edited by Bell Gale Chevigny (Old Westbury, New York: The Feminist Press, 1976), p. 58.

29. Anne Mellor makes a similar point in *Mary Shelley: Her Life, Her Fiction, Her Monsters* (New York: Methuen, 1988) when she asserts that the material conditions of her life forced Shelley to acknowledge that there was no place in middle-class British society for a woman like Euthanasia; "[the] absence from her novels of independent, self-fulfilled, nurturant women records Mary Shelley's

oblique recognition that such a woman does not survive in the world she knew" (210). For a discussion of the emancipatory potential of suicide in Staël's work, see Margaret R. Higonnet, "Suicide as Self-Construction," in *Germaine de Staël: Crossing the Borders*, edited by Madelyn Gutwirth, Avriel Goldberger, and Karyna Szmurlo (New Brunswick, N.J.: Rutgers University Press, 1991) pp. 69–81.

30. See, for example, in Germaine de Staël, *An Extraordinary Woman: Selected Writings of Germaine de Staël*, translated and introduction by Vivien Folkenflik (New York: Columbia University Press, 1987), the following essays: "Essay on Fictions," "The Influence of the Passions on the Happiness of Individuals and Nations," and "The Influence of Enthusiasm on the Enlightenment" from *De l'Allemagne.*

V

Ideological Interactions

Precursors and Epigones

9

David C. Hensley

Richardson, Rousseau, Kant

"Mystics of Taste and Sentiment" and the Critical Philosophy

> *Your Clarissa is, I find, the Virgin-mother of several pieces; which, like beautiful suckers, rise from her immortal root. I rejoice at it; for the noblest compositions need such aids, as the multitude is swayed more by others' judgments than their own. How long was* Paradise Lost *an obscure book? Authors give works their merit; but others give them their fame; and it is their merit becoming famous, which gives them that salutary influence, which every worthy writer proposes, on mankind.*
>
> —Edward Young to Samuel Richardson
> (November 5, 1749) *

In *Biographia Literaria* (1817), famously, Samuel Taylor Coleridge makes Samuel Richardson and his friends Edward Young and James Hervey responsible for developments that produced the German Gothic. According to Coleridge, Young's *Night Thoughts* (1742–1745) and Hervey's *Meditations among the Tombs* (1746), both of which Richardson printed,[1] belong together with *Clarissa* (1747–1748) as the main "*English*

---

* *The Correspondence of Edward Young, 1683–1765*, ed. Henry Pettit (Oxford: Clarendon, 1971), p. 337–38.

. . . *origin*"[2] of the rhetoric and aesthetic premises of *Sturm und Drang* drama and the writings of early German Romanticism. Coleridge's extraordinary claim is most explicitly conceptualized in his memorable description of "the loaded sensibility, the minute detail, the morbid consciousness of every thought and feeling in the whole flux and reflux of the mind, in short the self-involution and dreamlike continuity of Richardson."[3] This tribute to *Clarissa* not only calls attention to Richardson's peculiar literary style and its far-reaching effect on German translations and imitations; but it also addresses, as historical conditions, the forms of subjectivity and response in eighteenth-century German readers. In other words, while Coleridge's point is that German readers of *Clarissa* became rewriters of Richardson, he goes further by suggesting conceptual and affective indices of their rewriting.

Criticism since Coleridge has sometimes followed his lead in celebrating Richardson for having "helped usher in the Romantic Movement"[4] and indeed as "one of the first [r]omantic writers."[5] Occasionally, recent treatment of "Richardson's impact in Germany"[6] has been more specifically Coleridgean to the extent of describing Richardson as "one of the great influences on the German romantic movement."[7] But even in echoing this nineteenth-century view,[8] twentieth-century criticism has hardly ever reassessed Richardson's contribution to the basic assumptions, preoccupations, attitudes, and patterns of thought and expression that define either British or German Romanticism.[9] Only now, two decades into a major revival of interest in Richardson, are materials for evaluating Coleridge's thesis about *Clarissa* being collected for the use of scholars.[10] It seems strange to say, but we are just beginning to track the evolution of forms of cultural interaction that shaped the astonishing generative role of Richardson's fiction in modern European and especially German literary and intellectual life.

To align *Clarissa* with the introspective religious ruminations of Young and Hervey underscores Richardson's distinctive rendering of spiritual sensibility. In this way, with striking appreciation of the overt authorial aesthetic of Richardson's "Religious Novel,"[11] Coleridge implicitly locates the early romantic lexicon of *Clarissa*, as Richardson did, in "the *Christian System*."[12] At the same time, we can take the philosophical measure of Coleridge's claim by paraphrasing his famous tribute in somewhat more familiar terms. *Clarissa*, he can be understood to say, charts the struggle of self-consciousness to assert the absolute unity and purity of its "inmost nature"[13] despite being burdened and perplexed by the fallen multiplicity and conflict of experience that keep "thought and feeling" at odds by blocking the meditative fusion of imagination and everyday things.

Coleridge's conceptual synopsis of *Clarissa* responds to the paradoxical self-reflexivity posited by Richardson's artistic and interpretive conviction "that in the minutiae lie often the unfoldings of the Story, as well as of the heart." For Richardson, good reading is always rereading; it is an ultimately devotional attention of the imagination to the mass of "minute detail" with which the Lockean sensibility is "loaded." Reading *Clarissa* exercises "the whole flux and reflux of the mind," the infinite coiling in which interior life seeks to integrate "every" part of the divided self and world "to make one Whole."[14] Structurally and thematically, such totalization is both demanded and frustrated by the "double yet separate correspondence" (1:vi; 1:xiii) of *Clarissa*. At every level, the "unfoldings" of the narrative signify strife and division both within and between "the Story" and "the heart." In response to this allegory of the conflictual doubleness of all things in nature and the soul, Coleridge's understanding of the "self-involution" of *Clarissa* also seems to identify a paradox of colliding frameworks typical of romantic representation. *Clarissa* upholds the claims of both vitalism and realism; it figures at once an inner longing for unity and an uncompromising critique of the worldly ethical impasse of the divided mind.

If we add to these layered structural paradoxes Richardson's concern with genius and originality, the basic terms of a romantic aesthetic are authorized by the goal that Young describes as the organically proliferating "salutary influence" of *Clarissa*. Writing about *Clarissa* as well as his *Night Thoughts*, Young commented: "he that writes popularly and well does most good, and he that does most good is the best author."[15] Richardson and Young desired fame, and they were both pleased with the particular enthusiasm their works inspired in Germany.[16] The emphasis of Coleridge's judgment of *Clarissa*, despite its chauvinistic overtones, thus seems right. Richardson's artistic self-understanding *was* romantic. In addition, not only his authorial "*design*" (1:xi; 1:xv), but also the conditions of its mediation to Germany were crucially *spiritual*. Whether we approach Richardson's writing and the process of its transmission in terms of influence or intertextuality[17]—and however inadequate we may find the period category of "Romanticism"—the point is that literary history has canonized but largely neglected Coleridge's insight. Richardson's religious position and the secularization of its assumptions still constitute a rich and open textual field in which to analyze the specific formal and ideological conditions for the outgrowth of *Clarissa*'s "beautiful suckers" in German as well as British culture.

We may never be able to say whether Coleridge owes more to Plotinus or Jakob Böhme, to Immanuel Kant, F. W. J. Schelling, August Wilhelm Schlegel,[18] or indeed to William Wordsworth, in formulating his reaction to the "dreamlike continuity" of self-consciousness in *Clarissa*. But this ambiguity itself is appropriate and perhaps inevitable. Like Coleridge's own thinking, *Clarissa*'s concern with integrity of self and experience, with self-knowledge and communication, freedom, sympathy, and organic unity as contemplative and cognitive ideals, has complex affiliations with both ancient theology and modern philosophy. Niklas Luhmann notes, similarly, that "[m]ysticism and the Enlightenment thrived side by side" in the German contexts where Richardson's novels became powerful literary and social paradigms in the late eighteenth century. Luhmann's argument, however, does not reconsider the Richardson craze in Germany in relation to the irrationalistic religious and moral culture of pietism. Rather, in effect, Luhmann gives a selective and secular specification of Coleridge's judgment. He inscribes Richardson's effect on continental readers in the process of self-reflexive individualization that began in England and culminated theoretically in the new German "philosophical anthropology" associated with Kant's transcendental turn and the cult of romantic love.[19]

Recent studies of the pietistic side of Richardson's religious context invite reinterpretation of his fiction as an allegory of "Christian dialectic."[20] Such rereading seems likely to supplement Margaret Anne Doody's account of Richardson's attitude of Tory resistance as a theological and ethical as well as political and feminist critique of an increasingly rationalistic, commodified, Whiggish world.[21] So oriented, the study of Richardson's participation in the "new Christian dispensation" of pietism[22] could change our approach to his aesthetic program—its motivation, internal relations, and contribution to subsequent writing. It is already remarkable, for example, that Richardson's pietism and his impact on German Romanticism have received so little historical and theoretical analysis even separately, much less together. Here Luhmann's particular focus typifies a limitation of most Richardson criticism. For Luhmann suggests—just as many Richardson scholars have claimed or implied—that Richardson's novels should be considered among the historical analogues and causes of Kant's philosophy and as a key to the semantics of nineteenth-century romantic love. Both of these propositions are good starting points for further inquiry. But both claims, as advanced by Luhmann, simplify the process or inner logic of Richardson's legacy to German culture by bypassing the discursive medium of spiritual dialectics. In *Clarissa*, the function of that mediation at every level—rhetorical, epistemological, psychological, ethical, and theological—is a "trial" of readers both inside and outside the text; and its structure and results, like the fallen state of the divided mind, are always "mixed" (2:38; 1:265). In this context, then, *Biographia Literaria* may still set a challenging and indeed corrective critical standard.

Unlike Luhmann's secularizing socio-semantics, Coleridge's paradoxical view of *Clarissa*'s "self-involution" is attuned to the dialectical doubleness[23] of Richardson's religious conceptuality.[24] Hence, it is Coleridge who, with due ambivalence, can direct us to the historical paradox of Richardson's stupendous influence. *Clarissa* does articulate the basic agenda of transcendental philosophy and a new idiom of romantic love—but always together with a reactionary Christian critique of both of these liberating ideologies of modern, secular subjectivity.

Coleridge's dialectical ambivalence toward Richardson stands as a warning against what we may call the "Kantian misreading" of *Clarissa*. A separate essay is needed to describe this orientation in detail. It informs much of twentieth-century Richardson criticism. Even a schematic summary of its stance, however, will indicate the importance of reconceptualizing the relation between Richardson and the Enlightenment. In brief, the Kantian misreading (for example, Luhmann's) astutely identifies Richardson's specific and influential articulation of conceptual dilemmas later systematized by Kant. But Richardson's critics, instead of placing this recognition in relation to "the *Christian System,*" almost conventionally absolutize the "Kantian" moment, undialectically, as the philosophical touchstone of his fiction. The reductive selectiveness of this approach is the theoretically most rigorous way in which Richardson has been defined as a bourgeois ideologue. In practice, at least very often, it means that Richardson's endlessly reflexive and ambivalent but ever hopeful use of the letter form to interrogate the spiritual limits of self-knowledge and sympathy is reduced to a bleak field of cognitive or representational questions about objectivity and power, skepticism and domination. Likewise the Richardsonian ethic, with its peculiar emphasis on moral excess, the demand for reconciliation of virtue and pleasure as a communal project of brotherly love from which no one should be excluded, is converted into the austere negativity, individualistic rigorism, and formality of the categorical imperative. Finally, Richardson's paradoxical affirmation of worldly beauty and desire through an antitheatrical "Dramatic Narrative" (8:280; 4:554), the whole point of which is to celebrate the unrepresentable and infinite "inner light" of the soul's subjective will and divine life, is translated into the very sublime it criticizes, a self-endorsing aestheticization of spectralized subject-object relations. As this checklist suggests, the Kantian misreading turns the elusive Richardsonian alternative right back into Fielding's critical common sense, or at worst into the rake Lovelace's cynical terms of rationalization. From the perspective of *Clarissa*'s spiritual dialectics, it is a misreading in the strong sense of a partial truth that embodies a profound historical and theoretical error.

Ironically, this error means that Richardson's Kantian misreaders, like most other interpreters of English literature, have been disciples of Coleridge. They, too, have read *Biographia Literaria* and have noticed, as Coleridge did, that Richardson anticipated the conceptuality of Romanticism. But even critics who see Richardson as an early romantic have usually underestimated his novels as a source of romantic forms of thought. Their readings, like Luhmann's, do not work out the conceptual consequences of his allegory of radical dialectical doubleness shaping the turbulent life of the soul. Thus, they can hardly do justice to Coleridge's complex ambivalence toward Richardson. Instead, typically, the twentieth-century response to *Clarissa* underscores the dilemma of a "divided mind" statically torn between two worlds, represented by the inviolable freedom of an integral self pitted against the additive and deterministic causal plotting of human understanding. Judgment in both of these realms, respectively of value and fact, moral and natural law, is understood as dictating maxims and methods, and as laying equal but always separate claim to objectivity, and this entire antinomic structure is interpreted as if Richardson unequivocally assumed a totalizing organic unity. Certainly such an antireductive configuration is in play in Richardson before Kant, and Richardson's twentieth-century readers, partly following Coleridge, have rightly called attention to this historical parallel as important, even though the causes behind it remain to be investigated and may be found too manifold or diffuse for final definition.

Yet, once due acknowledgment has been offered to the historical discernment of Richardson's critics, we nonetheless confront a massive misunderstanding. It is a misreading, not of Kant and German Romanticism, but of *Clarissa* and Coleridge. It is a particularly ironic error, too, in that reading Coleridge, as Richardson's critics apparently have done so well, could have been just the means to prevent any assimilation or subordination of Richardson's achievement to the terms of the Kantian paradigm.

Coleridge's view of Richardson, after all, is a model for Mark Kinkead-Weekes's heuristic distinction between "two Richardsons,"[25] inseparable opposites who cohabit the novelist's "divided" personality. Almost as famous as the tribute to *Clarissa* in *Biographia Literaria* is Coleridge's denunciation of Richardson as "so oozy, hypocritical, praise-mad, canting, envious, concupiscent."[26] Obviously, this description does not apply to the untimely creative genius Coleridge admired, the politically courageous[27] as well as spiritually radical Christian writer who drew from the same dialectical springs as Coleridge himself did when he read Böhme in the 1780s and attended Johann Friedrich Blumenbach's lectures on physiology in Göttingen in 1799.[28] Coleridge was referring in disgust, rather, to the far more conventional social compulsions and apprehensions of the pragmatically calculating and circumspect tradesman—Kinkead-Weekes's "Mr. Richardson"—with his irrepressible celebration of the triumphant bourgeois will and his ambitious wish for his heroines, as for himself, to be successful in this world no less than hereafter. This Richardson, the self-made man who wrote *The Apprentice's Vade Mecum* (1734) and *Familiar Letters* (1741),[29] advocated a commonsense ethic of "independency"[30] in terms of credit, investment, and property; he located his values within the axes of "interest" and "disinterest" that gauge so much of eighteenth-century moral controversy leading up to Kant.[31] While always quick to invoke the realistic economic logic of prudence, however, Richardson was at the same time far more than a zealous Tory opponent of Whig patronage and patrician political control. Spiritually, as Coleridge must have seen, he was an ardent critic of the "narrow selfishness" (1:46; 1:34) of the entire system of material acquisition and exchange as an abuse of rationality that is the soul's worst enemy. In *Clarissa*, "independency" comes under continual scrutiny as a possible rationalization of the selfish desire for power that destroys "Unity and Love" (1:124; 1:92). Coleridge clearly suspected such structural bad faith to be lurking in the antinomies and paradoxes of Richardson's double position as the celebrated authorial subject of the "divided mind." Nevertheless, his ambivalence toward the prosperous City man as Christian author responds to a kind of nervous self-questioning implicit even in Richardson's claim that *Pamela* (1740–1741) taught Henry Fielding all he knew about writing fiction.[32] From this remark we may gather that Richardson felt Fielding's worldly critical standpoint was already inscribed in *Pamela* and *Clarissa* as an alluring half-truth, contained and overcome by the Christian dialectics of his novels. Similarly, we should keep in mind both Coleridge's recognition of Richardson's romantic aesthetic and the pietistic assumptions that made his writing at once a compelling source and an enduring critique of romantic ideology. Despite his moral misgivings, in seeing *Clarissa* as a great founding text of German Romanticism, Coleridge would have been the last to identify Richardson's positive contribution to German culture with *the* secular enlightened ethic, Kant's stoical formalism, which Max Horkheimer and Theodor W. Adorno, following G. W. F. Hegel, would later criticize as "the bourgeois philosophy."[33]

To a great extent, Richardson criticism has not seen, as Coleridge did, that Richardson, for all his bourgeois ideology, is more dialectical than Kant. It has not celebrated the productive anomaly of *Clarissa* in the eighteenth century (and now), its dialectical discussion of human life and "human nature" as dialectical. The difference between Richardson and Thomas à Kempis (2:175; 1:367) remains vast; *Clarissa* was not presented to the public as a mystical meditation. But it is remarkable that Richardson could succeed in convincingly reaching back at all to the Christian tradition of a dialectical "upward way" to "everlasting clearness."[34] He did so at a time when the tendency of secular thought culminating in Kant's philosophy involved a suppression of dialectic as "unclear" or categorially "confused" thinking. What this dismissive imputation of obscurity meant was partly that the dialectic of Christian inner light, with all too painful clarity, held together in critical tension the rival claims of happiness and virtue, feeling and knowing, instead of anesthetically separating these concerns as Kant's procedure of "purification" was supposed to do on the model of chemical analysis.[35]

The rest of this essay will argue that Kant himself was no Kantian misreader of Richardson. Like Coleridge, Kant seems to have recognized in Richardson the "morbid" early romantic self-consciousness of pietism and its dialectical resistance to enlightenment philosophy. Twenty years after the first publication of *Clarissa,* Johann Wolfgang von Goethe summed up the social anthropology of Richardson's German readers as "practically synonymous with 'Schwärmerei.'"[36] We can understand such "Schwärmerei" (fanaticism) as typical of the European response that led British literary history, gazing back through Coleridge, to view Richardson—by no means always favorably—as "the first sentimentalist."[37] Richardsonian "fanaticism" challenged categorial boundaries of established institutions and conventions by bringing the private Christian discipline of conscience together with a popular new dialect of courtship and interpersonal practices, indeed a paradoxically public cult of communal feeling. Kant, whose antipietism shares much with Goethe's subtle exposé of pietistic asceticism and mystical experience in the "Confessions of a Beautiful Soul" (1795),[38] repeatedly levels the charge of "Schwärmerei" at the entire Richardson craze. The following discussion will sketch the theoretical rift between Richardson and Kant. But it also aims to invite reflection on a probably significant conceptual interaction between Richardsonian "fanaticism" and the development of Kant's "critical system." The point here is to redraw, or at least to bring into bold relief, some underresearched "lines of cultural force in the age of Richardson."[39] In particular, a comparison of Kant's readings of Richardson and Jean-Jacques Rousseau should call attention to questions of historical mediation that still need to be explored and theorized before Coleridge's claim that *Clarissa* shaped German Romanticism can be turned into a basis for appropriately wide-ranging and detailed work in literary and cultural history.

A study of the relationship between Richardson and Kant could begin with the German reception of *Clarissa.* As Lawrence Marsden Price points out, the novel was almost immediately translated, and the main intellectual sponsor of this project, Albrecht von Haller (1708–1777), was also "the chief herald of Richardson in Germany." Though, according to Price, it remains uncertain to what extent Haller was directly involved in the translation of *Clarissa* begun by his colleague in Göttingen, the orientalist Johann David Michaelis (1717–1791), "it is generally assumed that the translation was undertaken on the advice of Haller," and "it certainly enjoyed his support from first to last." Haller, in any case, was Richardson's most important early reviewer in Germany, and his article on *Clarissa* in the *Bibliothèque raisonnée* of Amsterdam (1749), addressing his "most extensive laudatory account" of Richardson to a French audience, was notable enough to be translated the same year into English for the *Gentleman's Magazine* and to elicit from Richardson a response, printed as footnotes to Haller's review.[40]

The significance of Haller's evident mediatory enthusiasm for Richardson, however, emerges more profoundly from his placement of his first praises of Richardson in the most prestigious academic periodical of its time in Germany, the *Göttingische gelehrte Anzeigen,* which he edited.[41] Price notes that Haller himself emphasized the seeming eccentricity of this choice of critical setting in demanding that an exception be made for Richardson to the rule that "the discussion of novels . . . is not the ordinary function of learned journals." Haller, remarkably, was claiming that Richardson's fiction deserved serious philosophical and scientific attention.[42]

Such a tribute, strange as it may sound in Price's literary reception synopsis, becomes even more striking—but less odd—when we consider Haller's position in European intellectual life and especially in the history of science. According to Ernst Cassirer, Haller was one of the "men . . . who represent the entire scope and substance of contemporary German culture" in the eighteenth century. He was celebrated already during his lifetime as "the last great universal scholar in Europe."[43] As professor of physiology in Göttingen, particularly, Haller was by far the most advanced and influential biologist of his day in Germany.[44] It is thus highly significant, as Thomas O. Beebee points out, that "medicine and literature met each other on an equal footing" at Göttingen University when Haller discussed the possible continuation of *Clarissa* with his students during anatomy class.[45] Considered in this arena, the Richardson fever in Germany was always inseparable from the concerns of Haller's physiological research and theory, his focus on questions of final causes, subjectivity, cerebral localization (is the brain where the mind is?), and vitalism—many of the problems in natural philosophy that preoccupied Kant.[46]

The similarity between Haller's and Kant's concerns is no distant or accidental parallel. It is a classic episode of intellectual lineage that can be elaborated as an influence study starting out from a direct historical link. The Göttingen anthropologist and comparative anatomist Johann Friedrich Blumenbach (1752–1840), namely, was Haller's greatest follower and arguably Kant's most important source for the *Critique of Judgment* (1790) in both aesthetics and teleology. As Timothy Lenoir has shown, Kant's philosophy, which owed so much to Blumenbach's biological theory, led Blumenbach in turn to realize the consequences of his own conception of organic form in developing a "vital materialism" that sought to reconcile mechanical and teleological modes of explanation in a general theory of natural history.[47] For our purposes, we may note that Kant acknowledges the contribution of Haller's great disciple Blumenbach to his understanding of teleology in the third *Critique*.[48] With regard to the connection between Haller and Kant's aesthetics, we should also flag Haller's treatment of the beautiful and the sublime in his poetry, cited by Kant throughout his writings.[49] Kant specifically calls Haller "the most sublime of German poets"; indeed, Johann Gottfried Herder reports that Kant would speak "with poetical enthusiasm" in quoting from "his favorite poets Pope and Haller."[50] Simplifying this complex interaction to a general tendency, we might emphasize one theoretical continuity of particular ethical and spiritual importance. In basic orientation, the overlapping positions developed by Haller, Blumenbach, and Kant are all antireductionist, and in their case this means that emerging vital materialism was not only non-mechanistic, but also staunchly antivitalist and antimystical.

Blumenbach and Kant formulate their antireductionist program against a version of vitalism in which the bourgeois individualist mind, which they theorize in accord with the assumptions of modern natural science, "decays" into enthusiasm and mystical religion. Kant's critical philosophy, from this viewpoint, offers a way of deciphering bourgeois consciousness precisely to prevent it from decaying. A prime example of such decay for Blumenbach and Kant is Emanuel Swedenborg. Already in his precritical *Dreams of a Spirit-Seer, Illustrated by Dreams of Metaphysics* (1766), Kant attacks the dogmatic metaphysics or "fanaticism" (*Schwärmerei*) of Swedenborg's mystical religion and provocatively compares Swedenborg's visions with the "dreams" of rationalist philosophy.[51] Thereafter, according to Otto Schlapp, Swedenborg specifically figures in Kant among the "Schwärmer" who, as "failed geniuses," transmit the "matter" of imagination unformed by the rules of understanding; thus, typically, Swedenborg's "originality borders on madness."[52]

In the *Critique of Judgment*, Kant gives exactly this definition of "fanaticism." It occurs where the understanding is unsettled by the "disease" of "a deep-seated and brooding passion." Significantly, Kant defines fanaticism in relation to his severe denial of any moral value to works of fiction, above all novels and plays, that rely for their effects on the aesthetic subject's surrender to the power of sympathy. Such "*sentimentality*" (*Empfindelei*), writes Kant, is an indulgence in the "*tender*" emotions of a "weak" soul that is so "fanciful," or morally so deluded and enfeebled in its "sympathetic grief" over "fictitious evils," as to fall short of a claim to serious criticism; it "cannot even be called enthusiastic."[53] Against sympathy, which he believes is at best without moral worth, Kant is well known to uphold the stern virtue of apathy. His *Anthropology* (1798) contains a definitive endorsement of apathy as "an entirely correct and sublime moral precept of the Stoic school," "that is, that the prudent man must at no time be in a state of emotion, not even in that of sympathy with the woes of his best friend . . . because emotion makes one (more or less) blind."[54] It is just here, in Kant's rigorous bifurcation of feeling and knowing, the systematic exclusion of "Affekt" from ethics as well as science, that his antipietism may be said to focus in censure and repudiation on the "fanaticism" of the Richardsonian novel.

Taking our cue from Kant, we should reconsider together Richardson's interrogation of sympathy and Kant's intellectual descent from the eminent natural scientist who was Richardson's leading German fan. Richardson's pietism, though elided by Kantian misreadings of his fiction, appears to have been no secret to Kant. Kant, preeminently, was not a reader who would fail to notice—to condemn—the exciting and dangerous private, irrationalistic, and ultimately mystical play of spiritual dialectics. In this case, he did not need to read further than Haller's reviews to find a celebration of Richardsonian sensibility that might have been at least doubly perturbing to him. For one thing, Haller's admiration for "the pathetic"[55] in *Clarissa* correctly reflects Richardson's brilliant anti-Longinian anticipation and spiritual critique of Kant on the sublime—a point that could be developed in reassessing scholarly secularization of "the divine Clarissa" (1:199; 1:147). Haller, furthermore, in reference to Richardson's depiction of Clementina's love for Sir Charles Grandison, praises the "faultless" representation of the "nuances" of a "fanatical and enthusiastic" passion. He regards Clementina's feelings as a positively exalted capacity "above the sphere of ordinary lovers"; it is "a finer fanaticism [*Schwärmerei*], the source of all great joys and all great sufferings, as well as all great virtues." Haller's reaction to Clementina, in short, affirms the dialectical "concept of love as a high critique, a standard for happiness as for virtue."[56] Richardson's treatment of love as this elevated state of consciousness, according to Haller, will be incomprehensible only to the reader unable to love; and Haller underscores his own "fanaticism" by adding, "woe to him who does not carry this stamp of immortality, as Young calls it, in his breast."[57]

Kant, Cassirer suggests, may not have deserved Charlotte von Schiller's lament that his inability to love kept him from being "one of the greatest phenomena of mankind in general." But we know that Haller's sober *Schwärmerei* in recommending the critical standard of Richardsonian passion on the authority of Young could not have met with his approval. For Kant, Young and Richardson are "masters of the feeling-and-affect-laden style of writing" whom he pointedly indicts as "mystics of taste and sentiment." In other words, Kant the enlightened critic of "visionary" metaphysics recognizes well in Richardson an archaic dialectical adversary; and he rejects in him, as Rosemary Bechler argues Fielding did, the pietist who shares with Swedenborg a common source in Böhme.[58]

As a matter of intellectual honesty and professional tact, however, Kant's position with regard to Richardson must have been delicate. Not only was Richardson warmly promoted as a kindred spirit by Kant's esteemed scientific and philosophical forerunner Haller, but Kant also may have realized that his own work, in its boundary-drawing rigor, could contribute to making Haller's early romantic "fanaticism" culturally prophetic. Indeed, from the standpoint sketched here, though most of the channels and stages in this reception narrative are still unmapped, Kant's debt to the dialectics of pietism was clearly enormous, and the fact that he scarcely mentions *Clarissa* may confirm this thesis.[59] In Harold Bloom's terms, Richardson must have haunted the edges of Kant's thinking as a peculiarly vexing kind of precursor.[60] If Kant could not altogether avoid acknowledging Richardson—which would have been hard amid the long continental craze for *Sir Charles Grandison* (1753–1754)—it should not be surprising if his self-understanding in dealing with Richardson's paradoxical significance was expressed in uneasy ambivalence. Kant's response to Richardson elliptically endorses his bourgeois ethic but above all with emphatic directness rejects his pietistic imagination rooted in mystical dialectics. In other words, Kant's ambivalence toward Richardson is something like Coleridge's in reverse.

One way to reconstruct Kant's ambivalent attitude toward Richardson is to plot its displacement in his reaction to Richardson's great disciple Rousseau. Kant's sparsely furnished Königsberg study, decorated only with a portrait of Rousseau, may be said to emblematize the pervasive attempt in his writing to circumscribe and "purify" the ancestry of his philosophy. We know of Kant's anxious desire insofar as possible to order even the external details of his life to eliminate the possibility of inconsistent meanings as well as unpredictable events.[61] In the austere exclusivity of choosing Rousseau's portrait to mount on his wall as a salient touchstone and manifesto of intellectual alliance, Kant made one of many gestures through which he tried to exert self-interpretive control. However, in surveying the well-known everyday scene of Kant's work, we may still wonder at the choice of Rousseau as his foremost comrade in thought. It seems worth considering that, in this symbolic announcement of origins and common cause, Kant could have been guiding students of his philosophy away from more compromising affiliations. Cassirer emphasizes that Kant's identification and struggle with Rousseau were every bit as decisive for him as encountering David Hume.[62] Nevertheless, Kant's account of his positive critical engagement with Rousseau, his supposed overcoming of Rousseau's radical contradictions as a crucial step in his own philosophical development, may also function as a synecdoche for what might be dramatized as a more primordial Bloomian parricide. To see how plausible this hypothesis could be, all we have to do is to step up close enough to the icon Kant chose for his study to discern figures not of his choosing behind it— among others, prominently, Richardson.

Kant's assessment of Richardson and Rousseau reflects a glaring measure of *parti pris* in a reader who prided himself on his open-minded and impartial curiosity. His ambivalence toward Richardson leans obviously to the negative, and it appears in the course of his career to lean only further and further in that direction. But the ambivalence never goes away; it keeps reappearing as an implied acknowledgement of unwanted relationship that we can infer from inconsistencies and excesses in his effort to pay intellectual debts that history must collect for Richardson to Rousseau alone. Obtrusively out of keeping with his usual cosmopolitan generosity, he makes unpersuasive attempts—at first vacillating, then over-harsh and even abusive—to distance himself from any possible affinity with Richardson by condemning the English author's ethics of fiction together with his personal morals.

In Kant's early *Observations on the Feeling of the Beautiful and Sublime* (1763), he refers favorably to "the noble bent" of such "heroic virtue" as that of Richardson's Grandison, a literary example that he regards as morally superior to the "quiet and self-interested diligence" of unimaginative readers who identify with Robinson Crusoe's triumphs.[63] This verdict, we might say, sounds Kantian through and through. But by the 1780s Kant reverses his praise; according to Schlapp, he pronounces that "morally perfect characters like Grandison should not be the subject of the novel." Much as Goethe outright equated *Grandison* with "Schwärmerei," Kant derides Richardson's fabulously popular third novel as having debilitating and delusory effects on its readers, especially on daydreaming women, at the expense of useful civic and social, including marital and domestic, duties.[64]

In moral contrast to Richardson, Kant now presents himself as the admirer of Fielding "because of his good humor and healthy irony about vice"—an attitude it is much harder to reconcile with Kant's ethics than his earlier approval of Grandison. Haller's *Diary* (1787), in a dictum that sounds more like Kant than Kant himself on this point, disapproves of Fielding as "a Flemish painter." For Haller, whereas "the serious Clarissa" is "a masterpiece in the depiction of mores, of the way to think and express oneself naturally, yet wittily," Fielding paints "accurate rather than beautiful pictures," and the "entertainment" of the "events" in *Tom Jones* (1749) is made worthwhile only by Allworthy's "sublimity" and "the scattered observations on the excellence of religion." Kant's *Anthropology*, on the contrary, praises Fielding's parodic style as affording a "comical contrast" to "a heartrending novel like *Clarissa*." Such parody, adds Kant, is not only amusing but also morally useful, since it "strengthens the senses by freeing them from the conflict which false and harmful concepts have instilled into them."[65]

Kant's reversal of Haller's idealistic and piously prejudiced assessment to favor Fielding might seem only an act of fairness. In Kant, however, it stands out as oddly inconsistent. To support his rather forced commendation of Fielding, Kant invokes one of the favorite axioms of Haller—for whom the great originality of *Clarissa* lies in the probability with which Richardson "paints nature, and nature alone"[66]—in declaring that "the novel must be realistic . . . and depict the real."[67] Haller's praise for the realism of *Clarissa*, however, refers above all to Richardson's vibrantly unified religious depiction of "the interiority of common life" as the integral reality of the soul. On this pietistic reading, *Clarissa's* representation of everyday events is "probable" only insofar as it is "natural," and the naturalness of *Clarissa* inheres in its moving allegory of the *spiritual nature* of moral and psychological experience.[68] By contrast, Kant's prescription of realism is little more than a jab at Richardson and his imitators, whose works he dismisses as "chimerical and enervating." Kant, to be sure, encloses these evaluations in the parenthesis of his more general judgment that "novel-reading . . . weakens the memory and destroys character." Nevertheless, in his extended remarks on this theme he stresses one novelist in particular: Richardson.[69]

Kant's few but vehement anti-novelistic outbursts are characteristically aimed at the "masters of the feeling-and-affect-laden style of writing" who are the "mystics of taste and sentiment."[70] We already know that these "mystics" include Young and Richardson. Kant censures them with the *ad hominem* accusation that they are "actors" who can represent and arouse emotions because they have none themselves. In their dramatization of "assumed" or sympathetically imagined and impersonated emotions, the feelings they lack, according to Kant, are unequivocally moral. For Kant, "[t]he enthusiastic authors are often the most frivolous, the gruesome poets in themselves the funniest, and Young and Richardson people of not the best character." Once again, the seeming rancor of such a personal attack is hardly mitigated by Kant's addendum to the effect that *all* poets manifest the same unstable and untrustworthy theatrical deficiency of authentic character ("Poets in general are devoid of emotions of their own").[71]

Increasingly, Kant appears to identify the novel with a trivializing simplification of the sentimental project of *Grandison*. In effect, the *Critique of Judgment* parodies and suppresses the strenuous optimism of Richardson's culminating ethical experiment. The paradox of *Grandison* inheres in its recognition of evil together with an attempt to prevent the defeat of pleasure by virtue. In Kant's references to sentimental fiction, Richardson's brave but failing effort to negotiate an impossible compromise between goodness and desire is reduced to the weak and tender yearning of mere wish-fulfillment fantasy. It is important, remarks Kant, "for morality to warn us emphatically against such empty and fanciful desires, which are often nourished by novels and sometimes also by mystical presentations, similar to novels, of superhuman perfections and fanatical bliss."[72] Though Kant refers here to novels in general, the fusion of literary and theological censure (of fanatical novels and novelistic mysticism) characterizes his rejection of Richardson. In the same vein, speaking for "the stern precept of duty" in opposition to enfeebling sentimentality and *Schwärmerei*, Kant declares that novels are neither beautiful nor sublime.[73] Repeatedly in his later writings, Kant treats sentimental fiction and its effects as the literary culture of pietism, and he denies that its moralized aesthetic feeling has the least moral or aesthetic value.

Kant's moral caricature of Richardson is an important assumption rather than a convincing result of his strained reasonings on the novel. The insistence on an inter-authorial agon in Harold Bloom's criticism— which, like Kant's aesthetics, derives so much from Richardson and Young's theory in *Conjectures on Original Composition* (1759)—seems highly pertinent here. In accounting for Kant's disparagement and even vilification of Young and Richardson, it would not be farfetched to look for some crisis of anxiety on his part, and this response may have involved an unwelcome sense of indebtedness to these supposedly insincere mystical deceivers. In any case, Kant seems to repudiate them as endangering the whole way of thinking, and the way of life, that he is struggling to theorize in his later work, which he actually calls the "*one* true system of philosophy from principles," before which "there was as yet no philosophy at all."[74] Perhaps significantly, the transcript of Kant's

terms of repudiation in his lectures is so discomposed that even
Schlapp's devoted editorial commentary can do little more than call
attention to the apparent self-contradictoriness of his comments on
Richardson. Kant seems to claim, for example, that the artist "who has
no emotions of his own"—that is, no "serious" or moral feeling—and for
whom therefore emotion is a mere "play of the imagination," "can best
teach" others by moving them. But Kant also asserts that such artists
"produce nothing in matters of genius that would be instructive." The
latter view is the prevailing charge that Kant brings against Richardson,
and the reasoning behind it depends on the claim that Young and
Richardson—like Swedenborg, and in supposed contrast to Rousseau—
are "without principles."[75]

How, then, does Kant, as such an anxious and willful anti-Richardsonian
reader, deal with Rousseau's descent from the English model that Haller
stresses *Julie ou la Nouvelle Héloïse* (1761) follows?[76] In brief, he does his best
to ignore this connection by proceeding as if his opposed assessments of
Richardson and Rousseau were separate matters. His anti-Richardsonian
polemic on Rousseau's behalf is mostly indirect, and it can be summed up
as putting one inconsistent preconception into practice: Kant converts
Richardson's imputed vices into Rousseau's virtues.

Typically, in the same lectures where Kant condemns Richardson's
"feeling-and-affect-laden style of writing," he endorses the "blinding"
brilliance of Rousseau's rhetoric as comparable to "the sound and
tasteful writing style of [Joseph] Addison and Hume."[77] The incongruity
of the styles compared here may support René Wellek's judgment that
Kant's literary-critical opinions are "undistinguished in any way."[78] More
importantly, though, in reading Kant's literary criticism we should keep
in mind his typical demand for systematic lexical consistency and
coherence. Considering that elsewhere Kant commonly uses "blindness"
to figure the precognitive self-relatedness of feeling,[79] his comparison of
Rousseau's "blinding style" with the suave control of Addison and Hume
is a jarring conceptual inconsistency, particularly in supposed
contradistinction to the "feeling-and-affect-laden style of writing" that he
denounces in Richardson.

Another instance of such self-undermining rhetoric appears in
relation to Kant's most famous tribute to Rousseau's eloquence. "I
must," Kant exhorts himself, "read Rousseau until his beauty of
expression no longer distracts me at all, and only then can I survey him
with reason."[80] The theory of reading in this statement should be
understood together with Kant's criticism of Rousseau's stylistic
"enthusiasm":

Rousseau . . . shows much understanding in his writings but lets himself get carried away too much through his enthusiasm; but he also has very much that is well-intended and true, so that one must leave it to each individual to distinguish this from that which is enthusiastic.[81]

As in praising Rousseau's "blinding style," Kant again essentially converts his blame of Richardson—here directly extended to Rousseau—into an occasion for excusing the Richardsonian "feeling-and-affect-laden style of writing" in his favorite. In general, for Kant, "taste is corrupted by the enthusiastic and inspired style just as by novels and frivolities." But he seems to take enthusiasm in Rousseau, unlike Richardson, to be at worst *only* a failing of style, which should not keep the reader from discerning all that is "well-intended and true" in his writings. As Schlapp points out, Kant typically holds that "[m]any authors have lost the value of their philosophy by adulterating it with feeling and taste." Yet, he denies that Rousseau is one of these writers:

Rousseau is one of the greatest geniuses. But he mixes in his writings something novelistic, as a result of which his keen mind is not comprehended well by everyone, and the strength of his arguments remains unrecognized by a part of his readers.[82]

Readers who cannot see the truth in Rousseau, Kant implies, have mainly themselves to blame.

One such reader is definitely Haller. Citing Rousseau's advocacy of "stupid blindness about the works of nature," he condemns him as "the enemy of the sciences" and complains almost equally of his sophisticated ambiguity of moral argument in *La Nouvelle Héloïse* as having lost the "British simplicity" of Richardson. Kant, who often echoes Haller, might be expected to agree with his repeated criticisms of Rousseau as a spiritually questionable, politically irresponsible as well as ethically evasive, idiosyncratic enthusiast. Actually, though, just Rousseau's enthusiasm receives from Kant unstinting moral vindication.[83] Cassirer quotes Kant's express defense of Rousseau "against the charge of being a visionary":

I place Aristides among usurers, Epictetus among courtiers, and Jean-Jacques Rousseau among the doctors of the Sorbonne. I think I hear a loud mocking laughter, and a hundred voices crying, "*What visionaries!*" This ambiguous appearance of being a blind idealist in moral feelings that are in themselves good is *enthusiasm,* and never has anything great been accomplished in the world without it.[84]

Kant denies that the "blind idealist" Rousseau deserves blame for the "stupid blindness" Haller attributes to him. Rousseau, he claims, is indeed a "visionary," but of intellectually and politically constructive, even revolutionary genius.

Kant's enthusiastic justification of Rousseau's enthusiasm, however, finds no support in his treatment of this subject in *The Doctrine of Virtue* (1797), no matter how high an importance he ascribes there to "moral feeling."[85] Rather, his systematic thinking demands what Cassirer represents as his effort in general to make Rousseau's ideas his own by purifying them of just the "ambiguous appearance" he celebrates in defending their enthusiasm. Kant, that is, engages in an ambivalent double self-contradiction. On the one hand, in seeking to justify in Rousseau a paradoxical reliance on the power of sympathy that he deplores in Richardson, he grants, in effect, the fundamental (or "at least" stylistic) identity of his chosen intellectual model and comrade with the pietistic precursor whose influence on the partnership between "Rousseau and Kant" he would deny. On the other hand, to rationalize Rousseau for his purposes, he needs to suppress the effects of even this implicitly acknowledged stylistic dependence on Richardsonian sentimentalism. The upshot, it can be argued, is that, in undertaking the formal purification of Rousseau's thinking, Kant again clarifies nothing so much as Rousseau's continuation of Richardson's fictive ethical inquiry.

Cassirer, reminding us that Kant's "real genius lay in his ability to make clear and precise distinctions," shows him proceeding as an interpreter through Rousseau's works by eliminating their "ambiguities" one after another. As a reader identifying with Kant, Cassirer presents with some understandable condescension the paradoxical obscurities in Rousseau's writing that Kant "clears up" through the sort of reductive reflection he compares in the *Critique of Practical Reason* (1788) to chemical analysis. Rousseau, remarks Cassirer, "does not analyze ideas precisely, and he never moves within the limits of a fixed philosophical terminology"; he "never learned to speak the language of 'clear and distinct ideas.'"[86] On this reading, Kant extracts from the enthusiastically "blind" and stylistically "blinding" texture of Rousseau's confused brilliance a perspicuous construction conforming to the architectonic of his own philosophy. But Cassirer recognizes what is rejected through Kant's reduction of Rousseau to the theoretician who "set him right": it is the "dangerous charm" of Rousseau's "dialectic." This remark, significantly, is Cassirer's commentary on the revision of Haller's praise of Richardsonian pathos in Kant's great tribute to Rousseau's style as distracting his reason, while he reads, by so powerfully moving his sympathy.[87]

Kant's apparently illogical celebration of Rousseau at Richardson's expense fits coherently into the ambivalent mediatory pattern of his intellectual relations with Haller. His direct criticism of Richardson is remarkably—and perhaps tactfully—economical. Kant, of course, knew Haller's position, which was so important to the latter that he had his *Clarissa* review in the *Bibliothèque raisonée* translated into German to go in his *Kleine Schriften* (1756).[88] This programmatic review included the flat assertion that "all the readers whom we know concur in giving [*Clarissa*] . . . the first rank among romances"; and two years after the first appearance of his review, Haller proudly announced in the *Göttingische gelehrte Anzeigen* (1751) that "the general approval of Europe has justified our own [praise] of *Clarissa*."[89] When Kant makes Rousseau, not Richardson, the great genius—much misunderstood but, if purged of the misleading confusions of an enthusiastic style, *his* intellectual source, authority, and ally—he is declaring independence from Haller by reversing his evaluation of the two writers.

Characteristically, in his *Anthropology*, Kant again at first seems to assent to Haller's literary judgment by respectfully invoking Richardson's name as synonymous with the novel. Referring to "Richardson and Molière," he asserts that fiction, to be sure, is no "real" source for anthropology because it is "not based upon experience and truth." "Plays and novels"—like Swedenborg's writings—permit only "the presentation of man as if in a dream," and thus "they seem to teach nothing of the knowledge of man." Yet, despite the "exaggeration of character and situation" that he finds in Richardson and Molière, Kant says their works may serve as valid "aids" to the anthropologist. The "basic traits" of their characters, he acknowledges, "still had to be derived . . . from observance of the actual doings of Man. Exaggerated as these traits may be in degree, they must still conform to human nature."[90]

This seeming endorsement of the "basic" mimetic validity of Richardson's representation of human nature, nevertheless, is implicitly turned right around a few pages later in Kant's direct criticism of Haller. Kant focuses here after all on the "exaggerated" allegory resulting from the procedure of a habitual devout self-examination that corresponds closely to the moral and religious ordeal of conscience embodied in Richardsonian letter writing. "Albrecht Haller, an otherwise splendid mind," he writes, provides in the "diary of his spiritual life"—the *Tagebuch* that contains so much enthusiastic praise of Richardson and deprecation of Rousseau—an occasion for giving a warning against the excesses of an "anguished soul," namely:

> the . . . warning against engaging in deliberate observation and studied
> compilation of an inner history of the involuntary course of our

thoughts and feelings. The warning is given because deliberate observation is the most direct path to illuminism and terrorism in the
confused belief that we are open to higher inspiration and, without our
help, who knows why, are subject to unknown interior forces. In such a
situation, without noticing it, we make pretended discoveries of what
we ourselves have introduced into our own minds. (Kant, *Anthropology*,
pp. 16–17)

Cassirer comments that this intervention of Kant's against "every self-
tormenting dissection of one's own inner life" is aimed specifically at
"the regulation and mechanization of religious life" that Kant associates
with pietism as a formative institutional context or condition of his own
as well as Haller's thinking.[91] We can add that, in separating himself
from the rigidly coded introspective logic of pietism, Kant here impales
Haller on the same spit as Swedenborg.

The confessional anxiety in Haller's diary is unmistakable. But as
one of the great liberal rationalists of his age, and in his youth
apparently a freethinker, Haller might seem an unlikely offender for
Kant to consign to the company of his intellectual archenemy the
mystical "Spirit-Seer." From Kant's perspective, however, a dangerous
affinity between Swedenborg and Haller is confirmed by the latter's
symptomatic passion for Richardson. As in the agile satire of his *Dreams*,
Kant's criticism of Haller strikes several targets at once. As a disciple of
Gottfried Wilhelm Leibniz, Haller *is* a rationalist, indeed an extreme
rationalist—and Kant therefore regards him as a metaphysical dreamer.
But as a conservative and finally intolerant (hence anti-Rousseauist)
supporter not only of established religion, but also of the aristocracy
that still defends the church by persecuting and even executing
Schwärmer for blasphemy, Haller is for Kant also a religious and
political fanatic no less than the clairvoyant Swedenborg or the "mystic"
Richardson.[92]

In his antipietistic intolerance of intolerance, his own renowned
enthusiastic opposition to all moral and religious irrationalism, Kant
rejects as superstitious and "confused" Haller's and Richardson's
conscious exploration of unconscious moral as well as psychological
factors in experience. As a matter of definition, he banishes such
subjective factors from the legitimate cognitive domains of "experience"
and ethics. Haller may not be a mystic, but his enthusiasm for
Richardson bears out the worst implications that Kant draws from the
outpouring of his guilt-ridden pietistic conscience. In distancing himself
from these two mutually confirming symptoms of Haller's fanaticism,
Kant stands off in discreet but firm disapproval of the moral and
religious content of his thinking. The *Anthropology* strives to disassociate

him from Haller's self-deluding *Schwärmerei* as essentially no better than Swedenborg's, and Kant's respectful reproof suggests that Haller's implicit irrationalism is perhaps all the more dangerous because it emerges in the writings of such a spokesman of enlightened values.

The anxious cultural politics of this author-centered approach to Kant's tendentious treatment of Richardson and Rousseau could help to account for the self-contradictoriness of his judgments about them. Further research may succeed in arguing that Kant's sharp rejection of novelistic dialectics resists an indebtedness suggested by Haller's enthusiasm for Richardson. Certainly Kant's critique of poetic emotionalism in Richardson and his German admirers deserves more detailed study.[93] In this essay, we have considered his anti-Hallerian warnings against the debilitating effects of Richardsonian fiction.[94] The spiritual authority that Richardson and Haller so influentially ascribed to emotion—over against which, more or less, Kant seeks to vindicate Rousseau's enthusiastic form—does not satisfy the purely rational criterion of Kantian moral feeling, and it is for this reason that Kant "especially" names Young and Richardson as "bad subjects" among "the masters of the feeling-and-affect-laden style of writing."[95]

Kant was no Kantian misreader of Richardson. He never confused the absolute standard of spiritual sensibility in Richardson's novels with the antireductionist program of his own "critical philosophy." In comparing Richardson and Young as "mystics of taste and sentiment," he particularly questions their concern with the ethical importance of feeling. According to Kant, their "fanaticism"—an irresponsible "deliberate overstepping of the limits of human reason"[96]—is intellectually shallow, self-indulgent, and insincere. We have seen that Kant identifies fanaticism with the self-absorbed brooding of pietism and the deluded visions of theosophy. He implies that these religious attitudes misguidedly sanction an unfounded and equivocal appeal to "sentiment," in which emotion or sheer fantasy may replace true moral judgment. At stake therefore in Kant's reversal of Haller's praise of Richardson is nothing less than the moral law. In criticizing poetic emotionalism, Kant tries to clear a space for his own ethical position in contrast to the arbitrary outpouring or manipulative posturing of the uncontrolled sentimental imagination. For example, he minimizes the debt of his aesthetics to Richardson and Young's account of genius and originality in the *Conjectures*[97] by noting that "[i]f originality [of the imagination] does not harmonize with concepts, then it is [not genius but] . . . fanaticism."[98] It is against such disharmonious ambiguity or excess—a mark of the early romantic sublime—that Kant asserts his own sublime "law of freedom" in celebrating Rousseau as "the Newton of the moral world."[99]

"What always reconciled Kant again to Rousseau, with all his paradoxical and enthusiastic qualities," writes Cassirer, "was the fearlessness, the independence of thought and feeling, the will to the 'unconditioned' he there encountered."[100] "Independence," as noted earlier, is also an ethical watchword in Richardson. Clarissa's "Integrity" (3:256; 2:168) figures a discipline of conscience or self-critical moral reflection that is based neither on any external, conventional, social code nor on a concern for consequences. Kant, however, recognized that Richardson did not set out to vindicate an attitude of rational autonomy. In Clarissa's "close self-examination," she indeed judges her "motives" by innate "Principles." But in assuming that "[t]he heart is very deceitful" (4:97; 2:306), and that we should "look into ourselves, and fear" (3:345; 2:236), Clarissa's exercise of conscience is precisely the pietistic "fanatical discipline"[101] that Kant recalled from his youth. Likewise, the "Scandal" (6:195; 3:387) of Clarissa's "Triumph . . . over all her Oppressors, and the World besides, in a triumphant Death"[102] arises indeed from an individual's uncompromising decision of pure duty. But Clarissa's claim to have "got above all human dependence" (7:241; 4:205) is not primarily a self-legislating transcendental pronouncement. It expresses commitment, rather, to a process of purification that is spiritual. "GOD ALMIGHTY," she says on her deathbed, "WOULD NOT LET ME DEPEND FOR COMFORT UPON ANY BUT HIMSELF" (4:339; 7:421). As Richardson's friend William Law (1686–1761) writes, "Nothing hath separated us from God but our *own Will*, . . . [and i]t is this *Self* that our Saviour calls upon us to deny. . . ."[103] The pietistic dialectic of regeneration teaches renunciation of the very conditions of worldly philosophy.

Cassirer, like many other commentators, cites Herder's remark that Kant read all of Rousseau's writings, including *Émile* and *La Nouvelle Héloïse*, as philosophy.[104] Reading Cassirer reading Kant reading Rousseau is similar to reading twentieth-century criticism that reads Richardson through the lens of Kantian categories. Like Kant himself, however, we should not neglect the emphasis of Young's prediction that *Clarissa* "will probably do more good than a Body of Divinity."[105] Kant would have known Haller's reminder to the same effect in contrasting *La Nouvelle Héloïse* with *Clarissa*:

> One sees . . . that Mr. Rousseau wanted to fight against the death of Clarissa. But the dying Julie is a deist who feels no conscience and no decay [*Verderben*] and carries rejoicing to excess. Clarissa is rather more a Christian, less witty, and thus hopeful, without presumption. [In *La Nouvelle Héloïse* t]he thoughts about prayer are very inadequate, and Mr. Rousseau, like most philosophers of our day, does not feel human corruption [*Verderben*].[106]

Rational autonomy does not regulate the sensibility of pietism.[107] It may not be the "narrow selfishness" that Richardson criticizes, but it also bears slight resemblance to his spiritual standard of a return to "Unity and Love." Haller comments that Julie's moral misgivings and turn to religion make her "moving" and more natural than Rousseau's other characters, but that Rousseau's religion is still "too general."[108] For Kant, and for Cassirer's proto-Kantian Rousseau, "the fusion with the deity of the theosophists and mystics" is a "pathological" imposition on reason.[109] Richardson and Haller, however—as Kant saw—imagined Clarissa's hope for our "supersensible vocation"[110] as an everyday attitude but always mysterious and anything but purely rational.

NOTES

1. William M. Sale, Jr., *Samuel Richardson: Master Printer* (Ithaca: Cornell University Press, 1950), pp. 175, 218–21.

2. Samuel Taylor Coleridge, *Biographia Literaria*, edited and introduced by James Engell and W. Jackson Bate, 2 vols. (1983), in *The Collected Works of Samuel Taylor Coleridge*, 16 vols. (London: Routledge and Kegan Paul; Princeton University Press, 1969–), vol. 7:2, p. 212.

3. Coleridge, *Biographia Literaria*, vol. 7:2, p. 211.

4. T. C. Duncan Eaves and Ben D. Kimpel, *Samuel Richardson: A Biography* (Oxford: Clarendon Press, 1971), p. 609.

5. Margaret Anne Doody, *A Natural Passion: A Study of the Novels of Samuel Richardson* (Oxford: Clarendon Press, 1974), p. 153; see also pp. 105, 373.

6. Rita Goldberg, *Sex and Enlightenment: Women in Richardson and Diderot* (Cambridge: Cambridge University Press, 1984), p. 6; see Doody, *A Natural Passion*, pp. 369, 371–72.

7. Harold Foster, *Edward Young: The poet of the Night Thoughts, 1683–1765* (Alburgh, Harleston, Norfolk: Erskine, 1986), p. 343.

8. Alan Dugald McKillop, *Samuel Richardson: Printer and Novelist* (1936; reprint, Shoe String, 1960), p. 250, refers to Erich Schmidt, *Richardson, Rousseau und Goethe* (1875), and Joseph Texte, *Jean-Jacques Rousseau et les origines du cosmopolitisme littéraire* (1895), and points out that these classic influence studies canonize Richardson's fiction as the great English model of French as well as German literary Romanticism. McKillop himself, however, in canvasing the reception of Richardson in both Germany (pp. 251–65) and France (pp. 268–82), stresses Richardson's unromantic "Philistine rationalism" (pp. 251, 261, 275) and raises "a doubt as to just how much of Richardson is left by the time we get to Rousseau and Goethe" (p. 266). Similar skepticism seems to restrict very narrowly Richardson's role as a paradigm of nineteenth-century German romantic novels in Lawrence Marsden Price, *The Reception of English Literature in Germany* (1932; reprint, New York: Benjamin Blom, 1968), pp. 352–53.

9. One exception to this tendency is Jay Clayton, *Romantic Vision and the Novel* (Cambridge: Cambridge University Press, 1987), pp. 27–46.

10. Such research, which should substantially enrich our historical understanding of Richardson, is under way in *The Clarissa Project*, vols. 12 and 13, *The Critical Controversy—Historical Commentaries*, edited and introduction by Margaret Anne Doody and David C. Hensley (New York: AMS), forthcoming.

11. R. F. Brissenden, ed., *Samuel Richardson, Clarissa: Preface, Hints of Prefaces, and Postscript*, Augustan Reprint Society 103 (Los Angeles: University of California Press, William Andrews Clark Memorial Library, 1964), p. 4; John Carroll, ed., *Selected Letters of Samuel Richardson* (Oxford: Clarendon Press, 1964), p. 92.

12. Two versions of the third edition of *Clarissa* are cited in this essay: Samuel Richardson, *Clarissa. Or, The History of a Young Lady: Comprehending The most Important Concerns of Private Life*, edited and introduction by Florian Stuber, 8 vols. (New York: AMS, 1990); and Samuel Richardson, *Clarissa, or the History of a Young Lady. In Four Volumes*, introduction by John Butt (New York and London: Dutton-Dent, Everyman, 1965–1967). All references are to both Stuber and Butt, in that order, in the form "8:280;4:554" (the present reference). The text quoted is Stuber's. See also Brissenden, ed., *Hints of Prefaces*, p. 1; Carrol, ed., *Selected Letters*, p. 87.

13. Coleridge, *Biographia Literaria*, vol. 7:2, p. 147.

14. Carroll, ed., *Selected Letters*, p. 289.

15. *The Correspondence of Edward Young 1683–1765*, Henry Pettit, ed. (Oxford: Clarendon Press, 1971), p. 182. Hereafter cited as Pettit.

16. In 1757, Richardson remarked to Lady Bradshaigh that the Germans read his novels "wth strange Approbation" (Carroll, ed., *Selected Letters*, p. 336). To Young himself, in 1759, Richardson wrote that "[i]n Germany, they revere Dr. Young in his works more than they do those of any other British genius" (Pettit, ed., *The Correspondence of Edward Young*, p. 499). On Richardson and the Germans, see Lawrence Marsden Price, "On the Reception of Richardson in Germany," *JEGP* 25 (1926): pp. 7–33, and Price, *The Reception of English Literature in Germany*, pp. 190–215; and Eaves and Kimpel, *Samuel Richardson*, pp. 320, 413–16, 437, 491–93. For Young's effect in Germany, see studies such as Johannes Barnstorff, *Youngs Nachtgedanken und ihr Einfluss auf die deutsche Literatur*, foreward by Franz Muncker (Bamberg: C. C. Buchner, 1895); Walter Thomas, *Le poète Edward Young (1683–1765): Étude sur sa vie et ses oeuvres* (Paris: Hachette, 1901), pp. 502–20; John L. Kind, *Edward Young in Germany: Historical Surveys, Influence upon German Literature, Bibliography*, Columbia University Germanic Studies 7 (New York: Macmillan, 1906); Price, *The Reception of English Literature in Germany*, pp. 144–56, 289–92; and Foster, *Edward Young*, pp. 260, 299, 309–11, 329–30, 341–44, 387–88.

17. For a survey and analysis of the relationship between these approaches to literary history, see Jay Clayton and Eric Rothstein, "Figures in the Corpus: Theories of Influence and Intertextuality," in *Influence and Intertextuality in Literary History*, edited by Jay Clayton and Eric Rothstein (Madison: University of Wisconsin Press, 1991), pp. 3–36.

18. See Thomas McFarland, *Coleridge and the Pantheist Tradition* (Oxford: Clarendon Press, 1969), pp. 14, 35–36, 249, and passim.

19. Niklas Luhmann, *Love as Passion*, translated by Jeremy Gaines and Doris L. Jones (Cambridge: Harvard University Press, 1986), pp. 130–35.

20. See two articles by Rosemary Bechler: "'Triall by what is contrary': Samuel Richardson and Christian Dialectic," in *Samuel Richardson: Passion and Prudence*, edited by Valerie Grosvenor Myer (London: Vision; Totowa, N.J.: Barnes and Noble, 1986), pp. 93–113; and "Reading the Fire-Scene," in *Samuel Richardson*, edited by Harold Bloom (New York: Chelsea House, 1987), pp. 141–60. The most detailed synopsis of the "pietist form of life" in the inner Richardson circle appears in Simon Schaffer, "The consuming flame: electrical showmen and Tory mystics in the world of goods," in *Consumption and the World of Goods*, edited by John Brewer and Roy Porter, ch. 24 (London and New York: Routledge, 1993), pp. 489–526.

21. See Margaret Anne Doody, "Richardson's Politics," *Eighteenth-Century Fiction* 2:2 (January 1990): pp. 113–26.

22. Alan Dugald McKillop, "Richardson, Young, and the *Conjectures*," *Modern Philology* 22 (1925): p. 393. See also John A. Dussinger, "Conscience and the Pattern of Christian Perfection in *Clarissa*," *PMLA* 81:3 (June 1966): p. 243.

23. In light of Bechler's and Schaffer's research, an important philosophical congruence between Coleridge and Richardson should not be surprising. It results partly from Coleridge's subtle response to literary structures in *Clarissa*. But it could also reflect an informed inference about the principles of Richardson's pietism. Coleridge was in a good position to make such an inference because he shared intellectual roots with the pietistic inner circle of Richardson's friends. *Biographia Literaria* emphasizes his debt to the German mystic Jakob Böhme (1575–1624) (vol. 7:1, pp. 146–47, 161) and Böhme's British expositor "the pious and fervid WILLIAM LAW" (1686–1761) (vol. 7:1, p. 151; see McFarland, *Coleridge and the Pantheist Tradition*, pp. 35, 248–50). Coleridge may well have known that Law was the most esteemed theologian in the Richardson circle. In any case, Richardson and Coleridge both probably understood *Clarissa*'s basic principle of "a double yet separate correspondence" in relation to the double dialectic or *Contrarium* of the will and desire that Böhme and Law describe as the suffering and struggling state of division and conflict in the fallen soul. For an exposition of Böhme's "two dialectical schemas" and his dualistic doctrine of "the hostile and devouring *Contrarium* of being," see Alexandre Koyré, *La philosophie de Jacob Boehme* (1929; reprint, New York: Burt Franklin, 1968), pp. 367 ff., 394 ff., 489. Translations in this essay, unless otherwise indicated, are my own.

24. The conceptuality, or systematic interconnectedness, of spiritual concepts in Richardson's novels is an assumption of the dialectics of reading that he endorsed. Many of his most admiring contemporaries accepted this devotional and interpretive standard. For example, in a comment that we know Richardson approved, Phillip Skelton (1707–1787) asked, "Is *Clarissa* a mere Novel?" His answer is characteristic of Richardson's correspondents: "Whoever considers it as such does not understand it. It is a System of religious and moral

Precepts and Examples, planned on an entertaining Story, which stands or goes forward, as the excellent Design of the Author requires." (Brissenden, ed., *Hints of Prefaces*, pp. 7–8).

25. Mark Kinkead-Weekes, *Samuel Richardson: Dramatic Novelist* (Ithaca, N.Y.: Cornell University Press, 1973), p. 77 and passim.

26. *The Notebooks of Samuel Taylor Coleridge*, edited by Kathleen Coburn and Merton Christensen, 5 vols. (New York and London: Pantheon; Princeton, N.J.: Princeton University Press; London: Routledge, 1957–), 2:2471.

27. See Doody, "Richardson's Politics," pp. 117 ff.

28. McFarland, *Coleridge and the Pantheist Tradition*, pp. 35 n., 325–32; Coleridge, *Biographia Literaria*, p. 207.

29. *The Apprentice's Vade Mecum*, introduced by Alan Dugald McKillop. Augustan Reprint Society 169–70 (Los Angeles: University of California Press, William Andrews Clark Memorial Library, 1975); Brian W. Downs, ed., *Familiar Letters on Important Occasions* (London: Routledge, 1928).

30. On "independency" as as both an inner attitude and an outer benefit of prudence in Richardson's bourgeois ethic, see Eaves and Kimpel, *Samuel Richardson*, pp. 51–53, 56, 540; on its economic and political context, see John Brewer, "Commercialization and Politics," in Neil McKendrick, John Brewer, and J. H. Plumb, *The Birth of a Consumer Society: The Commercialization of Eighteenth-Century England* (Bloomington: Indiana University Press, 1982), pp. 198–200.

31. A survey of the eighteenth-century British philosophical debate about egoism from Hobbes to Kant appears in Bernard Harrison, *Henry Fielding's Tom Jones: The Novelist as Moral Philosopher* (London: Chatto and Windus for Sussex University Press, 1975), pp. 70–88. Harrison's study is a miniature Kantian misreading of Richardson. He squarely identifies the ethical concerns of "Richardsonian criticism" (p. 26) with Kant's. Moreover, with a Kantian bias of his own, Harrison reduces Richardson himself to the same position (p. 24).

32. Carroll, ed., *Selected Letters*, pp. 133, 197.

33. Max Horkheimer and Theodor W. Adorno, *Dialectic of Enlightenment*, translated by John Cumming (New York: Seabury, 1972), p. 96.

34. Thomas à Kempis, *The Imitation of Christ*, 3:64, in *The Consolation of Philosophy*, introduction by Irwin Edman (New York: Random House, Modern Library, 1943), p. 279.

35. See, for example, Immanuel Kant, *Critique of Pure Reason*, translated by Norman Kemp Smith (New York: St. Martin's; Toronto: Macmillan, 1965), p. 24 n., and note 86 below.

36. Price, *The Reception of English Literature in Germany*, p. 208.

37. Leslie Stephen, "Richardson's Novels," in *Hours in a Library*, 4 vols. (New York and London: G. P. Putnam's Sons, Knickerbocker, 1907), 1:80.

38. See Frederick J. Beharriell, "The Hidden Meaning of Goethe's 'Bekenntnisse einer Schönen Seele,'" in *Lebendige Form: Interpretationen zur deutschen Literatur*, Festschrift for Heinrich E. K. Henel, edited by Jeffrey L. Sammons and Ernst Schürer (Munich: Wilhelm Fink, 1970), pp. 37–62.

39. Pat Rogers, "'A Young, a Richardson, or a Johnson': lines of cultural force in the age of Richardson," in *Samuel Richardson: Tercentenary Essays*, edited

by Margaret Anne Doody and Peter Sabor (Cambridge: Cambridge University Press, 1989), pp. 203–22.

40. Price, "On the Reception of Richardson in Germany," pp. 8, 16, 19, 21–22; see Albrecht von Haller, *Bibliothèque raisonée* 42 (1749), and *Gentleman's Magazine* 19 (June and July 1749). Haller's review is reprinted in *Novel and Romance, 1700–1800: A Documentary Record*, edited by Ioan Williams (London: Routledge and Kegan Paul, 1970), pp. 130–41. See also Thomas O. Beebee, *"Clarissa" on the Continent: Translation and Seduction* (University Park and London: Pennsylvania State University Press, 1990), pp. 16–24.

41. On the importance of "Haller's journal" and his massive contribution to the *Göttingische gelehrte Anzeigen*, see Karl S. Guthke, *Haller und die Literatur*, Arbeiten aus der Niedersächsischen Staats- und Universitätsbibliothek Göttingen, vol. 4 (Göttingen: Vandenhoeck and Ruprecht, 1962), pp. 30–37 and passim; Christoph Siegrist, *Albrecht von Haller* (Stuttgart: J. B. Metzler and Carl Ernst Poeschel, 1967), pp. 38–44; and Karl S. Guthke, ed., *Hallers Literaturkritik* (Tübingen: Max Niemeyer, 1970), pp. 2–13 and passim.

42. Price, "On the Reception of Richardson in Germany," p. 17. See also the biographical introduction to *Albrecht von Hallers Gedichte*, edited by Ludwig Hirzel (Frauenfeld: J. Huber, 1882), pp. ccclxxii–iii n.; Guthke, ed., *Hallers Literaturkritik*, pp. 58 n., 66; and Theodor Wolpers, "Haller, das gelehrte Göttingen und Richardsons *Clarissa*: Eine literarische Rezeption und ihre Rückwirkung auf den Autor," in *Ausstellung Albrecht von Haller 1708–1777*, Arbeiten aus der Niedersächsischen Staats- und Universitätsbibliothek Göttingen, vol. 14a (Göttingen, 1977), p. 38.

43. Ernst Cassirer, *Kant's Life and Thought*, translated by James Haden (New Haven: Yale University Press, 1981), p. 17; see Richard Toellner, *Albrecht von Haller: Über die Einheit im Denken des letzten Universalgelehrten*, Sudhoffs Archiv Zeitschrift für Wissenschaftsgeschichte 10 (Wiesbaden: Franz Steiner, 1971), pp. 1–2.

44. I am indebted to Simon Schaffer's advice on the interaction between scientific research, philosophy, and literary criticism that can be understood as the standpoint of Haller's enthusiasm for Richardson. See Hirzel, ed., *Hallers Gedichte*, pp. clxxi ff., cclxxxviii ff., and essays by Walter Zimmerli ("Haller in Göttingen"), Hans-Heinz Eulner ("Haller der Mediziner"), and Gerhard Wagenitz ("Haller als Botaniker") in the exhibition catalogue of the [Göttingen] Niedersächsische Staats- und Universitätsbibliothek for the *Ausstellung "Albrecht von Haller, 1708–1777,"* im Foyer der Bibliothek, *12.12.1977-7.1.1978*. On Haller's views as a natural scientist, see especially Shirley A. Roe, *Matter, Life, and Generation: Eighteenth-century Embryology and the Haller-Wolff Debate* (Cambridge: Cambridge University Press, 1981); Shirley A. Roe, ed., *The Natural Philosophy of Albrecht von Haller* (New York: Arno, 1981); and Timothy Lenoir, *The Strategy of Life: Teleology and Mechanics in Nineteenth-Century German Biology*, Studies in the History of Modern Science 13 (Dordrecht, Boston, and London: D. Reidel, 1982).

45. Beebee, *"Clarissa" on the Continent*, pp. 17, 184.

46. For an introduction to these issues in the eighteenth-century philosophy of science from Kant's perspective, see Robert E. Butts, *Kant and the Double*

Government Methodology: Supersensibility and Method in Kant's Philosophy of Science (Dordrecht, Boston, and Lancaster: D. Reidel, 1984); and Clark Zumbach, *The Transcendent Science: Kant's Conception of Biological Methodology*, Nijhoff International Philosophy Series 15 (The Hague, Boston, and Lancaster: Martinus Nijhoff, 1984).

47. Timothy Lenoir, "Kant, Blumenbach, and Vital Materialism in German Biology," *Isis* 71, 256 (March 1980), pp. 77–108; Lenoir, *The Strategy of Life*, pp. 2–53.

48. Immanuel Kant, *Critique of Judgment*, translated and introduction by Werner S. Pluhar (Indianapolis: Hackett, 1987), p. 311. An indication of the extent of Kant's direct acknowledgement of Blumenbach is the list of references to him compiled in Katharina Holger and Eduard Gerresheim, ed., *Personenindex 2. Stufe zu "Kants Gesammelte Schriften," herausgegeben von der Preussischen Akademie der Wissenschaften, Band I–XXIII, und von der Deutschen Akademie der Wissenschaften, Band XXIII*, 6 vols. (Letters A-O), vol. 1 (1964) (Bonn: Universität Bonn, Philosophisches Seminar A, 1964–; manuscript photocopied for the Kantgesellschaft Landesgruppe Rheinland-Westfalen), pp. B 110–13.

49. See the Kant *Personenindex*, vol. 3 (1966), pp. H 14–18.

50. Hirzel, ed., *Hallers Gedichte*, pp. ccclii, cdxxiv, cdxxiv n.

51. On Kant's attitude toward *Schwärmerei* as a guiding thread running all through his works, see Butts, *Kant and the Double Government Methodology*, pp. 1–15, 282–318; on Kant's *Dreams of a Spirit-Seer*, see Cassirer, *Kant's Life and Thought*, pp. 77–92.

52. Otto Schlapp, *Kants Lehre vom Genie und die Entstehung der "Kritik der Urteilskraft"* (Göttingen: Vandenhoeck and Ruprecht, 1901), pp. 250, 251.

53. Kant, *Critique of Judgment*, pp. 133–34, 136, 137. See Immanuel Kant, *Kritik der Urteilskraft*, edited by Karl Vorländer (Hamburg: Felix Meiner, 1974), p. 120: "nicht einmal enthusiastisch genannt werden kann."

54. Immanuel Kant, *Anthropology from a Pragmatic Point of View*, translated by Victor Lyle Dowdell, revised and edited by Hans H. Rudnick, and introduced by Frederick P. Van De Pitte (Carbondale and Edwardsville: Southern Illinois University Press, 1978), p. 158.

55. Haller, in Williams, ed., *Novel and Romance*, p. 136.

56. Bechler, "Reading the Fire-Scene," p. 160.

57. Albrecht von Haller, *Tagebuch seiner Beobachtungen über Schriftsteller und über sich selbst: Zur Karakteristik der Philosophie und Religion dieses Mannes*, edited by Johann Georg Heinzmann, 2 vols. (Bern: 1787; Frankfurt am Main: Athenäum Reprints, 1971), 1:299; Guthke, ed., *Hallers Literaturkritik*, p. 111. Kant was well acquainted with Haller's diary (see Kant, *Anthropology*, p. 17).

58. Cassier, *Kant's Life and Thought*, pp. 413–14; Schlapp, *Kants Lehre vom Genie*, p. 299; Bechler, "Reading the Fire-Scene," pp. 156–60.

59. The index to Kant's works lists only one reference apiece to "Clarissa" (cited below in note 65), "Grandison," and "Richardson"—in contrast to more than twenty references by name to "Rousseau." See *Wortindex zu Kants gesammelten Schriften*, edited by Dieter Krallmann and Hans Adolf Martin, 2 vols.,

in *Allgemeiner Kantindex zu Kants gesammelten Schriften*, ed. Gottfried Martin (Berlin: Walter de Gruyter, 1967), Zweite Abteilung: Wortindex, 1:195,440, 2:763,768.

60. See Harold Bloom, *The Anxiety of Influence: A Theory of Poetry* (New York: Oxford University Press, 1973), and Harold Bloom, *A Map of Misreading* (New York: Oxford University Press, 1975).

61. A humanely humorous synopsis of Kant's quotidian regime appears in Wilhelm Weischedel, *Die philosophische Hintertreppe: 34 grosse Philosophen in Alltag und Denken* (Munich: Deutscher Taschenbuch Verlag, 1973), pp. 177–81.

62. Cassirer, *Kant's Life and Thought*, pp. 86–92; Ernst Cassirer, *Rousseau Kant Goethe: Two Essays*, translated by James Gutmann, Paul Oskar Kristeller, and John Herman Randall, Jr. (Princeton: Princeton University Press, 1970), pp. 6–18, 40–42.

63. Immanuel Kant, *Observations on the Feeling of the Beautiful and Sublime*, translated by John T. Goldthwait (Berkeley and Los Angeles: University of California Press, 1965), p. 70.

64. Schlapp, *Kants Lehre vom Genie*, pp. 170–72, 299. Kant's attack on the Richardsonian novel, as recounted by Schlapp, is bluntly antifeminist: "The man is unfortunate who has a novel reader for a wife; for in her thoughts she has certainly already been married to Grandison and has now become a widow. How little desire will she then have to go to the kitchen!" (p. 171).

65. Schlapp, *Kants Lehre vom Genie*, p. 299; Haller, *Tagebuch*, 1:59–62; Kant, *Anthropology*, p. 51. See *Kants Werke: Der Streit der Fakultäten, Anthropologie in pragmatischer Hinsicht* (Berlin: Georg Reimer, 1907), in *Kants gesammelte Schriften*, edited by Königliche Preussische Akademie der Wissenschaften, 29 vols. (Berlin: Walter de Gruyter, 1910–), Erste Abteilung: Werke, vols. 1–9, 7:163: "einen herzbeklemmenden Roman, wie Clarissa."

66. Haller, in Williams, ed., *Novel and Romance*, p. 132.

67. Schlapp, *Kants Lehre vom Genie*, p. 299.

68. Haller, in Williams, ed., *Novel and Romance*, pp. 132, 136; Guthke, ed., *Haller und die Literatur*, pp. 131–36, 150.

69. Schlapp, *Kants Lehre vom Genie*, pp. 170–71, 299.

70. Ibid., pp. 144, 299. See Kant's comments on the modern "moral fanaticism" of all feeling and sympathy oriented "novelists and sentimental educators"—condemned as "fantastic romancers"—in the *Critique of Practical Reason*, translated and introduced by Lewis White Beck (Indianapolis: Bobbs-Merrill, 1956), pp. 88–89, 158–61.

71. Schlapp, *Kants Lehre vom Genie*, pp. 143–44. Kant's affect-related usage in such passages is by no means always consistent. Here, for example, *Empfindung* (sensation) and *Gefühl* (feeling) seem all but . . . would be hard to distinguish them from *Rührung* (emotion). This ambiguity is compounded by Kant's depreciation of sensation, feeling, and emotion in contrast to the *moralisches Gefühl* (moral feeling). See Kant, *Anthropologie*, pp. 251 ff.; Kant, *Anthropology*, pp. 155 ff.; Rudolf Eisler, *Kant-Lexikon: Nachschlagewerk zu Kants Sämtlichen Schriften, Briefen und handschriftlichem Nachlass* (1930; reprint, Hildesheim: Georg Olms, 1961), pp. 3–4, 115–16, 175–77, 474; and George

Schrader, "The Status of Feeling in Kant's Philosophy," *Proceedings of the Ottawa Congress on Kant* (Ottawa: University of Ottawa Press, 1976), pp. 143–64.

72. Kant, *Critique of Judgment*, p. 420 n.; see p. 137.

73. Ibid., p. 133.

74. Immanuel Kant, *The Doctrine of Virtue: Part II of "The Metaphysic of Morals," With the Introduction to "The Metaphysic of Morals" and the Preface to "The Doctrine of Law,"* translated and introduced by Mary J. Gregor (Philadelphia: University of Pennsylvania Press, 1964), p. 3.

75. Schlapp, *Kants Lehre vom Genie*, pp. 143–44.

76. Haller, *Tagebuch*, 1:199; Guthke, ed., *Hallers Literaturkritik*, p. 80.

77. Schlapp, *Kants Lehre vom Genie*, p. 299.

78. René Wellek, *The Later Eighteenth Century* (1955), in *A History of Modern Criticism: 1750–1950*, 6 vols. (New Haven: Yale University Press, 1955–1986), 1:299.

79. See, for example, Kant, *The Doctrine of Virtue*, pp. 7–8, 32–33.

80. Cassirer, *Rousseau Kant Goethe*, p. 6; see also Cassier, *Kant's Life and Thought*, p. 88, and Schlapp, *Kants Lehre vom Genie*, p. 175 n.

81. Schlapp, *Kants Lehre vom Genie*, p. 238.

82. Ibid., pp. 48, 72.

83. Haller, *Tagebuch*, 1:101, 112, 200; Guthke, ed., *Hallers Literaturkritik*, pp. 61–62, 80–81, 155–57; see Siegrist, *Albrecht von Haller*, pp. 50–51, and Butts, *Kant and Double Government Methodology*, p. 287.

84. Cassirer, *Rousseau Kant Goethe*, p. 17.

85. Kant, *The Doctrine of Virtue*, pp. 70–71.

86. Cassirer, *Rousseau Kant Goethe*, pp. 19, 24, 25, 33, 45, 59; see Kant, *Critique of Practical Reason*, pp. 96, 167. This essay echoes Kant's attention and overwhelming commitment to clarity and distinctness (see *Critique of Pure Reason*, pp. 12, 373 n.). In his literary criticism, typically, Kant criticizes Klopstock for not achieving "an intuitive clearness" (Schlapp, *Kants Lehre vom Genie*, p. 170). It should be emphasized, though, that Kant at times also shows aesthetic appreciation for the obscurity of figurative language, and he even remarks that clarity "soon tires" the reader of poetry (Schlapp, *Kants Lehre vom Genie*, p. 298; see pp. 131–34).

87. Cassirer, *Kant's Life and Thought*, pp. 84, 87, 88, 235.

88. *Sammlung kleiner Hallerischer Schriften* (1756), 1:339ff.; second edition, 3 vols. (Bern: E. Haller, 1772), 1:293ff. For comments on the "obviously special importance" that Haller ascribed to his *Clarissa* review, see Price, *The Reception of English Literature in Germany*, p. 194; Guthke, *Haller und die Literatur*, p. 135; and Wolpers, "Haller, das gelehrte Göttingen und Richardsons *Clarissa*," p. 40.

89. Haller, in Williams, ed., *Novel and Romance*, p. 131; *Göttingische gelehrte Anzeigen* (1751), p. 605, cited in Theodor Wolpers, "Haller als Romankritiker," in *Albrecht von Haller zum 200. Todestag* (Göttingen: Vandenhoeck & Ruprecht, 1977), p. 45; Wolpers, "Haller, das gelehrte Göttingen und Richardsons *Clarissa*," p. 38.

90. Kant, *Anthropology*, p. 6.

91. Cassirer, *Kant's Life and Thought*, p. 18.

92. See Butts, *Kant and the Double Government Methodology*, passim; Hirzel, ed., *Hallers Gedichte*, pp. cxxv, cdxiii; and Karl S. Guthke, *Zur Religionsphilosophie des jungen Albrecht von Haller* (Turin: Edizioni di "Filosofia," 1970).

93. An investigation of Kant's reaction to the "chimerical and enervating" Richardsonian novel in relation to German literature might begin with his pointedly similar stress on the "chimerical emotionalism" (*chimärische Rührseligkeit*) of the poetry of one of Richardson's most influential German fans, Friedrich Gottlieb Klopstock (1724–1803) (Schlapp, *Kants Lehre vom Genie*, pp. 298, 299). See my essay "*Clarissa*, Coleridge, Kant, and Klopstock: Emotionalism as Pietistic Intertext in Anglo-German Romanticism," *Studies in the Literary Imagination* 28:1 (Spring 1995): pp. 134–42.

94. See notes 53, 69, and 70 above and Schlapp, *Kants Lehre vom Genie*, pp. 47–48.

95. Schlapp, *Kants Lehre vom Genie*, p. 299; on "moral feeling," see notes 71 and 85 above and Kant, *Critique of Judgment*, p. 128.

96. Kant, *Critique of Practical Reason*, p. 88. For Kant's treatment of fanaticism elsewhere, see Kant, *Critique of Judgment*, pp. 135, 241, 351; Kant, *Anthropology*, pp. 49, 62, 84, 98; Immanuel Kant, *Religion within the Limits of Reason Alone* (1793), translated and introduced by Theodore M. Greene and Hoyt H. Hudson (New York, Hagerstown, San Francisco, London: Harper and Row, Torchbook, 1960), pp. 62, 78, 105, 121, 162–63, 172; and Eisler, *Kant-Lexikon*, p. 485.

97. See Schlapp, *Kants Lehre vom Genie*, pp. 61–62 n., 305 n., 344, 352 n., 365 n., 411, 417.

98. Kant, *Anthropology*, p. 62.

99. Ernst Cassirer, *The Question of Jean-Jacques Rousseau*, edited and translated by Peter Gay (1963; New Haven: Yale University Press, 1989), p. 39; see pp. 58, 72.

100. Cassirer, *Rousseau Kant Goethe*, p. 17.

101. Cassirer, *Kant's Life and Thought*, p. 18.

102. Carroll, ed., *Selected Letters*, p. 87.

103. William Law, *Works*, 9 vols. (London: J. Richardson, 1762), 5:180.

104. Cassirer, *Rousseau Kant Goethe*, p. 14.

105. Pettit, ed., *The Correspondence of Edward Young*, p. 311.

106. Guthke, ed., *Hallers Literaturkritik*, p. 81.

107. See Friedhelm Radandt, *From Baroque to Storm and Stress 1720–1775* (London: Croom Helm; New York: Barnes and Noble, 1977), p. 13; and John Sitter, *Literary Loneliness in Mid-Eighteenth-Century England* (Ithaca and London: Cornell University Press, 1982), pp. 62–63.

108. Guthke, ed., *Hallers Literaturkritik*, pp. 80, 81.

109. Kant, *Critique of Practical Reason*, p. 125.

110. Kant, *Critique of Judgment*, p. 115.

10

Gregory Maertz

Reviewing Kant's Early Reception in Britain

The Leading Role of Henry Crabb Robinson

*Ich fragte Goethe, welchen der neueren Philosophen er
für den vorzüglichsten halte.
"Kant," sagte er, "ist der vorzüglichste, ohne allen
Zweifel. Er ist auch derjenige, dessen Lehre sich fort
wirkend erwiesen hat und die in unsere deutsche
Kultur am tiefsten eingedrungen ist. Er hat auf Sie
gewirkt, ohne daß Sie ihn gelesen haben. Jetzt brauchen
Sie ihn nicht mehr, denn was er Ihnen geben konnte,
besitzen Sie schon."*

—*Eckermann,*
Gespräche mit Goethe*

The mediation of German literature and thought is one of the defining features of British culture from the late eighteenth century to the decades following World War II.[1] During the Romantic Age this process occupied writers from all strata of the literary world, from leading poets and critics to professional reviewers and hack translators, and engaged all factions, including Tories, Whigs, and Jacobins. Moreover, if one surveys the review criticism of William Taylor, William Hazlitt, Thomas De Quincey, and Henry Crabb Robinson, clear parallels emerge between the increasingly sophisticated treatment of Immanuel Kant and the development of review criticism as a free-standing genre. Having evolved from mere appendages of the book trade to assume a condition of greater freedom, reviewers often chose to exercise their new-found independence in meditations on Kant.[2]

In addition, the reception of Kant reflects in microcosm the cultural politics of the post-revolutionary era, including the debate that arose over British cultural identity. The xenophobic, nativist position that may be inferred from the Kant criticism of Taylor, Hazlitt, and De Quincey and is echoed in the hostile reaction to continental influence that one encounters in the pages of the *Anti-Jacobin Review* and the *Edinburgh Review*, stands opposed to the cosmopolitan vision, based on cultural interaction, that was fashioned by Henry Crabb Robinson. From the war in the reviews canvassed in the present essay to the longstanding disciplinary rivalry between English and comparative literature in Anglo-American universities, extreme ambivalence, if not open hostility to continental influence, appears to be a characteristic expression of British culture and of Anglophiles living in former British colonies, and is only partly to be explained by the existence of real or perceived threats from across the English Channel.

The present discussion was suggested by and yet substantially departs from the methods and conclusions of René Wellek's *Immanuel Kant in England* (1931). More concerned than Wellek with the cultural politics underlying their interpretations, I begin by examining the Kant criticism of Taylor, Hazlitt, and De Quincey. Then I assess the merits of Robinson's "Letters on the Philosophy of Kant." It is my contention that these epistolary essays, which appeared more than a decade before Samuel Taylor Coleridge's *Biographia Literaria* and two decades before Thomas Carlyle's essays, translations, and reviews, offer an interpretation of Kant's thought of unparalleled discernment, coherence, and originality in the first two decades of the nineteenth century.

Scholars know William Taylor as a close friend of Robert Southey and the author of a reference work, *English Synonyms Discriminated* (1813), that Coleridge cites in *Biographia Literaria*, chapter 4. Contemporaries admired him as one of the most capable and prolific reviewers writing for the *Monthly Review, Monthly Magazine,* and *Critical Review.* Covering a broad range of topics, including ancient and modern history, linguistics and philology, theology and politics, travel and ethnography, philosophy and literature, his contributions to these periodicals run literally into the hundreds.[3] More than any other critic before Coleridge and Carlyle, Taylor is responsible for creating an audience for German literature and for encouraging the German studies of Walter Scott, Coleridge, Southey, Walter Savage Landor, Sarah Austin, and Robinson.[4] Besides reviews of Kant, C. M. Wieland, Johann Gottfried Herder, Friedrich Gottlieb Klopstock, Johann Wolfgang von

Goethe, Friedrich Schiller, August von Kotzebue, A. W. Schlegel, Johann Gottfried Eichhorn, H. E. G. Paulus, and Johann David Michaelis, Taylor translated Gottfried August Bürger's influential and widely admired "Lenore" (said to have inspired Scott's translation of Goethe's *Götz von Berlichingen* and his first experiments in the ballad form), Gotthold Ephraim Lessings's *Nathan der Weise,* and Goethe's *Iphigenie auf Tauris.* Taylor, who elevated reviewing to new respectability, was admired by his peers for the depth as well as the breadth of his learning, as the following comment by Hazlitt makes clear: "The style of philosophical criticism, which has been the boast of the *Edinburgh Review,* was first introduced into the *Monthly Review* about the year 1796, in a series of articles by Mr. William Taylor, of Norwich."[5] In addition to his innovations in reviewing, which anticipated the publication of long reviews in the *Edinburgh Review,* Taylor was also a forerunner of that class of professional reviewers who were able to support themselves solely by their writing.[6]

Yet, for all his importance as a literary innovator and early cultural intermediary, the opinions that fill Taylor's reviews have not stood the test of time. Quixotically, he remained all his life convinced that Wieland and Kotzebue, rather than Goethe and the German Romantics, represented the dominant tendency in German literature. Deemed utterly "preposterous" by George Saintsbury, the great Edwardian arbiter of taste, because they were already outdated when they appeared in a 1828–1830 collected edition, Taylor's articles on German thought and literature elicited the "good-humoured, judicious censure" in the review that launched Carlyle's career as a critic.[7]

Taylor's reaction to Kant consistently reflects the anachronistic tendency that detracts from his literary criticism in general. In a review of the German émigré scholar A. F. M. Willich's *Elements of the Critical Philosophy* (1798), one of the earliest systematic efforts to transmit Kant to Britain, he expresses profound skepticism toward ideas that seem superficially so foreign to the British philosophical tradition. Typically shallow is the observation that Kant "is nearly seventy-five years old: a singular period of life for the construction of a new system of philosophy!"[8] Taylor finds justification for his qualms in the hero-worship of Kant's German admirers: "His scholars, like the disciples of Plotinus, seem only in doubt whether to revere him as a sage or to worship him as a divinity; from the angelic and seraphic doctors of their forefathers, they turn with awe to this incarnate logos; and they want only the trumpet of Eloa to sound his name from sun to sun."[9] With characteristic British skepticism Taylor condemns the specialized vocabulary that accompanies Kant's "syllogizing" method because it permits "dialectic obscurity to pass for intellectual subtlety." Even the assistance provided by Willich's glossary of the critical philosophy is rejected because "these explanations have not rendered it much more intelligible."[10]

As a proponent of xenophobic cultural nationalism, Taylor demonizes Kant as a subversive outsider, whose teachings threaten to "overshadow the modern world" with "the same obfuscation of the public mind, which, by a similar process, the Platonists of Alexandria [the Sophists] superinduced on the antient [sic]."[11] Consonant with the editorial position of the *Anti-Jacobin Review* toward continental, especially German, thought, Taylor blames the post-1789 "general dissolution of morals" in France on the acceptance of Kant's "cloudy phraseology which may intercept from below the war-whoop of impiety, and from above the evulgation of infidelity." At home and abroad Kant's disciples have adopted this system as a "cypher of illuminism," a codeword for Jesuitical sophistication, that is, a method of conducting "public discussions of the most critical nature . . . without alarming the prejudices of the people or exciting the precautions of the magistrate." In addition, Taylor implies that there are parallels between Kant and "the philosophers of the Lyceum," both of whom seek to "entomb with reasonings the reason of the modern world."[12]

The vehemence of Taylor's animus against Kant was not out of the ordinary for his time. Indeed, it is typical of older professional critics, whose taste as well as political, religious, and other cultural allegiances were formed during the Enlightenment, to espouse a nationalistic and conservative ideology. But even in younger critics usually associated with Romanticism, such as Coleridge, Hazlitt, and De Quincey, hostility to German culture, whether embodied in Goethe or Kant, is not uncommon and yet, it is surprising, given that the literary apprenticeship of many leading romantic writers consisted of emulating, appropriating, and translating German literature and thought. A short list of these translators includes: Coleridge, Austin, Lord Byron, Percy Bysshe Shelley, Carlyle, and Scott. According to Leslie Stephen's entry on Scott in the *Dictionary of National Biography*, the translation of *Götz von Berlichingen* was published with the help of M. G. "Monk" Lewis, another English "Germanico," who took an active part in translating and adapting German plays for the London stage.[13] Without taking sides in the debate over Coleridge's alleged plagiarisms of Kant, Johann Gottlieb Fichte, Schiller and F. W. J. Schelling, it is nonetheless clear that, without the corroboration he found in German sources for his own aesthetic, religious, and metaphysical principles, British Romanticism would have "remained dumb in matters of the intellect."[14]

Hazlitt and De Quincey were also among those young writers who "Germanized" themselves, and set up shop as critics of German thought. Hazlitt published a long two-part review of Germaine de Staël's *De l'Allemagne*, her monitory appeal to a French audience that, to avoid censorship in Paris, was first published by John Murray in 1813. In harmony with Coleridge's recommendation of Kant as an antidote to eighteenth-century empiricism, Hazlitt describes the critical philosophy as a "formal and elaborate antithesis" to John Locke. Convinced of his superior grasp of Kant, Hazlitt notes that "the harmony of his style and the graces of her exposition" conceal "the abruptness of the reasoning."[15] In a subsequent review of Coleridge's *Biographia*, Hazlitt employs crudely dismissive rhetoric, an arrow drawn from the quiver of the *Anti-Jacobin* reviewers, to dismiss Kant's system as "the most wilful and monstrous absurdity that was ever invented."[16]

How is one to account for such a rash opinion that hardly seems worthy of Hazlitt's pen? Wellek is persuaded that Hazlitt's piece embodies "much more than a declaration of antipathy against technicalities the importance of which he did not grasp, but rather a grotesque example of misunderstanding which scarcely can be paralleled from the literature of the time."[17] A survey of contemporary critiques of Kant reveals that Wellek's confidence that this is an exception is misplaced. Indeed, few of Hazlitt's contemporaries would be spared the same embarrassment. It would be a mistake, for instance, to expect a lack of distortion in De Quincey's writings on Kant, since he established a track record for willful or unintentional misunderstanding in his reviews of books by German authors. Quick to exploit the public's growing fascination with German literature, which he considered "beyond all question . . . the wealthiest in the world," his contributions to a critique of German culture are nonetheless tinged with hostility.[18] In addition to a wrongheaded review of Carlyle's translation of *Wilhelm Meister's Apprenticeship*, he published some dreadfully inaccurate translations from the writings of Jean Paul Richter (which contrast with Carlyle's much more skillful versions of "Quintus Fixlein" and "Feldprediger Schmelzle"), a mean-spirited attack on Goethe's character (in which he adopts the moralizing tone of the *Anti-Jacobin Review*), a few fragmentary translations of Kant, and related critical-philosophical essays, including the first history of Kant's reception in Britain.[19]

In this piece, "Letter V: On the English Notices of Kant," the last installment in a series of "Letters to a Young Man whose Education has been Neglected," De Quincey expresses concern that the "gross misrepresentations" of other critics and intermediaries, including Willich, Coleridge, Dugald Stewart, and Staël, may have misled his addressee and undermined his advice "to take special notice of German literature, as a literature of knowledge, not of power." De Quincey considers it his "business to point out any facts which may tend to disarm the authority of these writers, just so far as to replace you in the situation of a neutral and unprejudiced student."[20] What follows, however, is not anything like an authoritative interpretation of Kant's thought, but merely a litany of errors, complaints, and disappointments. Dugald Stewart, who represented the academic establishment from which De Quincey, the ink-stained wretch, felt alienated, is reprimanded for his total neglect of Kant's importance to modern philosophy. As for the synopsis of Kant's ideas in De l'Allemagne, De Quincey reiterates the charge that Staël's penchant for simplification "has contrived to translate his philosophy into a sense which leaves it tolerably easy to apprehend; but unfortunately at the expense of all definite purpose, application, or philosophic meaning."[21] By contrast, Coleridge is criticized for insufficient clarity in chapter 9 of the Biographia: "by expounding the oracle in words of more Delphic obscurity than the German original could have presented to the immaturest student."[22] Because of a tendency to intertwine the thoughts of others in the fiber of his own intellect such a result is to be expected from him: "Mr. Coleridge's mind . . . never gives back anything as it receives it." De Quincey concludes that Coleridge "has unfortunately too little talent for teaching or communicating any sort of knowledge" and that "this indocility of mind greatly unfits a man to be the faithful expounder of a philosophical system."[23] There is no denying the accuracy of these charges. The vehemence of De Quincey's assault on Coleridge is motivated in part by disillusionment. Despite a supposedly more profound understanding of German culture than any of his contemporaries, Coleridge proved a less than reliable intermediary. Yet, in light of his criticisms of others, it is only fair to examine De Quincey's most extensive commentary on Kant.

Concerning a later article, "German Studies and Kant in particular" (Tait's Magazine, June 1836), Wellek insists that it reflects "a gross misunderstanding of the purpose of the Kantian philosophy" and a "certain fundamental insincerity in his relation to Kant." Despite evidence that he studied Kant in the original and therefore could claim an intimacy with German culture unmatched by his contemporaries, "this experience," Wellek suggests, "however actual and indisputable, remained only skin-deep, the expression of a mood, of a moment's despair and tedium." Unlike Coleridge and Carlyle, whose writings reflect genuine affinity with idealist philosophy, De Quincey has "no deeper relation to philosophical thought."[24]

Indeed, for an accurate, sympathetic contemporary analysis of Kant, one must turn to a figure whose writings on Kant predate those of

Coleridge, Hazlitt, and De Quincey. Celebrated in the literary *salons* of nineteenth-century Europe as the friend of Goethe, Coleridge, and William Blake, Henry Crabb Robinson is remembered, along with Benjamin Robert Haydon, as one of the most important contemporary chroniclers of the Romantic Age. Self-effacing in a way that focuses attention on his subjects, Robinson inverts the usual function of literary memoirs (by which, according to Goethe, one always learns more about the writer himself than any of his experiences), and provides greater scope for the reader to identify with the remarkable men and women whom he encountered over a long life devoted to literature.

Robinson was, however, not satisfied with his myriad activities as diarist, lawyer, traveler, patron of poets and artists, and ardent Germanophile. In addition to these credentials, he also sought to make his mark as a critic. Among the first to recognize the importance of Goethe's lyric and epigrammic poems, he published a series of three "Letters on the Philosophy of Kant."[25] These appeared from August 1802 to May 1803 in the *Monthly Register and Encyclopedian Magazine*, an upstart London journal designed to satisfy the increasing popular demand for news of cultural developments on the Continent. Familiar in tone, these epistolary essays were written during an extended period of residence in Jena and Weimar, where, thanks to a letter of introduction from William Taylor and his own gregarious nature, he got on well with the luminaries attached to the court of Grand Duke Carl August.

While it is true that many pilgrims from Britain and America flocked to Weimar, including Taylor, Lewis, R. P. Gillies, Edward Everett, George Bancroft, George Ticknor, Henry Wadsworth Longfellow and William Makepeace Thackeray, few visitors were treated with the high regard that Robinson enjoyed in the Goethe household. But this is just one of the advantages that he enjoyed over another Englishman who had taken up residence in nearby Goslar and attended lectures in Göttingen not long before this time. Exaggerating what was accomplished during his 1798–1799 residence in Germany in order to bolster his credentials as a mediator of German culture, is a standard feature of Coleridge scholarship. And while it is true that he acquired some German, read in the renowned Göttingen University Library, and heard lectures by leading scholars, including the great philologist Christian Gottlob Heyne, Coleridge's visit, as an intellectually formative phase in his life, pales beside Robinson's. In contrast to Coleridge's marginal existence in Göttingen, Robinson enrolled as a fully matriculated student at the University of Jena, learned to speak German with near-native fluency, and counted among his friends many leading figures, including Schelling, Goethe, Schiller, A. W. Schlegel, Wieland, and the Brentanos—Christian, Bettine, and Clemens. Indeed, Robinson's relationship with Schelling, who vied with Fichte and Arthur Schopen-hauer as Kant's successor in German philosophy, gave him unrivalled credentials as an elucidator of the Kantian system and helped him avoid the mistakes of Hazlitt, De Quincey, and Coleridge.

Due, however, to the vagaries of the publishing world, Robinson was prevented from exploiting his advantages as an intermediary between Britain and Germany. In the summer of 1803, the *Monthly Register* was taken over by a new editor-publisher and plans for more letters on Kant, along with a new series of letters on Goethe, were cancelled. This turn of events dealt a blow to the aspiring critic. In later years, when asked about his essays on German culture he replied with characteristic modesty that they "attracted no notice and did not deserve any."[26] The frustration of his literary ambitions could only have been intensified by his association with so many successful writers at home and on the Continent. But posterity has been kinder to this literary stepchild than its parent.

Wellek was the first twentieth-century critic to treat Robinson's "Letters on the Philosophy of Kant" as more than mere historical oddities: "They are extraordinarily accurate and vivid. They grasp the central problem of Kant's epistemology and try to give an interpretation of Kant's teaching which is by no means altogether usual and hackneyed today."[27] Robinson's use of the epistolary mode suggest parallels with Paul's evangelizing letters to the unconverted Hellenes. It is, in fact, his proselytizing that sets Robinson's epistles on Kant apart from the minor eighteenth-century genre exemplified by Charles-Louis Montesquieu's *Les Lettres Persanes* (1721) and Oliver Goldsmith's *Citizen of the World* (1762). Not interested in making satirical or moral comparisons between cultures or in recording impressions while abroad—Coleridge's observations in *Satyrane's Letters* (1798–1799) are entirely of the latter type—Robinson seeks instead to make converts to the foreign "creed." His purpose is similar to Staël's in *De l'Allemagne*: they both present the German ideology, headed by Kant's teachings, with its organic conception of mind and universe and its privileging of intuition and reason (*Vernunft*) over logic and the understanding (*Verstand*), as necessary therapy for their respective ailing national psyches.

This part of Robinson's discussion anticipates Carlyle's com-mendation of German thought and literature as a modern spiritual anodyne. According to Carlyle, "the higher literature of Germany . . . that wide-spreading, deep-whirling vortex of Kantism, so soon metamorphosed into Fichteism, and then as Hegelism, and Cousinism," contained "a new revelation of the Godlike." Carlyle saw in the growing interest in German thought a way of countering the leading tendencies of the age, "Pyrrhonism and Materialism," and making "Faith in

Religion" once again "possible and inevitable for the scientific mind."[28] Robinson considers it significant that German culture should have produced, simultaneously, "a great poet and a great philosopher."[29] Indeed, the appearance of Kant and Goethe together at the end of the eighteenth century embodies the reconciliation of poetry and philosophy. This observation was corroborated sixty-five years later as Robinson made the final entry in his journal. On January 1867, Robinson recorded his impressions of Matthew Arnold's essay, "On the Function of Criticism at the Present Time." Echoing Robinson's first letter in the series, Arnold writes that "the creation of a modern poet, to be worth much, implies a great critical effort behind it; else' it would be a comparatively poor, barren affair."[30] Reminiscent of Carlyle some thirty-five years before, who had urged readers of *Sartor Resartus* to "Close thy Byron; open thy Goethe," Arnold argues that Goethe's achievement as a poet will endure longer than Byron's because "Goethe's was nourished by a great critical effort providing the true materials for it, and Byron's was not."[31] Robinson notes his agreement with Arnold that the basis for Germany's modern cultural renaissance is precisely this reciprocal, mutually beneficial relationship between the imaginative and the critical faculties.[32]

Robinson's first letter (August 1802) opens with an account of the vertiginous effects of Kant's teaching on the mind of the author. His outlook, formed by Locke, Hartley, and the British empirical tradition, functions as representative of the romantic generation. The discovery of Kant shattered these enlightenment idols, leaving him with "no compass to guide me." Indeed, this letter reenacts the drama of his own conversion experience and the resulting crisis of intellectual disinheritance:

> I was, in the true sense of the word CONFOUNDED. In the critical school I found the first principles of Locke's philosophy, not refuted at length, but dispatched with insolent brevity, as too grossly false to require a minute refutation; my favorite authors not unknown, but known and almost despised; my own habit of thinking represented as the utmost reproach to a rational being; a sort of Esau-like relinquishing of our birth-right, the right to reason and determine.[33]

Although initially inclined to react with hostility to the "transcendental speculation" of Kant, he admits to having undergone a complete change of heart following long and "exclusive study." Thus, the "Letters on the Philosophy of Kant" should be read partly as intellectual autobiography and partly as a response to charges in the popular press that Kant and his followers had set out to destroy religion. Robinson asserts that, in contrast to the scepticism of enlightenment philosophers, Kant's teachings are not actually incompatible with religion. In a phrase borrowed from Goethe—and recycled in *Sartor Resartus* by Carlyle thirty years later—he derides such philosophical scepticism as "the *sans-*culottism of philosophy" and credits Kant with having revealed that systems based on "materialism and necessity" are in fact indistinguishable from "atheism."[34] Kant's method of disarming scepticism proceeds by "showing the precise limits of knowledge and the extent and degree of belief which we are compelled to give to notions that are susceptible of certain evidence." While thus affirming the power of man's intellect, Kant does not, however, undermine faith in a supreme deity. On the contrary, he "affirms the right, and even necessity of pure reason, of the belief in God and a future state; he asserts free will, repels the dogmatic notion of materialism, and indignantly rejects the notion of self-love as the basis of moral sentiment."[35]

While David Hume's scepticism, Robinson points out, is genuine, Kant only "seems to be hypersceptical"; he actually seeks to effect "a sort of peace and union" between philosophy and religion. Kant's attack on "scepticism by destroying dogmatism which generated it," a method which "cannot but terrify the orthodox," greatly appealed to Robinson, who was brought up in a dissenting household and was, before he left for Germany, a follower of William Godwin.[36] Therefore, somewhat paradoxically, Kant's "hyperscepticism" reveals that faith "is not merely a wish or a hope, but a confidence as strong and irresistable as knowledge itself." The "certainty" of faith, then, remains unchanged, but "the grounds of faith are reversed." Contrary to the popular contemporary caricature of Kant as "a reviewer of useless speculation, and . . . a descendent of the old schoolmen," he is actually "the direst foe of the metaphysicians, and possesses nothing of the schoolmen but their acuteness and profundity."[37]

As if in response to Taylor's paranoid anti-Catholic ravings in the *Monthly Review*, Robinson rejects any parallels between Kant and the "illuminati of the French atheists," including "that arch descendent of Loyola, the Ex-Jesuit Baruel."[38] Yet, in so hastily dismissing claims that Kant bears some responsibility for loosening the moorings of faith in what Carlyle called the "Atheistic Century," Robinson seems blind to the metamorphosis that Kant undergoes in his interpretation.[39] If only he had been more sensitive to the potentially devastating inferences to be drawn from Kant's teachings, he might have not so easily maintained his sangfroid in a controversy that roused F. H. Jacobi and Søren Kierkegaard to defend the prerogatives of faith against the *Zeitgeist*.

Robinson's views are generally in accord with Coleridge's analysis of British Associationism (while it is possible that Coleridge read the

"Letters on the Philosophy of Kant" in the *Monthly Register*, his review of British Associationism in the *Biographia* was certainly derived in part from J. G. E. Maass's *Versuch über die Einbildungskraft*), but rather than offering parallels to specific features of Coleridge's argument, it is the moral vision underlying Robinson's interpretation of Kant's teachings that anticipates the critique of the "consequences of the Hartleian Theory" in Chapter 7 of the *Biographia*. His polarization of German idealism and French materialism is part of the stock-in-trade of romantic ideology and the rhetoric he uses to demonize French thought is remarkably Carlylean in its vehemence: "The German school is one great antithesis to the French school. . . . This is a coupling of life and death together: between the French and the German schools there can be no peace, it is a war of extermination." Kant and German philosophy provide an "antidote" to "Locke full-grown" and the corrupt influence of materialism on ethics, religion, and art. In "this quintessence of French philosophy" only "the dregs of life are left, nothing but conscious organization and living mechanism."[40]

This is strikingly reminiscent of Staël's treatment of the opposition between French and German culture. She insists that the two nations occupy "two ends of the moral chain, because the former considers external objects the prime mover of all ideas, and the latter considers ideas the prime mover of all sense impressions. These two nations nevertheless enjoy rather good social relations, but there are none more opposed in their literary and philosophical systems."[41] Of course, any parallels with Staël are not entirely coincidental. August Wilhelm Schlegel, who traveled for a time as a member of Staël's entourage, was primarily responsible for her schooling in German thought and literature. But it is also true that Robinson, as a student of Schelling and as a foreigner, who had successfully come to grips with the most difficult aspects of German philosophy, was brought in by a mutual acquaintance, Carl August Böttiger, to serve as her special tutor.[42] In subsequent years, Robinson was convinced that proof of their collaboration is visible in the pages of *De l'Allemagne*. It is indeed ironic that Robinson, a British commoner and a Dissenter at that, should have been chosen to tutor Staël, a French aristocrat, whose work as a cultural intermediary exerted tremendous influence in Britain and the United States, not to mention France and Germany, whose culture she mediated for all the others. The mediation of a mediation (Robinson's) that in turn stimulated the efforts of other intermediaries, including Carlyle, Austin, Margaret Fuller, Ralph Waldo Emerson, George Eliot, and G. H. Lewes, *De l'Allemagne* supports the notion that romantic culture is the result of cultural interaction and the interplay of literary intermediaries in a cosmopolitan context.

Disguised as a letter from a British student in Jena to a friend back home, the second letter (November 1802) seems derived from Robinson's correspondence with his brother Thomas, to whom most of his private letters from Germany were sent. The main interest in this letter focuses on a comparison of the respective merits of Kant's and Locke's philosophical systems. Responding to accusations that he favored a system of "lyrical metaphysics," the student responds by offering a critique of materialism that is generically "romantic":

> And I pity you for having no metaphysics, only a mere physics. It is the essence of the sensible philosophy to degrade the mind into a necessarily passive machine. Locke, indeed, avoided this reproach by incurring a greater inconsistency: but the more celebrated of his followers have raised on his principles a system, according to which there can be neither poetry, religion, nor love.[43]

This invocation of the holy trinity of German Romanticism—poetry, religion, and love—is a reminder to us that Robinson attended Schelling's lectures in Jena. Schelling, as Wellek explains, "extolled poetry to be the truest revelation of the Absolute, it justified religion by philosophy and it found a new meaning for the mystery of love."[44] Although at times it seems that Robinson is less interested in the actual basis for Kant's notoriety—his revolutionary epistemology—he is so determined to remove the stigma of mysticism from German thought that he defends Kant's sometimes difficult technical vocabulary. Robinson's tolerance of jargon contrasts sharply with Taylor's dismissal: "In the glorious consciousness that his edifice would be lasting, he did not spare the trouble of forming an adequate scaffolding: he had thoughts which had never been thought before; and his new coin required a new stamp."[45]

From a defense of Kantian terminology Robinson moves to the question of whether a priori knowledge (metaphysics) is superior to a posteriori evidence (physics). He offers a commonplace paradox that illustrates how even the sceptical British mind has accommodated itself to the a priori: mathematics, the cornerstone of the experimental sciences, is actually "grounded on positions experimentally impossible." This paradox confirms that ideas are anterior to sense, since "the intellect or reason can think what the sense cannot behold."[46] In an actual letter to his brother, Robinson reinforces this point by comparing the subjective basis of knowledge to a magic lantern:

> In order to show the figures [projected by the lantern] there must be a bright spot on the wall, upon which the coloured figures are to be

exhibited. Without figures, the luminous spot is an empty nothing, like the human mind till it has objects of sense. But without the spot the figures would be invisible, as without an *a priori* capacity to receive impressions we could have none.[47]

The origin of knowledge as representation in the perceiving subject establishes the possibility of synthetic judgments and requires that the model of the mind based wholly on empiricism must be altered. Here Robinson's position coincides with one of the chief principles common to both British and German Romanticism, namely, that "the mind of man is essentially active, not the mere recipient of impressions."[48] The ultimate "basis of truth" is thus not confined to experimental science, but is found in metaphysics and its a priori conceptions, which are seen as "the essential laws of mind." By appealing to another proposition derived from mathematics, Robinson seeks to clarify the distinction between analytical and synthetic judgments and seeks to prove that to achieve any kind of result one must resort to synthetic judgments, for which there are, however, no proofs available in the world of experience:

> Beyond all doubt—analyze $2 + 2$ as long as you please; the result can never be otherwise than $2 + 2 = 2 + 2$; that the result is 4 is a synthesis of reason, for 4 does not lie in $2 + 2$, though we necessarily think so, for we confound our acquired synthetical knowledge with what lies in the simplest subjects.[49]

Consistent with the position outlined in this letter to his brother, Robinson seeks to convert the reader to his view that Kant's "Criticism of Pure Reason" provides one with a means of determining how "knowledge, *a priori*" arises out of the faculty of reason, what the extent of this knowledge is, and how to distinguish between "mere objects of experience" and "supersensible" objects. In case British readers object that all this is foreign mumbo jumbo, Robinson's fictional proselytizer notes that immediately as one seeks to ground the possibility of knowing upon "a system of *a priori* conceptions," one becomes engaged in solving the "sublime" problems of "the transcendental philosophy."

Robinson believes that Kant's epistemology has opened a new world of certainty to the notice of humankind. Unlike the contingent forms of certainty provided by empiricism, Kant's teaching offers a measure of certainty unavailable to "the school of Locke," which mistakenly "degrades rational truths to matters of fact: and Hume affirmed the truth, that facts afford no certainty, only probability."[50] By citing Hume, Robinson invokes the all-important affinity between Kant and British thought. (Indeed, among Kant's followers, Schopenhauer regarded Hume so highly that he learned English with the intention of translating *An Enquiry Concerning Human Understanding*.) In this light, the transcendental philosophy treated with such hostility by Taylor, Hazlitt, and De Quincey can be seen as the consummation of native British scepticism, only deepened and systematized by Kant.

Of the three letters published in the series, the third (April 1803) contains the most numerous examples and the most polished argument. Robinson begins by recapitulating the main issue of the previous letter: the proposition that there is "something in our knowledge which is not experimental." He insists that even in cases where the mind is the object of its own knowledge and thus becomes simultaneously subject and object, "it does not lose the priority of its nature." To lend support to this argument Robinson appeals to Spinoza, whose work he might easily have discussed with Goethe over dinner: "'*Substantia prior est suis affectionibus*': the substance is prior to the affections; the organ, to the sense; the basis, to the structure."[51] This is also the position of Fichte and Schelling. The issues that dominate an unpublished fourth letter—the status of time and space according to Kant and the ontological status of objects of subjective knowledge—are discussed next. Robinson defends Kant's assertion that the priority of the mind is demonstrated by "the nature of things" and time. Citing Fichte's refutation of Gottfried Wilhelm Leibniz, he insists that there are concepts, such as "the one, the same, cause," that do indeed enjoy independence from consciousness. As Robinson interprets Kant,

> the mind itself could not exist without external objects, which furnish us with the matter of experience, and are collectively the world. And when we consider the same representations in reference to the necessity of external objects they are *a posteriori*: but this distinction itself is purely logical or ideal.

In closing his argument, Robinson appeals directly to Kant, who describes this antithesis as the opposition of "matter (the a posteriori) and form (the a priori) in our representations."[52] Robinson's interpretation is at odds with Schopenhauer's insistence that it was Kant's "erster Fehler" (first mistake) that he failed to acknowledge the irrefragable priority of the subjective knower. "The world," Schopenhauer writes, "is my representation. . . . Therefore no truth is more certain, more independent of all others and less in need of proof than this, namely, that everything exists for knowledge, and hence the whole of this world, is only object in relation to the subject, perception of the perceiver, in a word, representation."[53]

There are no references to Schopenhauer in Robinson's volu-minous diaries or correspondence, even though Schopenhauer, along with Fichte and Schelling, Robinson's teacher, was Kant's leading follower, and no thinker of the time was more adamant in laying claim to Kant's mantle than Schopenhauer.[54] Robinson's "Letters on the Philosophy of Kant" lack Schopenhauer's brilliance and stylistic verve, but these modest little pieces are far superior to the philosophical criticism of Taylor, Hazlitt, and De Quincey, and they embody the most important attempt in the early Romantic Age to offer an accurate interpretation of Kant's "peculiar logical method." Published more than a decade before Coleridge's *Biographia Literaria* and more than two decades before Carlyle's German criticism, Robinson's epistolary essays lay the foundation for Kant's reception in Britain. Almost two centuries after their appearance in the *Monthly Register*, the sense of intellectual discovery and conviction that they convey remains fresh, as does the enthusiasm and missionary zeal with which a young Dissenter announced the "Copernican Revolution" in modern European philosophy that was set in motion by the writings of Kant.

NOTES

* Johann Peter Eckermann, *Gespräche mit Goethe*, April 11, 1827: "I asked Goethe which of the new philosophers he thought the best. 'Kant,' he said, 'beyond a doubt. He is the one whose doctrines still continue to work, and have penetrated most deeply into our German civilization. He has influenced even you, although you have never read him; now you need him no longer, for what he could give you you possess already.'" Unless otherwise noted, all translations are mine.

1. Important examples of work in this tradition include the following: René Wellek, *Confrontations* (Princeton, N.J.: Princeton University Press, 1965); Norman Fruman, *Coleridge, the Damaged Archangel* (New York: George Braziller, 1971); Lilian R. Furst, *The Contours of European Romanticism* (London: Macmillan, 1979); Geoffrey Hartman, *Criticism in the Wilderness* (New Haven, Conn.: Yale University Press, 1980); Rosemary Ashton, *The German Idea* (Cambridge: Cambridge University Press, 1980); James Engell, *The Creative Imagination* (Cambridge, Mass.: Harvard University Press, 1981); Mark Kipperman, *Beyond Enchantment* (Philadephia: University of Pennsylvania Press, 1986); and Peter Edgerly Firchow, *The Death of the German Cousin* (London and Toronto: Associated University Presses, 1986).

2. For an illuminating discussion of the relationship between the reception of German culture in Britain and the rise of review criticism, readers should consult John Boening's "Pioneers and Precedents: The 'Importation of German' and the Emergence of Periodical Criticism in England," *Internationales Archiv für Sozialgeschichte der deutschen Literatur* (1982): 65–86.

3. In addition to Boening's article, the best previous discussion of Taylor's involvement with German culture is found in Merton A. Christensen, "Taylor of Norwich and the Higher Criticism," *Journal of the History of Ideas* 20: 179–94. A complete list of Taylor's articles and reviews is found in *A Memoir of the Life and Writings of the Late William Taylor of Norwich*, edited by J. W. Robberds (London: John Murray, 1843).

4. For a description of Taylor's impact on his younger contemporaries, see *The Correspondence of Henry Crabb Robinson with the Wordsworth Circle*, edited by Edith J. Morley, vol. 1 (Oxford: Clarendon Press, 1927), p. 497.

5. "Mr. Jeffrey," *The Complete Works of William Hazlitt*, edited by P. P. Howe (1930), 11: 127; cited by James M. Good, "William Taylor, Robert Southey, and the Word 'Autobiography'," *The Wordsworth Circle* 12 (Spring 1981): 2.

6. For the evolution of periodical criticism in the eighteenth century, see John Clive, *Scotch Reviewers: The Edinburgh Review, 1802–1815* (Cambridge, Mass.: Havard University Press, 1957); Derek Roper, *Reviewing before the Edinburgh, 1788–1802* (Newark: University of Delaware Press, 1978); and James G. Basker, *Tobias Smollett: Critic and Journalist* (Newark: University of Delaware Press, 1988).

7. George Saintsbury, *A History of Criticism and Literary Taste in Europe*, vol. 3 (Edinburgh and London: William Blackwood and Sons, 1900–1904), p. 497.

8. *Monthly Review*, 28: 62.

9. Ibid.

10. Ibid., p. 63.

11. Ibid., pp. 64–65.

12. Ibid., p. 65.

13. *Monthly Review*, 11: 1072. Stephen also describes what must have been one of the great formative influences of Lewis's youth: "In the summer of 1792, he went to Weimar where he was introduced to Goethe. . . . His taste for German literature either took him to Weimar or was acquired there. In any case he became a good German scholar" (1071).

14. Wellek, *Immanuel Kant in England* (Princeton, N.J.: Princeton University Press, 1930), p. 139.

15. "Mme de Staël's Account of German Philosophy and Literature," *Morning Chronicle* February 3 and 17; March 3, and April 8, 1814). This formula would, with only slight alterations, be appropriated by Carlyle to express his animus against enlightenment utilitarianism. In Carlyle's admittedly idiosyncratic interpretation Kant's thought forms the "centre round which" German culture "turns." It has made "a Faith in Religion . . . again possible and inevitable for the scientific mind," and "for him that can read it, the beginning of a new revelation of the Godlike" ("Characteristics," *The Centenary Edition of the Works of Thomas Carlyle*, edited by H. D. Traill, vol. 26 (London: Chapman and Hall, 1896–1899), p. 41.

16. *Edinburgh Review* 28 (August 1817): 488.

17. Wellek, *Immanuel Kant*, p. 169.

18. David Masson, ed., *The Collected Writings of Thomas De Quincey*, vol. 11 (London: A. C. Black, 1897), p. 221.

19. *London Magazine* (July 1823), reprinted in *The Collected Writings of Thomas De Quincey*, 10: 64ff: "On the English Notices of Kant."

20. Masson, ed., *The Collected Writings of Thomas De Quincey*, 10: 65.

21. Masson, ed., *The Collected Writings of Thomas De Quincey*, 10: 72.

22. Masson, ed., *The Collected Writings of Thomas De Quincey*, 10: 77.

23. Ibid., 10: 77.

24. Wellek, *Immanuel Kant*, p. 180.

25. See Diana Behler, "Henry Crabb Robinson as a Mediator of Early German Romanticism to England," *Arcadia* 12 (1977): 117–55, and my article, "Henry Crabb Robinson's 1802–03 Translations of Goethe's Lyric Poems and Epigrams," in *Michigan Germanic Studies* 19:1 (Spring 1993), pp. 18–45.

26. Thomas Sadler, ed., *Diary, Reminiscences and Correspondence of Henry Crabb Robinson*, vol. I (London: Macmillan, 1872), p. 87.

27. Wellek, *Immanuel Kant*, p. 159.

28. *Centenary Edition of Works of Thomas Carlyle*, 26: 41.

29. "Letters on the Philosophy of Kant, No. 1. Introductory," *Monthly Register and Encyclopedian Magazine* (August 1802): 402. Hereafter cited as Letter I.

30. Matthew Arnold, *Lectures and Essays in Criticism*, edited by R. H. Super vol. 2 (Ann Arbor: University of Michigan Press, 1962), p. 261–62.

31. Arnold, *Lectures and Essays in Criticism*, II: 262.

32. Of relevance here is Saintsbury's inversion of Goethe's comment that his entire oeuvre consisted of "fragments of a great confession": "the whole of Goethe's work . . . may be said to be a record of his criticism" (III: 360–61).

33. Letter I: 411.

34. Ibid.

35. Robinson, *Diary, Reminiscences*, I: 74. Robinson's remarks call to mind the essential arguments of Adam Smith's *Theory of Moral Sentiments* (1759), and Hazlitt's *Essay on the Principles of Human Action* (1805), in which sympathy rather than self-interest is demonstrated as the prime motive for human actions.

36. Letter I: 416.

37. Letter I: 412.

38. Letter I: 413.

39. Thomas Carlyle, *Sartor Resartus* (Oxford: Oxford University Press, 1987), p. 140.

40. Letter I, 413.

41. Germaine de Staël, *De l'Allemagne*, vol. I (Paris: Garnier-Flammarion, 1968), pp. 46–47: "deux extrémités de la chaîne morale, puisque les uns considèrent les objets extérieurs comme le mobile de toutes les idées, et les autres, les idées comme le mobile de toutes les impressions. Ces deux nations cependant s'accordent assez bien sous les rapports sociaux; mais il n'en est point de plus opposées dans leur system littéraire et philosophique." Translation by April Alliston.

42. Robinson recalls his role in Staël's philosophical education in this way: "she had a laudable anxiety to obtain a knowledge of the best German authors; and for this reason she sought my society, and I was not unwilling to be made use of by her" (Robinson, *Diary, Reminiscences*, I: 93). See also pp. 92–97 for Robinson's insider's account of Staël's sojourn in Weimar.

43. Letter II (November 1802): 7.

44. Wellek, *Immanuel Kant*, 146.

45. Letter II: 8.

46. Letter II: 11.

47. Robinson, *Diary, Reminiscences*, I: 40.

48. Letter II: 11.

49. Letter II: 12.

50. Ibid.

51. Letter III (April 1803): 485.

52. Ibid.

53. Arthur Schopenhauer, *Die Welt als Wille und Vorstellung*, vol. I (Munich and Vienna: Carl Hanser Verlag, 1977), I, Par. i, 32: "Die Welt ist meine Vorstellung . . . Keine Wahrheit ist also gewißer, von allen andern unabhängiger und eines Beweises weniger bedürftig, als diese, daß alles, was für die Erkenntnis da ist, also diese ganze Welt, nur Objekt in Beziehung auf das Subjekt ist, Anschauung des Anschauenden, mit *einem Wort*, Vorstellung."

54. The first published discussion of Schopenhauer in Britain was John Oxenford's long review of the second edition of *Die Welt als Wille und Vorstellung* that appeared in the *Westminster Review* of April 1853. Oxenford writes: "We only wish we could see among the philosophers of modern Germany a writer of equal power, comprehensiveness, ingenuity and erudition, ranged on a side more in harmony with our own feelings and convictions, than that adopted by this misanthropic sage of Frankfort" (407).

11

Marc Katz

Confessions of an Anti-Poet

Kierkegaard's *Either/Or* and the German Romantics

*What seems less the picture of a living person than a
silhouette? And yet, how much it tells us!*

[*Was kann weniger Bild eines ganz lebendigen
Menschen seyn, als ein Schattenriß?
Und wie viel sagt er!*]

—*Lavater,*
Physiognomische Fragmente

Although Søren Kierkegaard began *Either/Or* in Copenhagen, he wrote the bulk of it in an apartment on Gendarme Square in Berlin, where he spent the better part of 1841 escaping the public fallout from his breakup with Regine. As a *Bildungsreise* [journey of education] the trip was unusual, in that he fed off and collected only negative impressions. The newly expanded avenues of pre-revolutionary Berlin seemed to him inhumanly wide. Faust's *Wintergarten,* an elaborate glass exhibition hall to which he was lured by advertisements in the local newspapers, offered "little to see." He heard F. W. J. Schelling speak at the university on the philosophy of revelation, but found his vaunted breakthrough to speculative authenticity unconvincing.[1] The lectures of the Hegelian K. F. Werder displayed the virtuosity of a carnival strong man lifting "paper-maché" weights; while those of Henrik Steffens, one of the last living

227

intimates of the Jena circle and a one-time popularizer of its program in Scandinavia and Northern Europe, sounded vague to the point of senility.[2] Indeed, the city as a whole appeared to him to be living off its dwindling idealist capital: "not only in the realm of commerce," he would later write, "but in the realm of ideas, our age is organizing *ein wirklicher Ausverkauf*" [closing-out sale].[3] Kierkegaard's own sense of belatedness vis-à-vis the German Romantics (above all, Friedrich Schlegel, Ludwig Tieck and E. T. A. Hoffmann) was nothing less than acute, since in his case epigonism was a function not simply of time but place. For years he had chided himself as a provincial and polemicized against Copenhagen as a cultural backwater colonized by German thought. His Berlin *flânerie* only drove the fact of his marginality home, so that while abroad he felt himself to be an illegible, virtually occult figure: "I walk down the 'Unter den Linden' . . . like a silent letter which no one can pronounce."[4]

And yet Kierkegaard did not stroll through Berlin simply to gather material for a pastiche. His literary epigonism—cultivated, exacerbated, and worked up into a virtual technique—was deliberate and seditious, a continuation of his difficult, early efforts to orient himself aesthetically. Much as he had done a few months before in *The Concept of Irony* (1841), Kierkegaard attempts in *Either/Or* to purge himself of the hermeticism of German theory, only this time on German soil, and within fiction itself. His border-crossing offers a literal enactment of Mikhail Bakhtin's cultural dialogic, in which a writer inhabits the conventions of a foreign literature without sacrificing a distancing point of view:

> *Creative understanding* does not renounce itself, its own place in time, its own culture; and it forgets nothing. In order to understand, it is immensely important for the person who understands to be located *outside* the object of his or her creative understanding. . . . For one cannot even really see one's own exterior and comprehend it as a whole, and no mirrors or photographs can help; our real exterior can be seen only by other people, because they are located outside us in space, and because they are *others*.[5]

If a writer simply empathizes with a foreign cultural tradition, the result is merely some form of imitation or hybridization. Retaining the perspective of an outsider, according to Bakhtin, is essential for real cultural dialogue, in that it allows a foreign author to recognize and play with the latent possibilites of a host culture through a "surplus" of vision. As we will see in the course of this essay, Kierkegaard, as an outsider, was able to follow through on the critical premises of two generations of German romantic fiction with a detachment and abandon beyond the reach of the most estranged of contemporary native writers (one of the reasons why he, even more than Heinrich Heine, has proven so consequential in the development of twentieth-century German literature). *Either/Or* is not, as Theodor Adorno maintains,[6] merely a counterfeit of German prose with a thin overlay of polemic, but rather, a simulacrumous whole, executed from a critical distance. Like those nineteenth-century physiognomists who delineated their subjects through the casting and tracing of silhouettes, Kierkegaard physiognomizes German romantic prose by creating a literary shadow art, one that is drawn at second hand, stylized to the point of transparency, and drained of all but a negative trace of substance. Critics have generally tended to attenuate Kierkegaard's radicalized way of seeing, maintaining that if he turns with such heat on romantic impulses in the first part of the book, it is only in order to give them domesticated form in the second. It is the argument of this essay, however, that *Either/Or*'s embrace of the mid-century bourgeois literary idiom is actually a deception from start to finish, and that the book adopts the alternate guises of aestheticism and Biedermeier—what Georg Lukács once described as the twin tactics of late German Romanticism—in order to see through and supersede both. The cultural border Kierkegaard works at is, at the same time, an *historical* cross-roads. Although Adorno maintains that Kierkegaard, in attemping to come free of German influence, ends up retreating even deeper into the nineteenth-century bourgeois "*intérieur*,"[7] it is fairer to say that Kierkegaard actually goes a step further: in *Either/Or* he dissolves the German romantic interior in abstraction, and in the process, leaves behind one of the earliest blueprints of the modernist aesthetic.

Victor Emerita, the pseudonymous editor of Kierkegaard's *Either/Or*, claims to have discovered the vagrant manuscripts that make up the book in the trip-drawer of a second-hand writing desk. Since they were either left anonymous or signed by untraceable pseudonyms, he has divided them into two thematically distinct parts. Each of the contributions for part one illustrates an example of what he generically terms "aesthetic existence" (I: 13). *Either/Or*'s purported editor, Victor Emerita, suggests that the manuscripts, whether anonymous or signed, have likely been written by the single unknown author A., a nameless pseudonym behind the pseudonyms whose collection of aphorisms introduce the book. A. serves in *Either/Or* as paradigmatically totalized aesthete. Quick-witted, dialectically skilled, prone to extravagant mood swings, and above all self-dramatizing, he has the tendency to melodramatic excess one associates with Christian Grabbe, Nikolaus Lenau, or Lord Byron, only *Either/Or* offers internalized melodrama, with A.'s histrionics played out as thought experiments. A. forgoes the autobiographical techniques of amassing detail and linear narrative, and instead lends his self-portrait coherence chiefly through literary analogy. As a self-styled Faustian doubter, "master thief," and reflexive Don Juan void of a center and inherent stability, he embodies that heightened sense of masquerade which Nina Auerbach observes as signaling the epoch of mid-nineteenth-century "hero manufacture."[8] Portraying himself in the form of an unfinished consciousness, A. invariably lets us "catch" him in the act of Gothic self-fabrication: "My care is my baronial castle, which lies like an eagle's nest high on the mountain peak among the clouds. No one can take it by storm. From it I swoop into actuality and seize my prey, but I do not remain there. I bear my booty home, and this booty is a picture I weave into the tapestries at my palace. I then live as one already dead" (I: 42).

The literary program of *Either/Or* is thus worked out as a late variant on that of Friedrich Schlegel's reflexively "hovering" poet from the *Fragmente*, without the belief that through the constant projection and negation of the authorial ego a poetry of poetry can lead to the threshold of the absolute. It is *Transzendentalpoesie* stripped of its moral *telos* and reduced to a technique which, if not quite mechanical, has been sparked and sustained by instrumentalized reason (one of the essays develops a method for staving off boredom comparable to advanced techniques of crop rotation). Where forty years before the programmatic voluptuaries in *Lucinde* had oscillated between pleasure and rumination on pleasure, A. luxuriates exclusively in the latter, his self-awareness potentiated to the degree that the external world goes into eclipse. Method bears both the discursive and the imaginative weight of *Either/Or*, since the book is less a passive reflection of the bourgeois *intérieur* than it is a deliberate account of the process of interiorization. The "still life" Adorno and others see in it (Susan Buck-Morss refers to its "eternally fixed" tableaux)[9] is ultimately nothing but an optical illusion. Kierkegaard's art, closely observed, shows itself to be one of separating gesture from body, and act from entity. To deny this is to deny the book its most fundamental form-giving principle: *kinesis* as consciousness. "What," A. himself asks, "is the most seductive moment? When the glance falters, when the foot hesitates, when the heart trembles, when the eyes drop . . . when the creation sighs, when the voice fails" (I: 436). The transposition of substance into movement is made articulate in *Either/Or* through constant reference to music— snatches of melody, observations on operatic performances, specu- lations on the nature of the musical erotic, and private piano recitals. The manner in which music nullifies space, Hegel observes, is unique: "Specific sensuous material . . . turns to movement, yet so vibrates in itself that every part of the cohering body not only changes place, but also struggles to replace itself in its former position."[10] Likewise, dogs, hunters, trees, and carriages are contained *in abstracto* within the welter of sounds penetrating A.'s rooms from behind the physically palpable barrier of closed shutters and heavy drapery. Once heard, the visible returns, only this time as a coporealized *principle* of perception:

> [In the middle ages], stronger than ever before the sensuous awoke in all its profusion, in all its rapture and exultation, and—just as that hermit in nature, taciturn echo, who never speaks to anyone first or speaks without being asked, derived such great pleasure from the knight's hunting horn and from his melodies of erotic love, from the baying of hounds, from the snorting of horses, that it never wearied of repeating it again and again and finally, as it were, repeated it very softly to itself in order not to forget it—so it was that the whole world on all sides became a reverberating abode for the worldly spirit of sensuousness. (I: 84)

Even in what is generally regarded as the most plastic of A.'s prose pieces, "The Diary of a Seducer," the conventions of a nineteenth-century German novella serve as a background for aesthetic procedure. As a seducer, Johannes is distinguished by his ability to filter experience through the most filigreed capacity for self-representation. As Johannes himself observes, he is an emphatically "Faustian" version of Don Juan. Kierkegaard was not the first to try and link the two legends in attempting to come to terms with the legacy of aesthetic Prometheanism. In "Don Juan und Faust" (1826), Grabbe had alternated scene by scene between what he termed "the absolute transcendental" and "the absolute sensual." Kierkegaard, who knew the melodrama intimately, follows Grabbe's lead and melds the two narratives in the figure of Johannes, his cerebralized seducer. Indeed, in the very act of analogizing himself, Johannes displays his superior style of irradiating the life of the senses with reflection, potentiating them into an abstract, hence "demonic," force in an exaggerated version of the kind of mediated or triangulated desire René Girard has shown to be an essential element of nineteenth-century bourgeois privatization.[11] Johannes's exercise of sexual power is decentered and diffuse. He insinuates himself into the life of the young middle-class Cordelia, first by indifferently crossing her path on her way to church, and later, by befriending her relatives and shadowing her movements through his system of surveillance. Since he wants not only to pique her imagination, but also hold it captive in a state of anticipation, he affects the suggestiveness of a wraith. He begins his account as the epitome of the voyeuristically detached mid-century narrator, fixing his eye on the intricacies of Cordelia's domestic life but for weeks remaining unseen himself. Although his domination of her is not sadistic in any formal sense, it displays and even foregrounds the ascetic discipline which informs all sadistic performance. Johannes does not submit to desire, but mythologizes desire and indeed, mythologizes himself as desire (the real object of the voyeur, Jacques Lacan notes, lies in the voyeuristic gaze itself, and cannot be seen: "the object he sees is nothing but a shadow, a shadow cast on a screen").[12] For her part, Cordelia is ravished not by a corporeal being but by a process of seduction, with Johannes's subjugation of her turning on how successful he is at remaining a liminal presence. The little that actually occurs between them is transformed in his letters to her, where he gives himself over to violent outbursts and passionate verbal displays—all of which are meant to conceal his inviolate capacity for self-control. Hidden behind the rhetoric, this repressive element in Johannes's performance serves as a means of expanding the scope of his private sphere and, through psychic friction, heightening his erotic response.[13]

The unexampled purity of Kierkegaard's virtuoso ideal is most clearly gauged late in the diaries, when Johannes visits Jutland to locate and decorate a oceanside cottage for one of Cordelia's retreats. Although Johannes does not plan on being there to meet her, he leaves precise instructions with his servant on how she should first be shown the premises. Nothing is left to chance; her impressions are choreographed in advance, down to the play of light off the borrowed piano. Cordelia, we are informed, will first enter through the sun room, which is described as having windows three-quarters of the way around. To one side there is a view of a still lagoon and woods, situated so that looking out from the cottage all contours vanish:

> One moves closer to the window—a calm lake hides humbly within the higher surroundings. At the edge there is a boat. It works loose from its moorings, glides over the surface of the lake, rocked on the surface of the lake which is dreaming about the deep dark solitude of the trees, one vanishes in the mysteriousness of the forest. (I: 442)

Across the room, the windows open up to the sea, offering sheer light and a limitlessness horizon. Decorative effects extend to nature: the shimmer is seen from behind the window, framed as a self-consciously romantic vista, a Turner-like view of the abstract sublime. Around the corner and to the back there is a small parlor, furnished by Johannes to resemble Cordelia's mother's, only with everything more atmospheric and exotic: "Matting woven of a special kind of willow covers the floor: in front of the sofa stands a small tea table with a lamp upon it, the mate to the one there at home. . . . On the music holder, the little Swedish melody lies open. The door to the hall is slightly ajar" (I: 442). In expected mid-century fashion, objects are drawn into an interior space and subjectivized into ornament. Yet, there are no static or "eternally fixed" interiors within Kierkegaard's purview. Under his gaze, rooms become mere portals, there to be passed through, and *to be seen* being passed through. A. leads the reader to see how Cordelia will enter, step back, circle around and visually absorb her surroundings. The cottage is thus not simply a station in Johannes's gradual seduction of Cordelia, but this seduction's own three-dimensional analogue. Walking from one room to the other in line with his cues, she will follow the path of her own aesthetic debauch, from enchantment and the piquancy of the poetic, to a domestic order in which she is no longer fully at ease. *Poesis* makes a near airtight conquest—and to drive the point home, Kierkegaard lets the episode dissolve into the purely figural: what Cordelia does once she gets to the cottage, or whether she even arrives in the first place is never revealed. Johannes literally sets a scene, then retreats to his rooms in the city to imagine the playing out of his private theatrical. In *Werther*, Roland Barthes writes, amorous adventures are so thoroughly worked over in the narration that even when described in the present tense they contain a "tone of remembrance."[14] For Johannes, trysts occur neither in the here-and-now, nor the past, but in a hypothetical present: "The illusion is perfect," he writes from his apartment. "She enters the private room, she looks around, she is pleased, of that I am sure" (I: 443). As both the seduced and the seduction are bracketed out, sensuality is sacrificed on the altar of erotic potential (a gesture later refined in Rainer Maria Rilke's notion of objectless, intransitive love), and the ascetic self-denial traditionally used either to impress the beloved or, according to Michel Foucault, heighten one's interiority, enters the realm of pure thought. Even when Johannes finally has Cordelia in the flesh, *in mente* he is absent: "How Cordelia preoccupies me! And yet at the time will soon be over. I already hear, as it were, the rooster crowing in the distance. Perhaps she hears it too. But she believes it is heralding the morning" (I: 435).

Yet, at the same time *Either/Or* absolutizes the idea of German romantic potency, it also draws it to a dialectical turning point. Like the seducer, the "authentic" poet assumes prolonged interests to be an inherent challenge to his status as a creator *ex nihilo*. In order to keep his creative dynamism as self-supporting as possible, A. gathers momentum from a restless succession of tropes, a poetic calculus in which the imagination is determined exclusively by function. For the *Frühromantiker* self-destruction and self-creation had been a necessary concomitant of a poet's autonomy, and therefore axiomatic for their literary programs. A., too, considers poetic disillusionment an essential mark of artistic prowess, only it manifests itself in his work less as a promise of autonomy and what Friedrich Schlegel had called "*unendliche Kraft*" [immeasurable Power] than an increasingly frustrating and ultimately insuperable obstacle. In each of the book's manuscripts, talk of literary genre, method, and vocation is inevitably eclipsed by his expressions of disconsolateness, so that what, thematically speaking, looks at first like center stage becomes an antechamber leading elsewhere: a youthful enthusiasm for art hints at going sour ("The First Love"); a vain attempt is made to keep creative inertia at bay ("The Rotation Method"); modern ennui is discussed obliquely, by way of historical comparison ("The Ancient Tragical Motif"). Poetic disillusionment is played with in different settings and at experienced at different levels of intensity according to the self-awareness of the pseudonym (a sequential ordering is abjured in order to present despair as an ongoing struggle). It is the nature of such reflexive despair that it interiorizes and, knowing no closure, feeds on itself in perpetual motion.

Kierkegaard's fictional pseudonyms hover, then, at the vanishing point where late romantic self-consciousness, having swallowed contingency but unable to find repose, becomes visibly transparent to itself. This clearly aligns *Either/Or* with the allegorized romantic retrospective at the close of Hegel's *Phänomenologie des Geistes*. If Johannes could be said to correspond to the self-defeating master in the master-slave dialectic, then A. bears the features of the Unhappy Consciousness. Indeed, A. is enough of an intertextual concoction to use Hegel's aesthetic critique as a form of self-reproach. "The Unhappy Consciousness, " he writes, "is an idea that can almost make the blood run cold, the nerves shiver, it can make a person tremble like a sinner" (I: 222). The difference between A. and the Unhappy Consciousness is, as Stephen Dunning observes, no more than a fissure, but it is a fissure of immeasurable depth.[15] Even pared down to where he is little more than a voice, A. is neither a fixed category nor archetype, but a particular personality moving within a specific context; and rather than indulging the hope of short-circuiting reflective despair through the dialectic of universal history, A. attempts to gain in self-awareness by enduring the discomfort of non-identity. He is an existential *incarnation* of the Unhappy Consciousness, and as such a walking rebuke to the kind of Hegeliansim Kierkegaard was hearing in Berlin in the lectures of K. F. Werder and Philipp Konrad Marheineke.[16]

Kierkegaard's journals from the period cultivate the same radically epigonistic perspective. Taken as a whole they form a virtual compendium of allusions and quotations drawn either from Hoffmann, Grabbe, and Lenau, or from those passages in the high Romantics which, in their volatility, have a decidedly "late" or posthumous cast. Kierkegaard projects himself through the repertoire of stock Gothic-revival figures: the Wandering Jew, the master thief, the villified eccentric. The mid-century cult of *Weltschmerz* was at its core a theatrical phenomenon (a "*Faschingsmummerei*," [carnival masquerade], according to Karl Immermann) in which the claim of authenticity was an essential part of the act. In its struggle against reification, "inwardness" had put itself at reification's disposal, first by making itself a subject of virtuoso technique, then by spectacularizing itself as *Zerrissenheit* [inner division]—a phenomenon which placed its nineteenth-century practitioners squarely in line with a developing publicity culture (it is no coincidence that *Either/Or*, this most "personal" of confessions, became a Danish bestseller, its notoriety increased by the pseudonymous fan dance with his identity Kierkegaard executed in the pages of the local press). Kierkegaard experienced the mid-century crisis of non-identity at second hand, through a lens of German writing. When he "laments" like Nikolaus Lenau or "broods" like Hoffmann or Bonaventura, he evolves a purely *adverbial* Romanticism. Indeed, what is remarkable about the early journals is the degree to which he is able to heighten the performative aspect of post-romantic melodrama. The focus is neither on the German literary reference or prototype, nor on his own biography, but on the isolated act of literary simulation.

Of the actual trip to Berlin, the journals provide only glimpses: mention is made of walks through the more desolate parts of the *Tiergarten*, immersion in the "human baths" of the marketplace, a visit to the theater, a view of the colossal opera house where "Don Giovanni" had recently been performed, and the decor of his apartment. Nothing of the texture of Kierkegaard's stay in Germany is registered, however, until the story "Repetition" is completed two years later. In this fictionalized account of his brief return visit to Berlin (which he made in the spring of 1843), Kierkegaard excavates, or tries to excavate, the experience of his first visit months earlier during the composition of *Either/Or*. Again, he takes the same apartment on the *Jägerstrasse*. He writes: "The recollection of these things was an important factor in my taking this journey. One climbs to the stairs to the first floor in a gas-illuminated building, opens a little door and stands in the entry. To the left is a glass door leading to a room. Straight ahead is an anteroom. Beyond are two entirely identical rooms, identically furnished, so that one sees the room double in the mirror."[17] Despite the precision of his recall, he finds that repetition is impossible without difference, however partial or invisible. Like Charles Baudelaire in "Le Cygne," Kierkegaard's *souvenir* turns out to be a sense of the irrecoverable. Speed, the intoxication of sheer number, the deferred promise of chance encounters, surface glitter, all testify to the discontinuity of metropolitan life. Kierkegaard experiences Berlin as a gaslit theatrical space, the locus for an urban Gothic in which the capacity for experience is fugitive: "Sitting in a chair by the window," he says, "one looks out on the great square, sees the shadows of passersby hurrying along the walls . . . one feels a strong desire to toss on a cape and steal softly along the wall with a searching gaze, aware of every sound. One does not do this but merely sees a rejuvenated self- doing it. Having smoked a cigar one goes back to the inner room and begins to work."[18] Indeed, the fact that Kierkegaard is an armchair flaneur is decisive, since it allows him the perspective from which to physiognomize his own imagined movements. In this way, Kierkegaard's gaze comprehends what Walter Benjamin calls the flaneur's "illustrative seeing" by rendering the ephemera of urban spectacle as shadow play. From above the *Jägerstrasse*, Kierkegaard writes, "a single shadow appears even blacker, a single footstep takes longer to disappear. . . . Once again one goes out into the hallway, into, the entry, into that little room, and—if one is among the fortunate who is able to sleep—goes to sleep."[19] Urban reveries are thus simulated to the point where they are fed by echoes (audible shadows), or shadows (visible echoes).

In short, it is Kierkegaard's approach in these early works to mock the increasingly melodramatic and vacant German idiom of disillusionment not through parody or distortion but by stylistic and psychological *amplification*. The tradition of romantic arabesque is given an additional, metacritical twist: the kind of self-reflexive prose originally plied by Friedrich Schlegel and Ludwig Tieck itself becomes an object of imaginative play. Kierkegaard displays a measure of what Seamus Deane has described as the "vicious virtuosity" of the colonial working the conventions of a dominant, metropolitan culture.[20] In the first part of *Either/Or*, Kierkegaard, like Heine, follows through on the consequences of Schlegel's original dicta of aesthetic self-parody, expanding the scope and heightening the vertigo. Kierkegaard's formal term for this maneuver is "reduplication" or "redoubling;" a pure expression of the desire to potentialize which in *The Concept of Anxiety* (1844) he equates with anxiety's very essence: anxiety is objectless because at bottom it is always anxiety about possibility per se (the sense of absolute potential cultivated by the *Frühromantiker* is, accordingly, not a compounded but a compounding anxiety). Reduplication is similar to other rhetorical tactics used by the Romantics in their agonistic attempts to emerge from one another's influence. It aims at completion like *tessera*, it purifies like *askesis*, and it has the same repetitive drive as *kenosis*.[21] Yet, Kierkegaard—his already highly developed sense of retrospective distance magnified by his extraterritorial remove—takes a broader compass by collapsing universal history in on itself. "Reduplication" aims not to undercut one or more particular precursors, but to break with the German project of revisionism in toto. In discussing the privileged view of the cultural outsider, Bakhtin suggests the analogy of the physiognomist:

> A special and extremely important feature in the outer plastic-pictorial seeing of another human being is the experience of the outward boundaries that encompass him. . . . The *other* is given to me entirely enclosed within a world that is external to me; he is given to me as a constituent in what is totally delineated on all sides in space. Moreover, at each given moment, I experience distinctly all of his boundaries, encompass him visually. . . . I see the line that delineates his head against the background of the outside world and see the lines that delimit his body in the outside world.[22]

It is along similar lines that *Either/Or* "silhouettes" the corpus of the German *Nachromantik* by stepping back and delineating its fringe experience. The fact that it was Heine who was the first to deliberately and consistently turn the tradition of German literary irony against itself is something Kierkegaard himself acknowledges: "Heine," he writes in his journals, "moves in contrast to irony, and by his teaching, elicits humorous sparks from it."[23] But where the Heine of the *Buch der Lieder* is partial and tentative in this regard, Kierkegaard is methodical, to the point of establishing late romantic non-identity as the sole form-giving principle of A.'s shadowgraphic prose.

In the second part of *Either/Or*, Kierkegaard takes an additional step in orienting himself with regard to German aesthetics, this one in the direction of Biedermeier domesticity. The two letters addressed to A. which compose the book ("The Aesthetic Validity of Marriage," and "Equilibrium between the Aesthetic and Ethical") are written by a *paterfamilias*, provincial magistrate and self-styled defender of "altars and hearths" who signs himself "Judge Wilhelm." As opposed to A.'s metropolitan writings, these letters issue from the still preindustrial Danish countryside (or at least from the countryside as imagined, in a highly denatured form, from Kierkegaard's apartment labyrinth in Berlin). Unfortunately, in treating the Judge either as a mouthpiece for neo-humanism or as an archetypal burgher "writing expansively from his ease,"[24] critics have tended to obscure his specifically Biedermeier features, namely, a phobia of aesthetic excess, and fear that behind the epoch's museal interiors and garden views there is a steady threat of fracture and decay (although Kierkegaard was unacquainted with much of German-language Biedermeier, he knew Annette Droste-Hülshoff,

Justinus Kerner, Hermann von Pückler-Muskau, and Johann Nestroy. Indeed, a production of Nestroy's *Posse* "Der Talisman" was a highlight of his stay in Berlin). As Friedrich Sengle observes, the Biedermeier has to be understood as a further phase in the anxious "*Gesamtbewegung*" [dynamic] of European Romanticism.[25] Like one of the tutelary figures who surface in *Maler Nolten* or *Uli der Pächter*, the Judge's aim is not to extirpate but domesticate romantic impulses in order to rob them of their subversive powers. His correspondence constitutes a dialogue in and of itself: A. is invisibly present in it, in its prolixity and nervous energy. While writing, the Judge finds his assured, patriarchal identity unsettled by thoughts of A., whom he analogizes with the mesmeric, the foreign, the protean, and the effete. A.'s theatricalism provokes the Judge into an anxiety of indeterminacy (A.'s appearance in the Judge's letters is *un-heimlich* [uncanny or un-homely] in the Freudian sense: a fear of what is most familiar masquerading as fear of the alien). There is more than a touch of sexual panic at work here. The Judge resists being cast in the role of the seduced, maintaining that he has no reason to fear A., and arguing that stability and constancy are an even match for A.'s agility and attractive melancholy. He refuses, he says, to be "carried away" by A.'s talents (unlike the young men and women whom A. draws into his circle via "telegraphic communications," II: 78). Nevertheless, the Judge feels himself compelled to voice his fascination with A.'s seductive powers—powers which he clearly savors while resisting: "[Your] despair is like a fire in the distance . . . it gives a flourish to the hat and to the whole body. The lips smile haughtilly" (II: 195). Eve Kosofsky Sedgwick has observed that the sexual paranoia haunting Gothic post-romantic fiction often played itself out through the rivalry of two highly individuated male protagonists, each reading the mind of the "feared and desired other."[26] The second part of *Either/Or* enacts a struggle to turn this kind of Gothic pairing into the hierarchical, stable relation of mentor and protégé found in a conventional Bildungsroman. The Judge anticipates A.'s objections to his entreaties, and these imagined objections shape the flow of the Judge's discourse into a series of ellipses within ellipses which follow the same kinetic, circular patterning A. traced out in his portraits of romantic type-characters. As the Judge sits down to write to A., his fear of psychological contagion crystallizes into a perfect image of Biedermeier compulsion—a burgher manically securing his threshold: "I have spent my evenings on this letter. I have not imagined you here in my house, in my room, but outside my door, from which I have almost tried to drive you with my sweeping" (II: 154). Out of the era's *Tugendwortschatz*, [vocabulary of virtue] Kierkegaard erects a rhetorical enclosure:

I listen to the little one cry, and to my ear it is not discordant: I watch
his elder brother grow and make progress; I gaze happily into his
future, not impatiently, for I have time enough to wait, and to me this
waiting is in itself a joy. My work has meaning for me, and I believe that
to a certain degree it also has meaning for others. . . . I love my native
country, and I cannot well imagine that I could thrive in any other. I
love my mother tongue, which liberates my thoughts: I find that in it I
can express extremely well what I may have to say in this world. . . .
Amidst all this, I live a higher life, and when it happens at times that I
inhale this higher life in the breathing of my earthly and domestic life,
I count myself blessed, then art and grace fuse for me. (II: 324)

This domestic arrangement, however, is more ephemeral than it
first appears. The Judge begins his disquisition in expected nineteenth-
century humanist fashion by stating that ethical actions follow ethical
intent; and although this smacks of Kantianism—ethical volition
(*Willkür*) as the sole reliable tie to transcendence—the Judge implicitly
discourages such comparisons by rejecting any sense of duty that derives
action from universal principles as being too form-driven and external
an imperative. In his participatory ethics the sheer event of choice, and
not a ruling concept, is crucial. The Judge's notion of ethical-aesthetic
"equilibrium" is worked out in emphatically functional terms. He
sketches a number of hypothetical domestic tableaux for A.—like the
married pair who, wanting nothing so much as to stave off routine,
encourage the accidental in life and studiously avoid the moment when
repetitiveness begins (II: 114); or the household in which the husband
and wife live on separate floors so that he can enjoy viewing her from
his window as if she were still a complete stranger to him. Yet, each of
these domestic blueprints is merely cautionary, a presentation of
aesthetic equilibrium solely through negative circumscription (indeed,
at one point the Judge blames A. for having forced him into distracting
scene painting). Like the Judge's notion of conjugal eros, the properly
oriented romantic libido "constructs" itself in strictly oppositional terms,
situated as it is in the struggle against the kind of sensual phan-
tasmagoria he, like A., has experienced most consciously through
exposure to German fiction. Indeed, references to A.'s German
readings are turned to polemical account, sometimes explicitly (the
Judge cites "Rolands Knappen" in inveighing against phantom
pleasures, and later, accuses A. of behaving like a Peter Schlemihl), at
other times subterraneously: long stretches of the Judge's tirade against
A.'s poet's existence are lifted almost verbatim from Kierkegaard's
critical analysis of Friedrich Schlegel and K. W. F. Solger in *The Concept of*

Irony. Polemically charged, the letters to A. take on imagistic coloration. Yet, when discussing the way in which artistic form may, as he puts it, "coalesce with the world," he draws us a blank. Since "the aesthetic" is spoken of only with regard to A.'s instability, the Judge in effect relinquishes the very word to him:

> In despair nothing perishes, all of the aesthetic remains in a person, only it is reduced to an auxiliary and precisely thereby is preserved. Yes, it is certainly true that one does not live in it as before. But from this it does not follow that it is gone. The ethicist only carries through the despair that the advanced aestheticist has already begun. (II: 229)

Kierkegaard's notion of equilibrium turns on a slight of hand: "All of the aesthetic remains in a person, only it is reduced to an auxiliary and is thereby precisely preserved." Yet, far from being solidified or substantialized,[27] the literary process remains as destabilizing for Judge Wilhelm as it does for A. or for A.'s German romantic prototypes. Judge Wilhelm has experienced speculative doubt too intensely to trust in Biedermeier gardens and idylls as a cognitive bulwark. For Kierkegaard, the kind of brittle, precarious poetic compromise with the senses that constitutes the work of a contemporary like Eduard Mörike or Adalbert Stifter is literally unimaginable. What distinguishes the Judge from A. is a subtle shift of perspective: the Judge actively wills his own imaginative defeat. Such is the "ministering role" of aesthetic experience. The visual imagination is transfigured ethically to the extent that it is resisted (like one of Ludwig Wittgenstein's proverbial ladders, it is climbed and kicked aside). Narrative progress in the book is deceptive; and the closure one expects in the Biedermeier is forestalled. Characters make headway only by realizing the extent of their romantic stasis. Like a multitiered chess game, the pseudonyms and the different degrees of self-consciousness they incorporate are present synchronically. To get one's bearings in his world, therefore, depends on seeing all occurences as simultaneous, and on seeing their interrelationship in what Bakhtin calls "the cross-section of the moment." *Either/Or*'s voices thus move in counterpoint. A's lamentations already contain the possibility—the need—of Judge Wilhelm; while aesthetic experience does not exist for the Judge beyond the category of "the aesthete." The Judge claims he wants to tie the imagination more firmly to the mundane, but this is mere subterfuge meant to draw A. along:

> Therefore only when I regard my life ethically do I see it with a view to its beauty, and only when I regard my own life ethically do I see it with a view to its beauty. And if you were to say that this beauty is invisible, I

would answer: in a certain sense it is, in another sense it is not, that is to say, it is visible in the trace it leaves in history, visible in the sense in which it was said *Loquere, ut videam te*. It is indeed true that I do not see the consummation, but the struggle, but after all, I see the consummation every instant I will, if I have the courage for it, and without courage I see absolutely nothing eternal, and accordingly, nothing beautiful. (II: 275)

If Kierkegaard's Biedermeier portrait is so spectral, it is because the "how" of reorientation fully eclipses the "what" of the contingent world. The book renders diaphanous what Nina Auerbach terms the moral "pantomime" of mid-century fiction.[28] The domestic plot is undermined not by being up-ended but by being seen through. The Judge's artlessness and hardiness appear as attitudinizing. Children, locale, domicile—all the basic elements of homebound existence to which he clings have no more sensuous solidity than do stage cues or compass points. Throughout the letters the Judge claims to read in his wife's presence the very source, the original text, of his rootedness and domestic bliss (she incarnates the "female" virtues which uphold both his household and his writing). And yet, the only time we glimpse her, when she accidentally crosses his field of vision as he works on the letters, she appears as a barely visible sign of his rectitude, a redemptive trace: "This feeling of having a home can come over me when I am sitting alone in my study . . . and there is a soft knock at the door and a head peeks through the door in such a way that one could believe it did not belong to anybody, and then in a flash she is standing by my side and vanishes again" (II: 83). The affirmative art of the Biedermeier, Adorno observes, is a "cipher" of romantic despair, its purported hardiness a "mask or ritual to keep life at a distance." The significance of a writer like Stifter, he goes on to say, lies in the fact that he began to push the art of the period to articulate self-consciousness: the late work abjures "blissful colors" and looks instead like a pallid "pencil sketch."[29] What distinguishes a Judge Wilhelm from German contemporaries like Stifter's Risach (or Mörike's Maler Nolten) is that his "equilibrium" is not a gesture or ethical posture which by virtue of time and struggle he hopes to talk himself into believing, but ethical posturing laid bare *as such*. Having both fulfilled and exhausted A.'s inner potential, Kierkegaard does the same to the Judge: he transforms him into an acute hypertrophy of the Biedermeier demand for balance and stasis and, as such, a manifest expression of its latent dissonance. The Judge later turns up in *The Sickness unto Death* (1849) in a discussion of hidden disillusionment. Although he goes unnamed, his features are familiar: "Our man in despair is sufficiently self-enclosed to keep this matter of having a self away from anyone—while outwardly he looks every bit a real man. He is a university graduate. A husband. A father. Even an uncommonly competent office holder."[30] The Judge's detachment from his surroundings is so all-encompassing that no visible sign is allowed to betray it (in being able to submerge his theatricalism, he is simply a better actor than A.). To the outside world, his bourgeois mask fits with virtual seamlessness. Inwardly he is as much a figure of "romantic despair" as A.

In short, by stylizing the literary maneuvers of both the mid-century aesthete and the Biedermeier burgher, *Either/Or* draws the imagination of the *Nachromantik* beyond itself. "You know very well, A. writes, that the most intense enjoyment is in the clutching of the enjoyment in the consciousness that it may vanish the next moment. Pursued by the police, by the whole world, by the living and the dead, alone in a remote room, Don Giovanni once again gathers together all the powers of his soul and once again raises the goblet" (II: 25). From its overall architecture, down to individual tropes, the book is played out at the point of tension where distant reflections of German aesthetic experience yield to the purely invisible. It is this inner movement which more than anything else explains the book's deep affinity with music: "In music," Hegel writes, "the negativity into which the vibrating material enters is on one side the negation of the spatial situation, a cancellation negated again by the reaction of the body, and the expression of this double negation, that is, sound, is an externality which in its coming-to-be is annihilated again by its very existence, and vanishes of itself."[31] Unlike contemporary, self-flagellating aesthetes such as Baudelaire or Edgar Allan Poe, Kierkegaard rarely spurs his suspicion of the visible by courting sin in luxuriant, charnel-tainted images. He is at once more susceptible and more insensate, since he can goad himself on and heighten his responses simply with the *possibility* of art. The book legitimates itself only in so far as it calls attention to its own highly elaborated semblance, a realization one acquires retrospectively, at the book's end. In so far as the reader shifts his or her perspective in this manner, the book offers itself as a participatory event. All points of *Either/Or* extend from this moment of recognition. Unlike Stifter's *Der Nachsommer*, the book's illusory character is neither mute, nor passive: and to trap Kierkegaard within his own romantic construct, as Adorno attempts to do, is redundant, since Kierkegaard does so himself: he dissolves the book's artifice through a sense of pure procedure in order to vindicate—if only negatively—the claim of the moment in historical time.

Writing *Either/Or* in the Berlin of the 1840s at the center of what was left of the idealist legacy, Kierkegaard developed an art of disillusionment purer and arguably more consequential than any of his German contemporaries. If German Romanticism was constituted by a series of border-crossings (whether between literary genres, languages, speculation and poetry, or the spheres of "art" and "non-art"), Kierkegaard, the alien epigone, turned this highly cultivated sense of transgression and "becoming" against itself and in the process superseded it. He was enamored of the legend of an elf who breaks the spell of a witch's song only when he learns to play it backwards on his flute. *Either/Or* employs a similar tactic. Each of the book's purported authors tries writing his way out of his epigonism, first by personifying, then second-guessing, or upstaging, his creative powers. A. tires of his pseudonyms. Judge Wilhelm damns A., and Kierkegaard implicitly mocks the effort as a whole. "Even if the book were totally devoid of meaning," Kierkegaard later observes in his diaries, "the simple fact of having written it would be the pithiest epigram I could put over the meandering philosophy of this generation."[32] In short, *Either/Or* marks the site where the posturing of the German *Nachromantik* translates into hypermodern gesture. Like the vanishing trick of the Cheshire cat, what lingers in the end is not so much an ironic grin, as the sheer, disembodied act of grinning.

NOTES

Page numbers in parentheses refer to Søren Kierkegaard, *Either/Or* [*Enten-Eller*], translated by Howard V. Hong and Edna H. Hong, 2 vols. (Princeton, N.J.: Princeton University Press, 1987).

1. Friedrich Wilhelm IV called Schelling to Berlin (along with Felix Mendelssohn, the Grimms, Tieck, and Cornelius) in hopes of rejuvenating the Romantic Movement under semiofficial Prussian auspices. See Mario Krammer, *Berlin im Wandel der Jahrhunderte* (Berlin: Rembrandt Verlag, 1956), p. 154. Kierkegaard's disappointment with Schelling's lectures can be traced through scattered remarks in his letters from Berlin. See Søren Kierkegaard, *Letters and Documents*, translated by Henrik Rosenmeier (Princeton, N.J.: Princeton University Press, 1978) pp. 89–143

2. Kierkegaard, *Letters and Documents* [Breve og Aktstykker], p. 107.

3. Kierkegaard, *Letters and Documents*, p. 107.

4. Kierkegaard, *Letters and Documents*, p. 151.

5. Mikhail Bakhtin, *Speech Genres and Other Late Essays*, edited by Caryl Emerson and Michael Holquist, translated by Vern McGee (Austin: University of Texas Press, 1986), p. 55.

6. Theodor Adorno, *Gesammelte Schriften*, edited by Rolf Tiedemann, vol. 2 (Frankfurt am Main: Suhrkamp, 1979), p. 15–17.

7. Adorno, *Gesammelte Schriften*, vol. 2, pp. 34–53.

8. Nina Auerbach, *Private Theatricals* (Cambridge, Mass.: Harvard University Press, 1990), p. 6.

9. See Adorno, *Gesammelte Schriften*, vol. 2, pp. 61–63; and Susan Buck-Morss, *The Origin of Negative Dialectics: Theodor W. Adorno, Walter Benjamin and the Frankfurt Institute* (New York: Free Press, 1977), pp. 176–77.

10. G. W. F. Hegel, *Werke*, edited by Eva Moldenhauer and Karl Markus Michel, vol. 15.iii (Frankfurt: Suhrkamp, 1970), p. 134: "Die Aufhebung des Räumlichen besteht deshalb hier nur darin, daß ein bestimmtes sinnliches Material sein ruhiges Aussereinander aufgibt, in Bewegung gerät, doch so in sich erzittert, daß jeder Teil des Körpers seinen Ort nicht nur verändert, sondern auch sich in den vorigen Zustand zurückzuversetzen strebt."

11. René Girard, *Deceit, Desire and the Novel*, translated by Yvonne Freccero (New York: Harper, 1965), pp. 3–8.

12. Jacques Lacan, *The Four Fundamental Concepts of Psychoanalysis*, translated by Alan Sheridan (New York: Norton, 1973), p. 182.

13. Following Foucault, John Kucich makes the point that veiled tactics of repression were common in Gothic melodrama: histrionism, he writes, was often a means of "estrangement and distance, of self-elaboration in isolation." See John Kuchich, *Repression in Victorian Fiction* (Berkeley: University of California Press: 1987), p. 41.

14. Roland Barthes, *A Lover's Discourse*, translated by Richard Howard (New York: Hill and Wang, 1980), p. 216.

15. Stephen Dunning, *Kierkegaard's Dialectic of Inwardness* (Princeton, N.J.: Princeton University Press, 1985), p. 78.

16. Kierkegaard, *Letters and Documents*, pp. 105–9.

17. Søren Kierkegaard, *Fear and Trembling [Frygt og Bœven]* and *Repetition [Gjentagelsen]*, translated by Howard V. Hong and Edna H. Hong (Princeton, N.J.: Princeton University Press, 1983), p. 151.

18. Kierkegaard, *Repetition*, p. 151.

19. Kierkegaard, *Repetition*, p. 152.

20. Terry Eagleton, Fredric Jameson, and Edward W. Said, *Nationalism, Colonialism, and Literature* (Minneapolis: University of Minnesota Press, 1992). See introduction by Seamus Deane.

21. Harold Bloom, *The Anxiety of Influence: A Theory of Poetry* (New York: Oxford University Press, 1973).

22. Mikhail Bakhtin, *Art and Answerability: Early Philosophical Essays*, edited by Michael Holquist and Vadim Liapunov, translated by Vadim Liapunov (Austin: University of Texas Press, 1990), p. 36.

23. Kierkegaard, *Journals and Papers*, vol. 3, p. 229.

24 Louis Mackey, *Kierkegaard: A Kind of Poet* (Philadelphia: University of Pennsylvania Press, 1971), p. 39.

25. Friedrich Sengle, *Biedermeierzeit*, vol. 3, (Stuttgart: Metzler, 1971), p. 1028.

26. Eve Kosofsky Sedgwick, *Epistemology of the Closet* (Berkeley: University of California Press, 1990), p. 187.

27. See Dunning, *Kierkegaard's Dialectic of Inwardness*, p. 101; and Mark C. Taylor, *Kierkegaard's Pseudonymous Authorship* (Princeton, N.J.: Princeton University Press, 1985), pp. 185–90.

28. Auerbach, *Private Theatricals,* pp. 14–15.

29. "Objektivität erstarrt zur Maske, beschworenes Leben wird zum abweisenden Ritual. . . . Blaß und fahl ist das Licht über seiner reifen Prosa, als wäre sie allergisch gegen das Glück der Farbe; sie wird gleichsam zur Graphik reduziert." Adorno, *Gesammelte Schriften,* vol. 7, pp. 346–47.

30. Søren Kierkegaard, *The Sickness unto Death* [*Sygdommen til Døden*], translated by Walter Lowrie (Princeton, N.J.: Princeton University Press, 1941), p. 197.

31. Hegel, *Werke,* vol. 15:iii, p. 134: "Da nun ferner die Negativität, in die das Schwingende Material hier eingeht, einerseits ein Aufheben des räumlichen Zustandes ist, das selbst wieder durch die Reaktion des Körpers aufgehoben wird, so ist die Äusserung dieser zwiefachen Negation . . . eine Äusserlichkeit, welche sich in ihrem Entstehen durch ihr Dasein selbst wieder vernichtet, und an sich selbst verschwindet."

32. Kierkegaard, *Journals and Papers,* vol. 5: 217.

Contributors

APRIL ALLISTON is associate professor of comparative literature at Princeton and author of *Virtue's Faults: Correspondences in Eighteenth-Century British and French Women's Fiction.* Other publications include a critical edition of Sophia Lee's *The Recess; or, a Tale of Other Times* (1783–85), and a number of articles on European women's writing in the Enlightenment and the Romantic Age. She is currently collaborating on a biography of James Fenimore Cooper and is also at work on another book, *Fictions of History: Gender and the Genres of Historical Narrative, 1650–1850.*

FREDERICK BURWICK, who studied German literature and philosophy at Göttingen and continued his work in Anglo-German literary relations with Gian Orisini at the University of Wisconsin, is professor of English and comparative literature at the University of California, Los Angeles. He is editor of *European Romantic Review* and author of numerous studies of language theory and perception theory in the eighteenth and early nineteenth centuries. Recent books include: *The Damnation of Newton: Goethe's Color Theory and Romantic Perception; The Haunted Eye: Perception and the Grotesque in Romantic Literature; Illusion and the Drama: Critical Theory of the Enlightenment and Romantic Era.* His latest book is *Romantic Madness and the Romantic Imagination.*

ANNETTE WHEELER CAFARELLI, an independent scholar working in New York City, has held Guggenheim and NEH Fellowships, is the author of *Prose in the Age of Poets: Romanticism and Biographical Narrative,* the forthcoming *Women and the Formation of Romanticism,* and is currently working on a book about the British literary marketplace entitled *Romanticism and Patronage.*

JAMES ENGELL is professor of English and comparative literature at Harvard University. He is author of *The Creative Imagination* and *Forming the Critical Mind,* as well as articles on eighteenth- and nineteenth-century literature. He edited Samuel Taylor Coleridge's *Biographia Literaria* and, more recently, *Coleridge: The Early Family Letters*.

LILIAN R. FURST is Marcel Bataillon Professor of Comparative Literature at the University of North Carolina, Chapel Hill. She has written extensively on European Romanticism: *Romanticism in Perspective, Romanticism, Counterparts*, and *Fictions of Romantic Irony*. She has also published *All is True: The Claims and Strategies of Realist Fiction* and a dual voice autobiography with her father, *Home is Somewhere Else*.

DAVID C. HENSLEY is associate professor of English at McGill University. He is the editor of volume 13 of the Clarissa Project, *The Critical Controversy—Historical Commentaries*, a collection of nineteenth-century responses to Samuel Richardson's *Clarissa*. He has published essays on *Clarissa* and the culture of pietism, and is writing a book that resituates Richardson's ethics and aesthetic theory in relation to English and German Romanticism.

ROBERTA JOHNSON is professor of Spanish at the University of Kansas. She is author of *Carmen Laforet, El ser y la palabra en Gabriel Miro*, and *Crossfire: Philosophy and the Novel in Spain, 1900–1934*. She has held grants from the Guggenheim Foundation, NEH, Graves Foundation, and the Comité para la Cooperación Cultural. She currently sits on the editorial boards of PMLA, *Siglio Veinte/Twentieth Century, Journal of Interdisciplinary Studies*, and is an associate editor of *Hispania*.

MARC KATZ is assistant professor of German at Scripps College/The Claremont Colleges, where he teaches courses on twentieth-century literature and culture. He works on urban and cultural theory, and is currently writing on representations of Berlin.

KARI LOKKE is associate professor of English and comparative literature at the University of California, Davis. She is author of *Gérard de Nerval: The Poet as Social Visionary* and articles on the aesthetics of the sublime and the grotesque. Her essay, "Sibylline Leaves: Mary Shelley's *Valperga* and the Legacy of *Corinne*," is related to her current book project on gender and transcendence in the writings of Germaine de Staël, Mary Shelley, Bettine von Arnim, and George Sand.

GREGORY MAERTZ, associate professor of English at St. John's University in New York, has published a number of articles on Romanticism and Anglo-German literary relations in the nineteenth century. The author of a forthcoming study of Goethe as a transgressive and normative cultural icon in Britain and America, he is currently working on two other books, *Forbidden Culture* and *Children of Prometheus*, as well as a critical edition of George Eliot's *Middlemarch*.

JOHN L. MAHONEY is Thomas F. Rattigan Professor of English and former Department Chair at Boston College. He is author of *The Logic of Passion: The Literary Criticism of William Hazlitt*, *The Whole Internal Universe: Imitation and the New Defense of Poetry in British Criticism, 1660–1830*, and *William Wordsworth: A Poetic Life*. He edited *The English Romantics: Major Poetry and Critical Theory*, *The Enlightenment and English Literature*, *Coleridge, Keats, and the Imagination: Romanticism and Adam's Dream* (with J. Robert Barth, S.J.), and, most recently, *Literature and Religion: Essays in Critical Theory and Practice*.

Index

251